Building Urban Little Schools

Where every child succeeds with dignity.

D1530858

Building Urban Little Schools

Where every child succeeds with dignity.

Robert E. Newman

Emeritus Professor, Syracuse University

BROOKLINE BOOKS • CAMBRIDGE, MA

Copyright ©2000 by Robert E. Newman

Library of Congress Cataloging-In-Publication-Data
Newman, Robert E.
    Building urban little schools, where every child succeeds with dignity/ by Robert E. Newman.
    p. cm.
ISBN 1-57129-076-1
1. Education, Urban–United States. 2. Alternative Schools–United States. 3. Education–United States–Experimental Methods. I. Title.

LC5131.N49 2000
371.04–dc21

                          00-010676
                             CIP

Published by
BROOKLINE BOOKS, INC.
P.O. Box 381047
Cambridge, Massachusetts 02238-1047
ORDER TOLL-FREE: 1-800-666-BOOK

to Katherine

Contents

Supplemental Articles

Acknowledgments

Thanks, Harry Schwarzlander for all your thoughts and wise perspectives which now enhance the book. Your wisdom comes though to me from what you say but also by the way I see you living your life.

Thanks, Barbara Elander for fine-tuning the first complete draft, line by line, and coming up with so many useful suggestions.

Thanks, Jeff Bitner, Beth Ruffo, and the crew at Syracuse University's faculty computing center for all your help.

Thanks to Milt Budoff at Brookline Books, for suggesting changes leading to the book's last revisions.

And a very special thanks to Katherine Hughes, my wife, for your editing of draft after draft. Thanks not only for noting what seemed awkward, but for writing out how it might be said better. And thanks for keeping the book to its point while guarding against cynicism, blaming, and unnecessary compromise. Because of your respect for the reader's ability to think for her or himself, this book shows more and preaches less.

From Failing Schools to Our Best Schools: An Introduction

In this book I speak to people concerned about children growing up in failing urban schools—people who take seriously the principle that every single child matters without reservation, despite how life often seems cheap amid the hopelessness, violence and fear rampant on many central city streets. The Urban Little Schools I propose can make that belief in the value of every single child a reality in their schooling.

This Urban Little Schools idea, explained with nuts-and-bolts detail in the book, is a fundamental change from conventional education practiced in failing urban schools. In conventional education, students have to adapt to the school's system or lose out. Many students find this a difficult way to learn. In Washington, D.C. for instance, more than a third of the students drop out of school before graduation. In the proposed Urban Little Schools, the school adapts sensitively to each child so all can qualify for college or a more appropriate next step.

In the book I write from my experience making school work for each child. For ten years I directed a small experimental elementary school which was the forerunner of the Urban Little Schools explained in this book. It was neither a conventional school nor was it some version of an alternative free school. It was a flexible school which made learning work for each of its students because sensitive teachers knew how to individualize and because they acted in harmony with each child. I designed the book's secondary

Urban Little Schools, to complement and extend the basic features pioneered in the experimental elementary school.

Students in the proposed Urban Little Schools each will be guided one to one by a teacher who can help them take increasing responsibility for their own learning. In this process students will learn to judge themselves realistically as they come to know their unique strengths and accept themselves honestly. Guided by this clear sense of self they won't need to follow the peer group, the gang, or find themselves turning to drugs or other artificial sensation and delusion to feel significant.

The book proposes Urban Little Schools (ULS) to be parent-choice alternatives within public school districts striving to meet the challenge of education in our cities. They will be evaluated regularly and rigorously both as to students' academic attainment and their character growth. Urban Little Schools needn't cost districts more than most now pay per-pupil. The new schools also could be private schools. Whether public or private schools, they could be Charter Schools.

The book not only explains the ULS idea but it is written to be a handbook for those who wish to begin pilot schools within our cities. It lays out specific plans and guidelines for such key things as how elementary ULS teachers can help children to know writing as a vital and creative part of their thinking and likewise how they can help children find books, reading and libraries compelling ways of learning on their own. Another example of the book's how-to-do-it contents is how secondary teachers can guide each of their students to become job-wise as the young people work with principled employers on school-coordinated jobs. The book lays out what secondary teachers need to know in order to do this, such as how teachers can help students become adept at learning the next school-coordinated job quickly and thoroughly as part of what it takes to be prepared for success in the ever-changing market economy.

Failing Urban Schools: A Definition

When I say "failing urban schools" I am referring to schools where most children leave not prepared to hold their own in our modern highly competitive market economy; where most poor children are not prepared to make it out of the poverty cycle. This failing schooling is particularly dangerous to so many of our city poor children who have two strikes on them in the first place. These children risk a life diminished by poverty and societal neglect as they grow up in the violent no-hope-for-the-future street culture of many urban neighborhoods. They need our best schools, not our worst.

In the failing urban schools I speak of, children are offered essentially only one way to learn—the uniform curriculum with its prescribed methods, sequences, materials and pacing. Some take to it and learn quickly, the majority muddle through or are flat-out losers in this fateful learning game.

In this system, young children in failing urban schools typically find themselves sorted out on a continuum from winners to losers by the time they reach seven or eight years of age. They soon discover themselves informally embedded in one of their school's three overlapping categories with the top level category offering a minority of children an avenue to a decent life; the lower two categories hold no such promise. The school sends the majority of its poor children back to poverty and to its minimum-wage and menial jobs.

Children in the top level category find teachers treating them as school winners. Maybe as many as one fourth of a school's children end up in this winner group. More often in many city schools where I've worked, the number is closer to ten or fifteen percent. Children who are seen in this top category find it easy to do the prescribed lessons and tests fast and accurately without much teacher help. From their earliest days in kindergarten, these top children sense that their teachers feel they are on the road to college or other advanced training after high school.

At the other end of the school's continuum are the losers. These are children who find they get the low marks even if they try hard. As they become older, they often seem embarrassed by such things as their halting reading of the simple books used in the school's beginning reading groups, where most others read more fluently. They find themselves being sent to the remedial teachers regularly. A teacher might describe one of these loser children euphemistically to his parents as a "good boy, but a bit slow." In many city schools this bottom group might be ten to twenty percent of first, second or third grade classes.

The majority of children find themselves somewhere in between the losers and the winners on the school's continuum. For them school is a place where they come to see themselves as "just ordinary," at best. In these failing schools children thus run a more than fifty percent risk of learning to see themselves as lackluster diminished persons.

In failing schools most children, even some of the winners, find the learning program less than inviting. Needless to say, most children in these schools find that their hearts are not in their required academic work. One reason is that children are schooled in situations too impersonal for teachers and children to listen to each other responsively, too inflexible for the child and teacher to work together in adapting learning to the child even if the teacher were unconventional enough to individualize. In these schools, children are pressed through the sequenced curriculum in factory-like institutions which live and breathe uniformity for children and teachers alike. Children learn to do exercises to please teachers; that, as opposed to using their skills such as writing and reading, for the kinds of independent learning which might invite students to engage and probe the intriguing worlds of ideas and possibilities.

Another reason many children in failing urban schools do not put themselves wholeheartedly into their schoolwork is that being a good student—pleasing the teacher—is often seen as less than self-respectful according to the urban street code which is the prevailing influence on children's peer groups in many inner city schools. This street code mentality tends to become set into many children by the time they reach about eight-years-old. The omnipresent street code teaches that real self-respecting strong young people don't dutifully please the teachers. The code teaches that one shouldn't abase oneself by being seen as meekly following directions in order to get good grades. On the contrary, the code instructs that a strong young person is the one who earns respect by being accepted as a cool confident member of a high status peer group or gang which challenges outside authority, not bows to it. The street code impacts particularly on boys; but increasingly its influence is extending to girls.

Typically, children in failing urban schools don't have a trusting one to one relationship with any teacher which is strong enough to help the children stand up as their own persons, despite how other children are following the street code's dictates. I am speaking of a one to one relationship with a teacher who a child admires—a relationship grounded in shared respect where two people can listen to each other. With this kind of a relationship, children can learn to pilot their own ships despite the threat from other children dominated by the street code.

Instead of helping teachers to establish these supportive relationships, the system in failing urban schools, places the teacher in the role of judge who hands out the grades, as the authority separated from the children who is hired to control groups of children, who is expected to make children work or feel the results of school failure. In rare instances a "bright" top level student might achieve a supportive relationship with a teacher. But in most cases, responsible urban students at school are left without support to live in the shadow of the ever-present risk of being picked on or beat up by the other children caught up in the urban street culture.[1]

Teachers come to be disheartened and cynical in these failing schools where they can see the system is not working. If teachers have seniority they can get transferred to a school in a more privileged part of town. It's hard for teachers to keep any sort of enthusiasm for their teaching when disruptive children require most of their attention. The threat of failure doesn't hold disruptive children in check as it tends to do in the more affluent neighborhood schools. Teachers become conservative when it comes to trying ways to diversify their teaching to meet the needs of each child because individualization might threaten the teacher's tenuous hold on control in the classroom. On the other hand, uniformity promises order. And order is the number one goal.

And finally, failing schools are part of an obsolete conventional urban schooling system. The system isn't even teaching its winners, its college bound students, what they need in order to rise to the top in the new market economy. To get ahead in the modern world of work, they will need to be independent, but the school's system is geared to teaching them to be dependent. The urban systems' "high ability students" learn that in order to move up in their careers, they should find out what their bosses want specifically and do just that without further question—as they have been taught to do in order to get good marks from their teachers in school. But that doesn't fit them for the highly competitive world of work which requires constant innovation plus the skill and will to use your ability with ingenuity.

To get ahead in modern America, employees must know how to define nagging problems as well as to carry out their solutions. Employees who get ahead have to be self-reliant, versatile and know how to work effectively with others to solve problems. Then, on top of all that, like it or not, in order to survive in the market economy, modern employees must know how to take care of themselves. They need to respond proactively to technological changes and corporate restructuring in a new "lean and mean" world of work. They have to know how to upgrade their skills and often learn whole new careers.

As I think of this new "lean and mean" world of work, I am struck by how the conventional teaching-learning system in failing urban schools doesn't prepare young people for it. I am concerned how the conventional system doesn't help young people learn to encourage trusting relationships in the workplace. Schools don't help young adults to succeed with integrity in the world of work.

Preparing young people to succeed with integrity in the market economy is quite possible. The Urban Little Schools proposed in this book are designed to help each young person succeed with lasting self-respect. Secondary ULS students spend about a third of their time working on paid and unpaid jobs alongside successful honest people in their community who work in different sectors of the economy. Throughout their ULS education, they learn how to work closely one to one with their teachers in honest and open relationships. These young people learn how to make trust and listening-to-the-other-person work in solving problems and carrying out their solutions. In this process they can see themselves becoming job-wise and capable of learning what they need to do to accomplish what makes sense to them in their lives.[2]

Reforming Failing Urban Schools

The Urban Little Schools' approach to school reform is fundamental redesign of schooling grounded in the philosophy that every single child is of ultimate worth. In this new schooling each student's education fits the individual child. It is planned and guided in one to one trusting teacher-child relationships where students learn increasingly to take responsibility for their own learning. This redesign is not the quick-fix hodgepodge of new features now being prescribed as remedies for failing urban schools.

The quick-fix approach to improving failing urban schools doesn't change the conventional schools' uniform teaching system and its teacher's role of teaching to the group. In this book I argue that the conventional uniform teaching-learning system where teachers are kept from responding flexibly to each child, is at the root of the urban schools' failure. The redesign proposed in this book changes the basic teaching-learning system and the nature of the student-teacher relationship to where schooling fits every child. It is a fresh and wholesale change clearly based on deeply held respect and caring for every child.

To explain the difference further, let me contrast these two approaches to changing failing urban schooling—Urban Little Schools redesign vs. quick-fix reform—by citing examples in each case. First, I shall inventory and identify some of the current proposals for quick-fix reform of failing urban schools. Following that, and in contrast, I shall lay out some of the key elements in the Urban Little Schools design, showing how it starts afresh with a fundamentally new schooling approach.

The Quick-fix Approach to Urban School Reform

Here are some of the proposals now being used or being offered to fix failing urban schools:

- Raise the pay of inner city teachers and give them more decision-making power.
- Add more teachers in the lower grades.
- Replace teachers whose classes aren't delivering good achievement test scores.
- Turn operation of failing schools over to for-profit management.
- Train idealistic college graduates to teach in difficult schools.
- Break up larger schools to smaller units.
- Come down hard on children who disrupt, including administering amphetamine-type drugs or antidepressants to children labeled by school psychologists as afflicted with Attention Deficit Disorder. [3]
- Use closed circuit TV surveillance to make corridors safe and metal detectors to disarm gun-carrying children at the school's single unlocked door.

- Keep cumulative profile records on children reported to have expressed dark destructive thoughts.
- Raise academic standards which pupils have to meet to progress to the next grade level and to graduate.
- Have teaching geared specifically to prepare children to pass mandated achievement tests.
- Require that children do more homework and make failing children attend summer school classes or repeat their grades.
- Have military schools as a high school parent option within the school district, where children do close-order army drill, wear regulation uniforms, and learn with military discipline.
- Increase the number of preschool classes for those children seen as likely to fail the early grades.
- Start more after-school tutoring centers to help children with homework.
- Use more phonics to teach reading.
- Teach children to estimate answers as a guide to their arithmetic calculations.
- Provide instant remedial help for children who don't do well in a lesson.
- Bring in volunteer tutors and "mentors" from the community.
- Involve parents in school decision making.

So many of these quick-fix suggestions attest to the crisis situation in which urban teachers are struggling to teach and in which children are receiving an inadequate start in life. Some of these proposals are of obvious value, some long overdue.

Some quick-fix remedies seem of dubious value such as the current talk of raising academic standards in already failing urban schools where children are not now helped to meet the present standards. Current plans to raise academic standards for urban children, call for testing students periodically and rigorously. This means that teaching will be even more geared specifically to what is written into the achievement tests, with dire consequences for children, teachers and schools who don't measure up. In this clear example of quick-fix reform, test-prep mentality will permeate into an already inadequate teaching-learning system driving failing schools even further from being relevant to their children's needs and to the world in which their children live.

The Urban Little Schools: Basic Schooling Redesign to Meet the Urban Challenge

In contrast to the quick-fix approach, the Urban Little Schools idea explained in this book offers both critics and school people alike, a clear plan for school redesign along fine tuned individualized lines. In the ULS process, every urban child masters the basic skills to at least the academic standards that are required by the proposed new statewide testing programs. Further, students master the fundamentals while using them to communicate and calculate in real situations, not just to pass achievement tests. In addition, each Urban Little School is held accountable for students' character growth.[4] The plan's design makes sure each student succeeds with dignity and self-reliance, while learning how to learn and to be job-wise.

Now let's consider this proposed Urban Little Schools idea and how it starts afresh with a basic integrated design grounded in the fundamental belief of the value of each child. Here is a thumbnail sketch of the ULS design to extend and integrate the short references to the Urban Little Schools made earlier in this chapter. The design will be explained at length in this book:

The basic goal of the Urban Little Schools is that each child will have an even chance at further education and worthwhile jobs; each of the children will be enabled to have a decent life where they think and act without blind obedience to convention. That means not only will the children leave as academically independent and job-wise people, the children will leave Urban Little Schools able to be their own persons. I am speaking of young adults who are coming to understand and accept themselves enough to follow their hearts honestly, despite perhaps, shallow TV role models or the pull of the urban street culture.

Urban Little Schools elementary children have as long as it takes to learn to use the basic skills independently. That is because of the school's individualized learning system guided by teachers who work one to one with their groups of twelve children from five-to-twelve years of age. It's seen as perfectly natural if one child might take a year or two longer than another to learn the fundamentals. These parent-choice schools are just a few doors down the block or around the corner from where their forty-four children live. All children start at five-years old—before they might become conditioned by the street code or by conventional schools' ways.

As they spend about twelve hundred hours in paid and unpaid jobs alongside different community people of integrity, high school age ULS students learn how to be job savvy. Secondary ULS teachers plan one to one with students in their multi-age groups of no more than twelve students. Students learn traditional high school subjects independently, largely in self-directed learning centers, helped by tutors. As in the elementary Urban Little Schools, secondary young people can remain, without stigma, as long as it takes to be prepared for college or a more suitable next step; no losers.

Urban Little School teachers make it their priority to be aware and sensitive to each child's differences. This fits hand-in-glove with living in the city, where diversity is the norm. Children of different ages, learning styles, economic privilege and ethnic backgrounds learn side by side in ways which fit each child. Each of the children's learning emerges as one to one the teacher guides children to take responsibility for their learning. Children regularly conference and exchange written journals with their teachers. In this schooling process children learn to think, ask questions, analyze problems, find solutions and to be easy with the tools and skills of independent learning. These include using the computer, the library, and figuring out what's needed for a new job. Children can use this self-directing process and their tested wisdom, in their own lives too. Being true to yourself isn't a cliché in the Urban Little Schools; it's the way you live at school. Thus children learn to pilot their own ships with increasing sureness—learn not to follow the crowd unquestioningly to drugs, violence, gangs or teen pregnancies.

Parents can come together at their nearby Urban Little School. This sense of community can help them count on each other, can help them work together for a safe orderly neighborhood.

Urban Little Schools are proposed as autonomous parts of existing school districts, costing districts no more than most now pay, per child. These schools also can be private, fully independent of local school district control. Pilot Urban Little Schools can start as public or private Charter Schools.

The Urban Little Schools Design is a Practical Plan to Bring the Best Education to our City Children

My "Professional Journey" memoir, after this introductory chapter, traces how I evolved the individualized way of schooling eventually called the Urban Little Schools design; then how others and I developed the concept.

The memoir explains the forerunner of The Urban Little Schools proposed in this book—our experimental Syracuse Institute for Enabling Education (SIEE) elementary school which I directed for ten years in Syracuse, New York. Our experimental school eventually enrolled forty-plus children. The secondary schooling described in the book is a logical extension of this experimental elementary school. I directed our SIEE School from 1970 to 1980, during the period when alternative "free schools" were being started in almost all American cities. Our experimental school, however, was not a "free school."

The prevailing "free school" doctrine of the time said that if left to themselves in a loving intriguing school setting, most children would choose what was best for their own growth. This was described in books such as A.S. Neill's *Summerhill*. [5] I disagreed with the doctrinaire over-simplification expressed in most "free school" books of the time. My experience taught me that for some children this theory was spot-on true. I saw how schools such as Neill's, saved many children who had not fared well in the conventional school's uniform rigidity and lack of response to individual differences. But I was convinced that this was not something to be mandated for all children. I observed that most school children moved ahead best within an individualized learning program, with definite behavior boundaries set by a sensitive listening teacher according to what best fitted each child.

In our experimental SIEE School we did that. We had the best of both worlds—best of the "free school" and the traditional. Love was in the air, children learned in the ways suited to each of them. The children had the security of knowing that the teacher was in charge and boundaries would make sense for all. Our teachers knew each child sensitively and thus could work out individual learning and behavior limits which fitted each child. Intriguing learning opportunities abounded at our school. Each child's basic learning was chosen and sequenced in one to one planning guided by the teacher but sensitive to the child's inputs. And some learning at our school was not all that exciting, such as doing textbook exercises in math. But children at our school could see how such routine work was necessary and how it was in step with their prior knowledge. Children could see themselves learning well.

Thus, our teachers made it their business to listen to every child, but not in response to the classic "free school" question "What do you want to do today?" We seriously listened in order to tune in with each of the children as we sought to answer questions such as how they saw their worlds, what aroused their curiosity, what they seemed to care about deeply, and where their vulnerabilities apparently lay. Then, the teachers in a trusting one to one relationship with the child, worked to fashion learning tuned to the child. Increasingly, in this process children were helped to listen to themselves, to take part in planning the specifics of learning which fitted themselves. Our children could do this because they learned to work with their teachers with openness. Children soon found that our teachers accepted them as they were. Our teachers habitually didn't remind children how they weren't measuring up. Instead, children found they were being helped to appreciate what they were accomplishing and to judge themselves against goals which they understood and which made sense to them.

Our small experimental elementary school had a deep effect on both the adults and so many of the children involved. It has been so heartening for me to follow most of our children, during the last fifteen years, as our former students moved through their lives in differing ways, almost always with marked and independent honesty.

Of course it is difficult to ascribe clear cause and effect—how our SIEE School might take credit for what happened to the children later in their lives. Some of what happened was due to children's families, subsequent schooling and to their other formative experiences. But it was easy for us, teaching at the school, to see how children who stayed at our school for enough time, left able to succeed at college or in other further training.

They left with a sense of who they were as strong individual people. These conclusions are all the more satisfying when I think of the number of our children who came to us, especially during our school's first years, after having a difficult time in the local conventional schools.

Most of the teachers who started this experimental elementary school with me were thirty- to forty-year-old students from a state-funded teacher training program I directed at Syracuse University. This program is described in the memoir. Almost all of the trainees had school-age children of their own. They were helped to train themselves to become teachers who they might want for their own children—teachers who could fit learning to each child. In our training program, teachers tried out individualized learning for themselves. They were helped to plan their own training step by step. In the program, we used many of the same educational ideas teachers might use later with their own students, such as how each teacher-to-be had an essentially non-judgmental one to one relationship with the training program's director, me in this case. Many of the teacher recruitment and training ideas in the ULS design came from what I learned in that teacher training experience.

From my "Professional Journey," the book moves on, to offer the reader another chance to explore the practical promise and soundness of the ULS Idea—why Urban Little Schools will help every child succeed with dignity. Readers spend time as invisible observers at a "how it might be" elementary Urban Little School situated in a remodeled house in a declining part of town. In the "how it might be" secondary Urban Little School, located in formerly unused rooms in an urban church building, readers can see how one to one, the young people are helped to plan in ways so they can get the most from their working for principled community employers and from their learning of traditional high school subjects in the ULS Self-directed Learning Center.

Later chapters talk about the practical nuts and bolts of starting Urban Little Schools—how natural-listener teachers might be recruited and trained, how they could learn to individualize each child's learning, how quality pilot schools might be started within a host public school district, and then how all of this could be facilitated by a strong backup organization which handled the strict annual or biennial evaluation.

To What Extent Does the Climate of Opinion Among Voters in America Today Support the Establishment of Urban Little Schools?

As I read the signs, this is a time when the majority of voters are coming to be receptive to fundamental redesign of urban schooling, such as the Urban Little Schools Idea. A few years ago this might have seemed an unnecessarily complete change. As I sense the mood, the voting public is ready to allow starting afresh in city schooling first, because efforts so far have been largely ineffective. The problem just won't go away. Second, the majority of voters are willing to consider redesign because failing urban schools threaten the culture of contentment within which most of the people who vote, live.

The threat comes because the failing schools are adding to the numbers of poor people who have to stay in our cities' worst environments. This increases what some call our society's underclass—where life seems cheap, where daily young people shoot each other, where the street culture often is so scary many more-privileged Americans simply avoid that part of town, deny its presence.[6] But the underclass threat to complacency is harder and harder to disregard by the privileged when underclass-style casual violence spills over to the suburbs' culture of contentment. The threat of violence spill-over is heightened each time the television news shows graphic pictures in sensational stories such as news accounts of children attempting to gun down schoolmates in privileged middle class schools.

I'll elaborate now why I see this kind of bad news coming together with some important good news, to open public sentiment to the idea of complete redesign of failing urban schools—to bring our best schools to our worst neighborhoods.

First the bad news. One in five children grows up at or below the poverty line, in the USA today.[7] That's the highest poverty rate in the Western industrialized world. Sixty percent of children in Detroit live in poverty, forty four percent in New York City, according to recent figures. That is a 33.8% increase in the last twenty years.[8] Add to this how the gulf between rich and poor in the US has grown dramatically, leaving central cities and close-in suburbs as places where increasingly children grow up often without hope and without significant connection to the world of the economically privileged. In the words of John Kenneth Galbraith, "The present and devastated position of the socially assisted underclass has been identified as ... the most serious social problem of the time, as it is also the greatest threat to long run peace and civility." Galbraith adds, "...the possibility of an underclass revolt deeply disturbing to [the majority of the voters] exists and grows stronger." [9]

Now, some important good news. We are moving to support redesign of failing urban education through state and federal governments' Charter School policies. The Charter School movement is growing, providing practical hope. Let me explain the Charter School possibility here:

States with Charter School enabling legislation, agree to remove hamstringing regulatory and governance requirements and at the same time provide state funding for promising innovative schools. In most states where Charter School status is granted, individuals, private groups or local school systems may submit proposals. Federal grants send money to states to aid in their financing Charter School plans, particularly the startup phase.

By early 1998, the Charter School concept had been embraced by about 30 state departments of education. Typically Charter Schools could be run by public school districts or by private groups. There were then more than 700 Charter Schools operating. As of late 1998, five percent of the school children in Washington DC attended Charter Schools. As this book goes to press, there are over 1700 Charter Schools up and running. In 1999 New York State, one of the last major holdouts, passed Charter School enabling legislation for one hundred Charter Schools despite coolness from many local leaders of the powerful American Federation of Teachers Union in the New York City area. It seems almost a certainty that by the end of the year 2000 almost all of the states will have embraced the Charter School idea.

The new Charter Schools vary widely, as do the states' requirements and guidelines. For example, in Arizona a Charter School can be a for-profit enterprise. Then there was the original Arkansas legislation which required teachers' union approval of all applications and that only local school boards might apply. In the first year only one inquiry was recorded in Arkansas. On the other hand, New Jersey began by permitting applicants to go directly to the State Superintendent, bypassing the unions and local authority.

There, hundreds of applications were received by New Jersey's department of education, within two months after its new Charter School law was passed in 1996. In some states, only minimal funding is advanced for startup expenses. On the average, Charter Schools have been funded at about 80% of the per-pupil funding spent by the local public schools.

Should Urban Little Schools be Autonomous Parts of Existing School Districts or Should They be Private?

Enabled, perhaps, by Charter School status, Urban Little Schools could either be publicly sponsored—parts of public school districts—or they could be fully private and not under the control of elected board of education members.

In the short run, in most cases, it would be simpler and therefore easier to set up private Urban Little Schools separate from the public systems. It would be easier because then there would be no problems of negotiating a contractual relationship with the district—no problem agreeing on a contract which insured Urban Little Schools' autonomy; no problem, either, with having to mesh into a public school system's often entrenched bureaucracy; and there would be no problem co-existing with the district's teacher union which has to protect the jobs of its marginal teachers as well as its good ones.

All this notwithstanding, I strongly advise that every effort be made to have Urban Little Schools part of public school systems, perhaps started by the school systems as Charter Schools in states which have this enabling legislation in place. All the illustrations and descriptions throughout the book are written with the idea in mind that Urban Little Schools are autonomous parts of urban public school districts. Then public control of education could extend to the Urban Little Schools, as I think it should.

Public control of education is not only a cherished tradition, it is one of the best ways we have of keeping vital grass-roots democracy alive and well. Public education, however, won't make democracy work just because the voters elect the school board members. An education fitting for our democracy has to develop skilled and responsible young citizens who know how to listen and respect others and who don't blindly follow the crowd. Students can learn these skills and live these values in the proposed Urban Little Schools. If the Urban Little Schools were part of our public schools we would have the best kind of education for democratic citizenship and social justice coupled with the best in our tradition of publicly controlled schools. If the Urban Little Schools were part of established school districts the result should be stronger local public schools as well as stronger Urban Little Schools.

The public schools could be proud of their ULS component which was effective in helping all students toward a life of honest success. This would aid the local Urban Little Schools to develop with less tension than if they were seen by the city's school district as a competitive threat. The school district would be more inclined to incorporate some of the ULS ideas in their urban schools if those ideas were growing within the district. Also, other school districts would be more likely to copy the plan into their own systems.

In addition, if the Urban Little Schools were an alternative within a host city school district, many more parents would feel secure about sending their children despite the differences between Urban Little Schools and the education parents had gone through themselves. In addition, the resources of the public school district could be used for development of Urban Little Schools. For example some of the district's pre-school teachers could be recruited to be the first pilot Urban Little School teachers.

The Urban Little Schools could work both independently and under the authority of the local board of education, with the relationship facilitated by a detailed contract between the ULS backup organization and the host public school system. A ULS backup organization would oversee the new Urban Little Schools. The backup organization would train its own teachers, plan and equip neighborhood school sites, and develop independent learning materials. With its own funding from grants and other sources, the backup organization would be powerful enough to detach its Urban Little Schools from the local school system if all else failed, assuming a way could be worked out to continue the per-pupil funding, such as grants to parents.

Notes

1   For more on the street code and its place in the life of inner city children, see the participant observation study by the ethnologist Elijah Anderson (1999). *Code of the Street: Decency, Violence and the Moral Life of the Inner City*. New York: W.W. Norton. Also see Geoffrey Canada's description of how it was to grow up switching between the urban street code and the traditional moral work-ethic of his mother's family, in *Fist, Stick, Knife and Gun: A Personal History of Violence in America* (1995). Boston: Beacon Press.

2   See pp. 69–79 in Chapter Two for more comparison of how the ULS way is a fundamental change from the conventional teaching-learning process with its traditional teacher-student roles.

3   Estimates are that 12% of American school children take Ritalin, Prozac or similar drugs. The percentage of urban minority children on these drugs is much higher. (*The Christian Science Monitor,* November 19, 1999, p. 1.)

4   For specific detail see Supplemental Article #2, "The Academic and Job-related Exit Requirements List," and Chapter 10, "Beyond Rhetoric: Specific academic, job-related and character goal criteria against which each Urban Little School can be judged."

5   Neill, A.S. (1960). *Summerhill: A Radical Approach to Childrearing*. New York: Hart Publishing Co.

6   Most writers distinguish between "the underclass" as opposed to "the working lower class." "The underclass" is defined as those people of poverty who because of failing schools and other reasons, tend to find themselves and their children locked into the world of menial, unpleasant, demeaning jobs and in the process can lose hope; "working lower class" people are defined as upwardly mobile, staying with the dirty jobs as a stepping stone out of poverty.

7   From the June 17, 1999 report from The National Center for Children in Poverty, Columbia University as cited in *The Christian Science Monitor*, June 18. 1999. (The national poverty line is drawn at $16,400 annual income for a family of four.)

8   The National Center for Children in Poverty, Columbia University, *News and Issues*, Winter 1996-1997, pp 1-2.

9   Galbraith, John Kenneth. (1992). *The Culture of Contentment*. Boston: Houghton Mifflin, pp. 170 and 180.

2

The Genesis of the Urban Little Schools Ideas — A Professional Journey

A Schooling to Fit Each Child

I got the idea of a schooling based on a one to one teacher-child relationship, when I visited one-room schools in the California foothills. In these one-room schools, the teacher worked with about twelve children from five-through twelve- or fourteen-years-old.

I felt particularly welcomed in the one-room schools because I brought along my snake show which taught the children how snakes lived. At that time, the mid 1950s I was enrolled in nearby Chico State College's graduate teacher preparation program.

When I arrived for a snake show, all of us went out in the schoolyard. I put one of the harmless snakes, which was coiled around my arm, down on the dusty packed dirt of the schoolyard. As it moved away I pointed to the piles of loose dirt behind where the snake's coiled body had pushed. Then I showed the other way snakes moved—"walking" by moving their ribs together and opening them again. To explain this I had stapled small bits of wood to an old black sock. I pushed the bits together and moved them apart like the snake did with its ribs attached to the large transverse scales on its underside. At some point we stopped and quietly watched a snake who was entwined around my arm. I explained how the snake seemed contented and relaxed because it had absorbed the heat from my body.

By that time the children and I seemed relaxed with each other too. I felt good when I left at the end of the morning, visiting with the children and teacher while they got on with their schoolwork. I had interested children in snakes as fascinating creatures, not just something to torment or kill. Also I had learned how it was for them in their one-room school.

Visiting one-room schools opened an exciting possibility for me. I began to imagine myself as teaching in one of these schools. If I taught in a one-room school, I could make sure that each child would succeed. I could be there for every child over the long haul; maybe for two, three or five years or more. I could get to know each of the children and their families. I could work together with each child and set up the kinds of learning which the child needed to succeed. I might have to be strong and restraining with one child, but could be permissive with another who needed to venture forth. Each of us could accept ourselves as we accepted each other. Forty years later I designed a schooling for urban children based on these principles. I called it the Urban Little Schools Idea—what this book is about.

After my two graduate semesters of teaching methods and psychology courses at Chico State's teacher education program, I asked to do my student teaching in a one-room school. It was a school for sawmill families' children located on a mountain road near the Feather River Canyon.

One day a board member of another one-room school district, sixty miles north of San Francisco, came and spent most of the day. Before leaving he offered me the teacher's job in his one-room school—Alpine School. I accepted. In my two years at Alpine School I turned possibility into reality. I made the exciting possibility of individualized learning which I sensed as I visited one-room schools with my snake show, come to life in my own one-room school. That was in the mid fifties. I was twenty-six then.

Alpine School was situated on a road that dead ended to a dirt track three miles up the valley from our ninety-year-old white wooden schoolhouse. At the end of the paved road the brush gave way to a few redwoods and other larger trees. Further over the hills in an easterly direction lay the Napa Valley wine country. A few miles to the south of the schoolhouse was the Valley of the Moon, where Jack London lived and wrote.

I taught fourteen children, first grade through eighth grade, the first year at Alpine School. The second year we had twelve children, from first through sixth grades. I learned how it was perfectly natural and very sensible to listen seriously to Dave who was fourteen and by then had put together his own truck whose power he had geared through two Ford Model A transmissions, hooked up in tandem.[1] Dave lived on a mountain top ranch with his mother. Then there was Janet whose parents had cows down the valley along Mark West Creek, about a half mile from the school. She was just beginning school, at six-years-old.

And there was Jimmy. When I first began as the teacher, community people lowered their voices when talking to me about Jimmy. I got the picture. He was the school's "dumb kid," a ward of the county living with an older couple down the road. These people took good care of him. I like to think that by the time I left Alpine School, two years later, Jimmy was on his way to go through life with newly-felt self-respect. At least I was sure that Jimmy had a sense that his teacher believed in him. After a short time it was obvious that he liked me and the feeling was mutual. Jimmy could see that he was learning, too. He could see his progress in becoming an independent reader and writer and in figuring arithmetically. School no longer was a place where he'd find out daily that he didn't measure up. On the contrary, school was a place that made him feel good about himself—for good reasons which he could see.

As I lived with Jimmy and the others at Alpine School, I found twelve to fourteen interesting people. When I visited each of the children at their homes, they took me on walks to special places in the countryside around their homes. I found that I was accepted by every one of the parents. Their respect felt good. They talked of valuing the school not only for their children's education but as a center where they had a link with the others in and around Alpine Valley. I don't think they saw me judging them or their children. I didn't use grades or other symbols to show who was better than whom. I was there to help each of their children grow to be the capable decent persons they had it in them to be—people who knew that they were significant as they fitted themselves into right places in life. Our trusting relationship became a hallmark of good teaching for me. I built it solidly into my design for the Urban Little Schools along with over three decades of other experience about how a teacher can reach each student.

In Alpine School it simply felt natural to me to help each one of the children orchestrate their unique pattern of human essentials in ways so they would succeed and so those around them would be helped. I began to see how children had different learning styles, too. Some were mainly intuitive in the way they read difficult words, for instance. They looked at the print and out popped the correct word from their mouths; others seemed to rely heavily on decoding words and doing spelling logically—using the sounds of the consonants and vowels to unlock and spell unknown words. Of course you had to fit learning to each child. How could you teach in any other way? It not only made sense to teach in tune with each child; it was the only decent thing to do.

I found that it came natural to me to want to appreciate each child, too—to provide a mirror for every one of the children which showed them to be the special persons they were. Often I'd find myself lightly referring to some special thing about this child or that one, as we lived together in our little world. Some needed a hug, too, but in those days I hadn't yet learned that I not only could hug others but needed hugs myself. One child in our school needed to know that I was strong enough emotionally to keep him in control—strong enough not to let him do what later he might have felt rotten about doing. Children had to feel safe to be themselves in our school. That meant that I had to make sure our boundaries were fair and were kept by us all.

We shared each of our worlds, in our one-room school. I invited all the children to share their interests and they did. I shared my interests with the children, too.

For example I always had been fascinated by ships and harbors. So one day, all the children, three parents and I drove to San Francisco and were treated to a tour of the liner Lurline, then in the Matson Lines' Pacific Coast to Hawaii service. It was gleaming white after just having been restored to its old grandeur from the previous few years when it served as a troop ship during World War II. We were met at the top of the gangplank by one of the ship's officers. He gave us a complete tour which included our little column threading its way through its cavernous engine rooms. Then we drove down the waterfront about a half mile to the fire department docks. We ate our lunches on the top deck of one of the city's most powerful fireboats. We could look up at the underside of the Bay Bridge while we enjoyed the smells and sights of the harbor. A few feet from where we were eating, on both sides of us, the fireboat's water monitors stood at the ready to shoot streams of water higher than the top deck of a ship as big as the Lurline.

Back at Alpine School we recreated the whole San Francisco bay, in relief, on a table surface that took up about a fifth of our school. I read books to the children about ships; the county librarian filled our school with more books. It made me feel so good to watch the children proudly explain our harbor to parents and guests.

Then I enjoyed helping the children to invent plays and do other things which brought our little out-of-the-way community together. We put on Christmas plays each year for the people in and around Alpine Valley. Parents made the plays occasions when all could linger over pot-luck dinners. I used this experience when I designed the elementary Urban Little Schools to be places where parents and others living nearby could learn to know and depend on each other.

Our school plays benefited from the range of children's ages. This gave us wide dramatic possibilities. With a one-room school you have children big enough to act as adults and others are small enough to pretend to be toddlers. I remember one of our plays had Santa come to a toy shop where he made all the toys come to life for the night. As we put the story together, children chose toys each wanted to become. Then, at the end of the play Santa left in a specially prepared rocket which worked. Well, it worked so long as the child behind the curtain snapped the rocket's tow string at just the right moment in our drama.

And at Alpine School I learned a lot about how to build each child's independence in reading and writing. I had to teach myself how to teach children to read. I had to, in order to figure out the next step for each child so it would fit into what the child already had learned and would fit the child's learning style. At Chico State I had learned how to teach reading by taking children through the reading textbooks and using the exercises specified in the teacher's manuals for the textbook series. It was based on having classroom teachers fit all their children into three groups: a top group for children who learned easily with the system, a middle group for those who took longer to learn but eventually did, and a bottom group who didn't seem to take to the system.

According to this system, which is still used in about half of the primary grade classrooms in America, the teacher begins by explaining the seatwork exercises to be done by each of the three groups' children at their desks. These exercises lead children to practice the new words and expressions introduced that day in the reading textbooks, along with phonic elements which need to be practiced. Then while the children in two of the reading groups are doing their seatwork, the teacher hears each child in the remaining group read out loud a paragraph or so from the textbook, round-robin style. Every child reads orally, this way, each day. Every textbook story is progressively more difficult than the last. The stories are dull and shallow, because they are constructed as vehicles to emphasize the new words and elements being taught that day, rather than written to be captivating for their young readers. The most common series of textbooks in use when I began teaching was William S. Gray's series which began with the "Dick and Jane" stories.

Early on, as I observed teachers using this system, I noticed many of the less able children in each group often seemed to be embarrassed by their halting and stumbling as they read out loud while others who didn't falter when they read, followed in their textbooks. That didn't make sense to me. The system obviously didn't fit some children while it was not challenging for some. Children had only one way to learn regardless whether the system was the best for them. Then too, if I were a parent, I wouldn't want my little girl or boy to come to school each day and see they didn't measure up, to learn that books and reading caused them to be embarrassed in front of their schoolmates. Neither would I want my child to feel superior at the expense of the struggling readers.

But the system was simple and easy for teachers to manage. Almost anyone could learn to do it by watching a demonstration for a couple of hours. You didn't have to know what children needed to learn in order to read independently; only how to follow the system described step by step in the teacher's manual. The manual even told the teacher the exact words to say to the children.

Never mind that most children in this system learned books and reading were dull; never mind some children learned books and reading caused them to feel inadequate in their and others' eyes. Never mind the children. The system was easily manageable for even an inept teacher.

When I began at Alpine School I knew this system for teaching reading didn't make sense if you cared about each child. There was no doubt in my mind that there must be a better way. With only my fourteen children from six- to thirteen-years-old, I could try out a new and individualized approach to the teaching of reading. Individualizing was the only way to go; the range of needs in my class was too great to use group-based ways of teaching reading even if I had been inclined to do so.

The task was clear. I had to teach myself to teach reading to fit every child—so each child succeeded. To do this I had to find out what children needed to know in order to get on their own and then how to help them practice until they became fluent. Beyond that I needed to help the independent readers use their reading to learn and to enjoy books and reading. To teach myself the needed subject background I studied the teacher's manuals of the reading textbooks, located in the bookcase next to my desk. Along with instructions for each lesson, the manuals had summaries of the subject content that was being taught at each level. I had a full set of these standard teachers' manuals for all elementary curriculum levels because we enrolled children in all the elementary grades, one through eight the first year. By going through these books I gleaned the essential elements the textbook writers felt children needed to learn. I then applied this knowledge to what I figured each of the children needed to learn next as I worked with them one to one. The beginners read aloud with me, one to one, every day. No child read out loud while another child followed in a duplicate copy of the reading textbook.

I gave top priority to reading and writing, as these were the basic skills each child needed for independent learning. In arithmetic also, I focused on what each child needed in order to succeed.

With this one-room school experience, I was able to see how it was quite possible for a teacher to make sure that every child succeeded with dignity and what's more, each of the children knew they were succeeding, all along the way. My way was practical and possible.

I was developing some of the elements I later included in the Urban Little Schools design, but of course for me, a beginning teacher at that time, this wasn't a way to reform schooling, it was just teaching in a way that made sense. My job was to help each child learn the basics and I was doing it in a school where each person mattered.

I next taught in a suburban elementary school near Stanford University. While at Alpine School, I had been invited by a senior professor at Stanford's School of Education, Paul Hanna, to join his doctoral program. Unbeknownst to me, one of his former students, our county supervisor, had recommended me.

During the intervening summer I looked for a teaching job near Stanford. I knew I needed to be able to keep on responding to each child as a unique and special person and was intrigued with how I might do this with a class more than twice the size of the one I had at Alpine School. I found the job I wanted, working for a principal who was a fellow student at Stanford, Claude Norcross. Claude let me do things my way after he saw that I could manage my classroom of sixth graders. The first two years at Ladera I taught sixth graders, the last year I was one of the school's two second grade teachers.

At Ladera I taught classes of just under thirty children. I had to invent ways to reach each child—as I had been doing at Alpine—but do it with more organization and efficiency. For example, in our second grade, I had each of our fledgling readers using library books to practice their reading instead of the Scott Foresman "Dick and Jane" reading series then in use in the school. I got the idea of each student practicing in a book which was right for the child from a teacher's article Claude gave me. For my children to practice, I used the "easy reading" books the county had set aside for the remedial reading teachers who worked with older children who were seen as "behind." Most of these books had inviting story lines and were easy enough so the children could read with the speed they needed to develop reading fluency. For children who weren't independent enough to read the "easy reading" books, I assembled a mini-library of pre-primers, the first slim booklets in a reading textbook series. They could choose their reading books from this shelf. I helped most fledgling readers begin the first page or so in their books so they would sense the setting, plot line and so they knew the names of the characters. In our second grade classroom, I arranged the seating so those children who needed my help with an unknown word could get it quickly and keep reading fast enough to let the story's context help the child figure out harder words after an initial quick sounding-out.

In my second grade class, children wrote in ways that encouraged them to do it creatively yet not be held back by lack of spelling and form knowledge. Typically I would read each of their stories to the class without mentioning the author. For me this was an essential. What children were writing deserved to be taken seriously and this was one way I could do that. But it was a challenge for me to help each of the writers so they would feel that their piece was worth being listened to. In most cases I was undoing what the child had learned in first grade—that writing was to please the teacher, was an exercise that usually resulted in red marks on your paper.

Already, on entering my second grade class, about one out of five of my children had writer's block. They would stare at the blank piece of paper unless I got them started, unless I got them in touch with a story idea which might catch them up. Often, for these children, I would write their first few sentences from dictation until I felt they were off on their own. I did this without calling attention to the child I was helping because it was a part of my talking with many of the children about their stories, as I circulated around the room helping children spell words.

I think our daily Newstime sessions helped a lot here. I wrote in front of the children each morning, sparked by stories from the children's lives which they would volunteer in these sessions. When I was at a loss for words, I would ask for help from the children. Putting thoughts and feelings into words sometimes isn't as easy as falling off a log.

At the end of that second grade year I felt so good about how the children were learning to read and write. No child made less than a year's progress in the school's reading curriculum. Many jumped ahead two or more grade levels. Every single child wrote stories to be proud of—lots of them. At the end of the year we were surprised by Arthemise Samuelson, our school librarian, who in a special all-school award assembly gave us her new citation for the class which took out the most books from the library—more than twice as many as any other class. [2]

I continued to develop these ideas for individualizing children's learning of reading, writing and use of the library (explained in Supplementary Article #3) after I left Ladera School and began at Stanford, full-time as a graduate assistant supervising elementary teacher trainees.

Young People Who Think and Act on their Informed Independent Judgment

As important as was learning to read and write at one's own pace and in a way that excited each child, an even more important goal was beginning to arise within me. That was to begin children toward thinking for themselves in effective ways rather than their blindly following their peer groups or conventional wisdom. This goal is now implemented in the Urban Little Schools' design explained in this book.

From my study at Stanford, I began to feel a growing commitment to the idea of every child using reading and writing for individual thought and inquiry. I wanted them to use these skills and their excitement derived from writing and reading to help them become aware of themselves and to understand our world's current problems.

But why didn't I see the schools doing this in a high priority way? After the Great Depression struggle and World War II bloodshed many voices could be heard exhorting the schools to prepare citizens who could and would help us prevent the next needless destruction of life and hope. But I didn't see the bland language arts and social studies teaching in public schools preparing citizens to do this—to understand and cope with a fast changing and ominous world. History and civics textbooks, for example, were dull and tedious; they lacked sharply delineated descriptions of problems past and present. Why? To explore this question, for my doctoral dissertation topic I chose to study the circumstances around why the *Building America* social studies pamphlet series was withdrawn from the schools in the late forties. The thirty page pamphlets used *Life Magazine* style photo-journalism to present vividly the history and issues behind particular social problems. They were published monthly, at first by the Society for Curriculum Study and then by the National Education Association and used in junior and senior high social studies classes. Millions of pamphlets were bought by schools.

My dissertation, after two years' study and many interviews, documented how the pamphlets were withdrawn from the schools as a result of calculated innuendo publicized by the press. The charge was that the booklets were "a communist conspiracy" of progressive educators. For evidence, the books' detractors took passages and illustrations out of context, which gave an erroneous idea of what the publications were saying. Also, material was taken from booklets published in the early thirties and then was used to substantiate the claim that *Building America* was written contrary to current public policy—after the earlier policy had changed. An example was the "Russia" booklet published during the War when we were allied with the Soviet Union. The booklet described the Soviet Union as a dictatorship but also talked about its advances in universal education and healthcare. But after the war such an evenhanded description didn't fit with the growing sentiment that the Soviet Union was our enemy. [3]

School boards canceled subscriptions to the monthly pamphlets as a reaction to the *Building America* booklets being tried as "communist tools" in the courtroom of the press, with no evidence that could stand up in a court of law. Almost no administrators or teachers who used the pamphlets fought back. The pamphlets disappeared from the schools. Bound volumes of the booklets were pulled from school libraries simply because of the allegations and sensational charges published in the newspapers. I remember reading the meeting minutes of one school board, stating simply it was withdrawing the books "because they are controversial."

This study sobered me, as might be imagined. I learned how vulnerable our schools were. From my research I learned how groups who wielded power in our society, relatively easily could cause meaningful content to be withdrawn from the current and past history that was being taught to young people in our schools.

At the same time my research illuminated and defined sharply the basic question as I came to see it. This was: Given the difficulties I learned from my study of *Building America*, how might our schools best equip young people to become instrumental in a society which could withstand with vigor whatever the next economic dislocation, war, or other crisis might be?

A part of the answer was that we had a universally accepted source of understanding and content—the library—which could help young people become independent thinkers. This could be so if schools taught so young people became excited about the library's breadth of content, its variety of points of view, and the depth of its collection. Then the library would become a place where young people wanted to go to satisfy their curiosity, to follow ideas, to entertain themselves, to feed an awakened desire to know. In the process each of them could become skilled at individual inquiry as they came to know the library like the back of one's hand. This library-centered idea is now one of the basic elements in the Urban Little Schools design.

At San Jose State College, where I taught as an education professor while finishing my dissertation at nearby Stanford, I was able to weave together the two strands which were to undergird a library-centered individualized elementary schooling. In teaching the history of education I focused on what it might mean if Americans had an education which equipped them to understand the great issues of their society. In my children's literature class I taught teachers-to-be how to use a children's library and its books to make learning to read an adventure of substance and reward. I emphasized how they might help children grow to be adults who used books and reading to find out, to immerse themselves in the lives and times of people. I helped each of my students introduce inviting books to children.

As a laboratory, we organized a program for San Jose community children who could read but didn't choose to do so for recreation. The sessions met at the college's library. My children's literature students worked there with one or two children apiece, introducing the youngsters to inviting children's books which I knew could be helpful in opening up the pleasure of reading for oneself.

During this time, I was learning right alongside my students. My children's literature course prompted me to read piles of children's books I hadn't read up to that time. As I found gems, I would bring them into class and share them with the students in my lectures.[4]

Each Step Informs the Next Step

I took my next job, after I received my EdD degree from Stanford, with the idea that maybe I could build that library-centered elementary school where all children learned in ways that best fit each of them. After my initial explorations with Frank Chase, the dean at The University of Chicago's

School of Education I felt I might do that on the job he offered me at the University's venerable Laboratory School.

I was appointed vice principal of the Laboratory School's Lower School and after one year became the principal. We had about four hundred children in the Lower School. Many were the university's faculty children. Others were from families in the local neighborhood who wanted to stay in the city but didn't want their children going to the local Chicago schools. The university underwrote a significant part of the cost of the Lab School. The Lab School was free to do what it wanted without anything but perfunctory regulation from the Illinois State Education Department because it was a private school, because it was famous for experimentation and because it had the prestige of the University of Chicago behind it. Our teachers did not have to have teaching credentials and there were no other restrictions imposed by the state.

The school was begun by John Dewey and his wife Evelyn, at the turn of the century. John Dewey's thinking, in *Democracy and Education* [5] spoke to my own ideas. He wrote about how a school might educate children to think about the great problems of the times. He wrote about school children who could learn so that they would be able to define and redefine problems for themselves and then be able to think and act as citizens on the basis of a belief in the dignity of each person. The school he talked about would nurture each child, help each one of them, step by step, to learn how to think for themselves in penetrating ways. [6]

I arrived at the Laboratory School full of enthusiasm for building a library-centered school but short on experience in working to bring that about in an established organization. By the time I left, in three years, I had learned that I was both an effective education inventor and a capable administrator. But I had also learned that school administration wasn't my cup of tea. I didn't want to spend so much of my energy to make an organization run smoothly. Also I didn't like administrative politics where being open and trusting often seemed naive. Some of the Lab School's administrative tension arose because most of my fellow administrators saw the school as an elite prep school. I saw it as a center for school experimentation. Yet I accepted my administrative role in order to work step-by-step with teachers to invent a schooling that fitted each of the children as they became excited about books, reading, writing and the library.

The teachers and I had plenty to be proud of. In the three years I was at The Lab School. We had made some important changes in children's learning of reading and writing. Here are examples of these changes:

(1) I hired hard-to-find teachers who could pilot the plan for a library-centered school where children learned in ways that fit each child. When I arrived at the Lab School, I made it my highest priority to find new teachers who lived with children in ways that fit the kind of teaching-learning I wanted to bring about. There were several openings because of the Lab Schools' high teacher turnover rate caused by graduate students' wives leaving when their husbands got their degrees. I looked for experienced teachers who might want to come despite how they would have to give up their tenure and other job security they had on their public school jobs, to join us at the Lab School. That was a big order—finding magnificent needles in the haystack of teachers out there. So I decided to advertise nationally for people who listened to children, who wanted their children to read and write with relish as the children moved through an individualized program which responded to each of them individually.

One of these new Lab School teachers was Eileen Tway. I flew down to Cincinnati after Eileen responded to my ad in *The Saturday Review of Literature*.[7] I spent a morning in her classroom. Was I glad I came! In a few minutes it settled over me that I was watching a teacher who listened to each child in her classroom—a person with a constant and pervasive sense of how the children were getting on with their individual lives—as the best kind of mother does with each child in her family. So of course this teacher knew what to say to each child, what special boundaries or other unique plans should be implemented for certain children, where to lead the class as a whole. What she said and did reflected her awareness of each child. I was seeing a teacher who hadn't compromised her responsiveness to each child in order to control the class. Control came out of being in touch sensitively with each child. Being in harmony with each child was at the heart of it all.

I spoke to the principal about how impressed I was. He valued Eileen and hated to think of her leaving but didn't want to stand in the way of her receiving this appointment at the prestigious Laboratory School. Eileen took my offer of teaching third grade after we had a long talk about what she wanted for each child and what I wanted. She wanted to be where what she was doing with each child, might spread to other teachers.

(2) With examples such as Eileen at the Lab School, other teachers could see what I had in mind and person by person many on our staff followed suit. By the time I left, most of our Lower School teachers were using children's books extensively in their teaching of reading rather than using traditional reading texts. That meant a switch from a uniform group teaching approach to an individualized reading program. This was particularly noteworthy as just down the hall and around the corner was the university's reading and language arts center originally started by William S. Gray, creator of The "Dick and Jane" reading textbooks.

(3) Also by the time I left the Lab School in three short years, it had come a long way toward being a library-centered learning place. The Lower and Middle School library was completely remodeled and enlarged. The new layout was much easier to use, much more inviting to children. It was a child-friendly place and was fast becoming the vital hub of the school. The library's acquisitions budget was increased dramatically. Staff was added.

We organized a paperback bookstore in the Lower and Middle Schools' lobby where our children entered the building. It was staffed and run by parents and cost the Lab Schools nothing. The little store was bulging with paperbacks for children, started with liberal donations from the major publishers and distributors. The publicity was good for their sales during those years when children's paperbacks were just beginning to come out enmasse. The publicity was good for the Laboratory Schools' image, too.

The enthusiasm spread to teachers, to children and to parents who opened their pocketbooks for children to buy books. During my last year at the Lab School, the little store sold 8000 new and used books to Lower and Middle School children. Our tiny powerhouse bookstore became well known across the country after being lauded in a double page *Saturday Review* feature story showing pictures of children absorbed in decisions as to what book to buy as they stood in mountains of inviting paperbacks. Our school was awash in books and the children were choosing to read them. Those highlights make me feel good when I think back at the changes that I helped bring about during my three years at the Lab School. But increasingly I was becoming restless. Despite trying not to, I became involved in the sticky politics of our administrative group.

I felt I needed to find a new job where I could be free to build on what I had learned so far. I liked the freedom given to professors at universities and I wanted to work where I would feel a warm welcome to get on with my work as an educational inventor. I wanted to develop further my ideas for an individualized schooling where every child would have an even chance to succeed both at school and later on jobs—ideas which eventually were incorporated in my Urban Little Schools design. I hoped to find a job where I might do that.

How to Train the Teachers

I found that job at Syracuse University. There, I was assured that I would be given a great deal of freedom to develop my ideas. During my interviews at Syracuse, I talked about helping children to learn in ways that fit each of them. Could I continue my work to develop schooling where each child successfully could learn to read and write, could enjoy books writing and reading, and so all children could use their skill independently in their lives? I was promised that I would be able to work with the teachers who were out in the schools. Also I was given the expectation that probably I could be funded with grants to develop my ideas. These promises and possibilities worked out to be fact.

I received a grant to develop a partnership teacher training program at Syracuse. Partnership teacher training was to train two half-time teachers for one classroom—one for the morning and the other for the afternoon.

The New York State Department of Education, which was offering the grant, wanted someone to train well educated mothers for teaching on a partnership basis during those days of baby boom teacher shortage. They wanted a program which would fit this population of people and meet the need for more teachers. The rest was open.

I could do teacher education so it focused on each teacher trainee as an individual in the same way I hoped their teaching children would do. My trainees might become teachers who thought of each child first and conventional tradition in teaching, second. Having two teachers who knew every child in their classroom would make it easier to be aware of the child as a unique person. There would be two perspectives on each child, two people to discuss how best to help the child.

Partnership teachers, who were parents themselves, would have the predisposition to carry out a schooling they wanted for their own children—an education which fitted each one of their children carried out by teachers who listened to children. They could approach children's learning as sensitive loving parents might think of educating their own children.

In order to recruit people who were good listeners, I asked my friend and colleague Dick Pearson who trained school guidance counselors, to select trainees for our new program as if he were selecting the kind of people who might become the best counselors. We had a good sized group from which to select because our offer was attractive. Our grant paid for all the training. We offered parents, whose children were now in school, a chance to get their teaching credential, to continue their parenting during the days, plus receive a master's degree free of cost. In the end we had about one hundred people apply and selected thirty-three. All were women. Almost all had school-age children. Only two men had applied.

I designed the keystone for the whole training program to be a one to one responsive link between the program's director, the role I took, and each of the trainees. I wanted my role to reflect the role that I wanted these trainees to adopt when they worked with their own students.

The first four half-time semesters—two university academic years—were planned around this intensive one to one relationship of each trainee and her teacher. I planned that each trainee and I would exchange a substantial journal every other week and would have a face-to-face conference during each intervening week. In these weekly contacts I would help each trainee learn how to learn the kind of teaching that might best fit with her experience, goals and nature. The teacher-to-be would share in the planning and then carry it out herself. In the process she should learn a lot about how to guide her own learning in ways that fit her prior experience and that were consistent with who she was as a person. This individualized teacher training concept is now built into the Urban Little Schools teacher training plan explained in Chapters Nine and Twelve.

Our five semester, half-time partnership training program built up to the last semester where I would find a job for each of our teacher education students as a paid partnership teacher or in another paid half-time teaching assignment. During this fifth semester each one would have my continued one to one support while on the job.

But what about grades? Grading students in the usual way, would simply be out of the question. Each student needed to think for herself while planning and carrying out her own program—not work to please me for a grade. The two of us had to proceed with a trusting relationship as we planned and as she carried out the plan. This was the kind of trust that made it OK for both of us to be open in our conferences and journals. We could be honest about our occasional self-doubt. As I saw it, if I were to judge students in the traditional university way—grading students as to who pleased me most, who was better than whom—I stood a strong risk of casting a subtle chill on this essential trusting working relationship between each student and myself. I had to neutralize the grading role.

I decided to announce to the trainees before the program began that I would give every one of them a "B" grade each semester. This would satisfy the university requirement for grades, satisfy the School of Education master's degree program's requirement for a minimum "B" average, and satisfy our program's need for a working relationship of trust. The last thing I wanted to encourage was more "find out what the teacher wants and give it back to him, explicitly" mentality, which I assumed was ingrained in many of these good people we had selected for our program. I assumed this because they all had made it successfully through a schooling to please the teacher, all the way from kindergarten through their college bachelor's degrees. I titled the new program, The Mid-career Training for Partnership Teaching—MTPT for short.

But we didn't have even one local area classroom where I could show my teachers-to-be how they might teach children in an individualized responsive way. Nor did we have a book for our trainees to read which would give them a practical description of such a teaching-learning way.

Bit by bit it became clear to me: I would have to set up an unconventional individualized schooling for children in the schools. The needed demonstration would show our teachers-to-be the down-to-earth practicalities of what I meant, with real live children. Then they could see how they might do what they were learning to do in their own educations but do it in ways appropriate to children in a public school classroom. How could I possibly set up such a demonstration classroom taught by local teachers who didn't understand what I was talking about?

A light went on inside. What about Eileen Tway who I had brought to the Lab School? I called her and told her about the plans for our MTPT Program. Then I sketched the idea for her involvement which had come to me: She could be hired as a graduate assistant working for our MTPT Program. That would provide free tuition and a small income. Then she could get further income by working as a partnership teacher in a school nearby. I would find another graduate student for the other half of the partnership—a graduate student who could show teachers how to individualize in mathematics as Eileen showed teachers how to individualize in reading and writing. In the process she could get her doctorate. In our MTPT Program she could participate in training teachers to do what I knew she could do so well with children. This would help her later teach her own teacher trainees as a professor of education who had graduated from Syracuse University. She agreed. [8]

I talked with a principal I knew about Eileen and the idea of our Program's taking over one of her second grade classrooms with Eileen and a math teacher who also had a proved elementary teaching record, teaching as a partnership. The principal was Marian Beauchamp, who administered a "middle class" school on the fringe of Syracuse. She agreed in principle. I decided to go ahead even if we didn't have it all firmed up. Luck was with me. Marian became assistant superintendent in that district the next year. Thus I had a person at the top who was on our side.

I also discussed the idea of a demonstration center, with Jack Murray, the principal of Seymour School, an inner city school at Syracuse. I had taught a workshop for teachers at Jack's School during the summer before. I liked him a lot when we worked together then. He came across to me as a down to earth person and someone with whom I could work well.

As we talked, neither Jack nor I had a clear idea how we might work it all out—how we might carry out a partnership training program for individualized teaching of children in his school. We both trusted that the two of us could work out the plan because we shared the vision of helping each child succeed, step by step. We were sure of each other's capability and we could count on each other.

We never did come up with a smooth plan before the Program began. We would work it out step by step. After my Lab School experience I found it easy to trust this way of innovating and it seemed to fit Jack's style. Anyway it simply was impractical to try to involve the district's bureaucracy with our fledgling ideas. We knew the administrators "downtown" would want definite ideas and final plans to discuss. But as I said, both Jack and I wanted to see what developed at each step of the way and bit-by-bit make plans and figure out solutions based on what was needed to move things ahead to the next stage. This was a process guided by our conviction that it was possible to train teachers who would be able to make sure every single child succeeded as an independent learner and as a self-respecting person. We knew that once we had teachers able to do this, we could focus on to the next step: to design classroom teaching and learning situations where they could be helped to do what they were trained to do.

Jack resolved the problem of how much and what to say to "downtown" by simply not involving the administrative bureaucracy with any of the fledgling ideas which we were discussing about how we might merge our MTPT Program with Jack's Seymour School.

Jack had the kind of clearness and faith that I have not often found in school administrators. Most with whom I had worked were cordial but had learned to play it on the safe side in order to survive and be promoted in their often stressful jobs. Perhaps some of Jack's willingness to take risks for the sake of children, came from being on the edge of death when he was a sergeant tank commander during the African campaign in World War II. A German hand grenade exploded inside his tank and blew him all apart . But somehow, as they do in the M*A*S*H show on TV, the medics got his broken body out of the wreckage and the field doctors put him back together again. He returned home at about thirty, to be a school principal with the financial security of a full disability pension from the Veterans Administration and a clear sense of what mattered most in life. Jack died in the late 1970s.

We launched our MTPT Program in 1967 with the thirty-three women we had selected. In our one to one conferences and in our lengthy journals, each person in the Program and I not only talked about what the next training steps might be for her, we talked about the Program—what we might do in our

Wednesday morning group training sessions and in the other Program activities. So much of what emerged as group activities came about because of the weekly intensive contact I had with each of the people in the Program.

As mentioned earlier, during the first four half-time semesters, each person in the Program prepared to teach elementary school children in a responsive individualized way. Each trainee learned the basic idea by using it herself—by doing it in her training program while she learned the nuts and bolts of individualization for children. Then in the fifth, and last semester, each trainee would try it for herself in a paid job with children, working half-time as a partnership teacher or in another half-time role in the schools.

During the first year, my immediate goal was to introduce our trainees to how they might teach children responsively in the schools. I wanted our trainees to see how this might fit within a broader context of helping each child to develop integrity and independence of mind. As some of the content for students to learn, I put my extensive library of books about psychology and history of education out to become our program's library. Then too, Eileen and I introduced many of our favorite children's books, which trainees might read themselves and might read to children. Thus each trainee was responsible for reading children's books and adult books then discussing her thoughts and experience arising from this reading, in her twice-monthly journals. Often in my journals or conferences I would suggest additional readings, to trainees.

In some of our Program's Wednesday morning group sessions, Eileen and I showed how teachers might find out the specific skills each child already possessed for reading and writing independently. Then Eileen and I taught trainees so much of what we had learned as we helped children take the next best step for each of them on the road to becoming a thoughtful independent reader and writer. During these Wednesday sessions also we had many guest speakers explaining everything from how to analyze children's status in mathematics, to helping children come to understand themselves as growing people.

People in the Program spent a great deal of time out in the schools during this first year, particularly in Marion Beauchamp and Jack Murray's schools. In these schools they worked with individual children, practicing how to analyze a child's writing and reading status, helping beginning children to learn phonic and common word elements. Trainees did such things as introducing inviting easy to read books to those children who were at the place where they needed the practice, and discussing good children's literature with those children who were fluent readers.

During the first year of the Program, I worked out the specifics of the second year. I found a graduate student in the mathematics education program, Leon Graebel, who was interested in doing his dissertation around the idea of individualizing children's learning to compute. I suggested that he work out a way to analyze what each child needed to do to move ahead in skillfully adding, subtracting, multiplying and dividing. Leon did that and we duplicated his materials for analyzing each child's status, for our trainees. He liked the idea of working in Marian Beauchamp's school afternoons in partnership with Eileen who would teach in the mornings.

During this second year, Eileen and Leon's partnership would give me a strong assist as they demonstrated in their shared classroom what it might be like if teachers taught children in individualized ways so that each could succeed and each child felt the teacher was in his or her corner. Even though we had no books or audio visual materials to explain this, teachers-to-be would see it in action in Eileen and Leon's partnership.

But what about this kind of a demonstration with inner city children? Increasingly our trainees wanted to learn more about helping less privileged children to use the schools as a way out of the poverty cycle. Most of our students, during the first year of the Program, had chosen to spend a great deal of time observing in Jack's Seymour School, located in a poor part of town. This was during the time of President Johnson's "War on Poverty."

As that first year progressed, Jack and I realized that we needed a hands-on situation where the trainees could practice how to individualize, especially in reading and writing. Trainees needed a classroom where they could learn the heart of it: listening to each child, knowing where the student was on the road to becoming a fluent writer and reader, and knowing what to try next to help the student ahead. Trainees needed to participate in a classroom rich in language experiences for children—where each child would get lots of practice writing and reading in meaningful ways, lots of practice using language mechanics and conventions. Then, ideally, trainees needed to take part in teaching which orchestrated all this so every child might leave the classroom at the end of the school year with an exciting place in her or his life for reading and written expression. And we would need this kind of a demonstration classroom at Seymour School, when school began in September, just a few months away.

None of the teachers at Seymour were individualizing along those lines. All the teachers took the children through the school district's uniform curriculum which sorted the children into levels or "instructional groups" in which all in each group were supposed to do the prescribed exercises the same way and at the same pace.

I decided to teach the classroom myself. I would introduce our people to individualizing with inner city children, by running a demonstration classroom at Seymour School. Jack assigned me, as the teacher of record, to Room 205, starting in September of our Program's second year.

Jack handled it, within the system, in a very low-profile way. He simply didn't tell the school district people "downtown" that he needed a teacher to fill a third grade vacancy until I was ensconced in that third grade class-room and had already begun. Maybe he mentioned it casually to someone on some layer of the downtown bureaucracy, but essentially he kept all the levels of administrators in the dark until it was too late to change what we had launched.

Now, as I am writing this, what Jack did seems unbelievable from what I know of school bureaucracies. And especially from what I remember about the assistant superintendent for curriculum and instruction who had the overseeing responsibility for Jack's school. He was known far and wide as a bureaucrat's bureaucrat. He seemed reluctant to move to anything new which might be difficult for the least able teacher to handle. He almost never began any new project until it had been proved beyond the shadow of a doubt. He had gone up through the ranks taking care of himself and his people. They always seemed safe within the bureaucracy and firmly in con-trol of what happened in their schools—no big failures. Not much could go wrong because his administrators didn't take risks.

So, without making sure the assistant superintendent knew what we were going to do, we did it. I was responsible for teaching twenty-eight third graders in Room 205 along with teaching eight partnership teacher trainees in the morning and another eight who came in the afternoon. Each group of three or four children thus had two teachers who worked in partnership.

Over the summer I had made semi-partitions around the perimeter of Room 205 so that each of the morning shift of eight teachers could work with her own little group of children. Then their afternoon partners took over in that partitioned space. Partners varied their shifts so each of them could experience the morning and the afternoon routines.

In the middle of each morning I taught the whole class in our Newstime which was the centerpiece of our morning program, taking about forty-five minutes. The children sat on a soft rug we put in the middle of our classroom. I rigged a microphone plugged into the classroom record player so when I was down on one knee next to a child who wanted to share news, everyone in the room heard every word each of us spoke. I wanted to show our trainees how Newstime could be the best reading and writing learning time during the day—especially if the interviewing teacher listened carefully, asked questions of children who contributed and then responded to each child's "news" by writing thoughtful reactions in large print. Sometimes the teacher might simply write a restatement of what had been said. Often the writing would be laced with humor and emotion. Trainees saw what an important learning time this was for every one of our third graders. Some of these inner city children, who were not yet savvy about reading and writing, learned how reading and writing was talk-written-down—important talk that meant something to the child and to me. Others learned about punctuation, spelling, form and other conventions. We all saw how writing might capture key human emotion, exciting thoughts and could help us all laugh at ourselves from time to time. Many of our children came from homes where reading and writing were seldom in evidence. I wanted them to see how they could be caught up in writing and reading, which distilled the stuff of life and relationships, and have it all mirrored on sheet after sheet of writing that emerged from my sharing with children there in front of the group. We taped all these sheets to the walls of our room. Children then could take the sheets home. It was a special treat to walk out of our room at 3:00 with a roll of the morning's Newstime sheets tucked under your arm. [9]

Room 205 was a learning place for the sixteen people from our Program as well as for the children. Our teachers read inviting children's books to their children. They often exchanged journals and conferenced one to one with each of their children. Children dictated their journals to another teacher if they couldn't write well enough to put down what they wanted to say to their own teacher. Our MTPT trainees could focus particularly on how to help each child become independent in writing and reading. In this environment, our teachers could learn how to listen to children, to find out what particular children needed to learn and then step by step work out with the children how they might be successful in doing that. Our MTPT people also got to know the children's parents, usually going to the homes of the children with whom they worked closely. They had learned from Eileen and me how they might find out quickly what a child's next step should be in learning to write and to read. Much of the teaching of the regular phonics combinations and the most common words was done in games. [10]

Our trainees analyzed each child's status in learning arithmetic fundamentals, with Leon's materials. The trainees made sure children mastered one step before going to the next. They followed the sequence in the school district's mathematics curriculum.

During our noon break in Room 205, the morning group of trainees and I would eat lunch together with the incoming afternoon crew. So often the morning group and I were high from our intensive time working with the children. This resulted in plenty of laughs, easy emotion and spontaneity breaking out from us in the morning crew and infecting the afternoon people. By the time the children had returned, the eight afternoon people had set aside the rest of their lives and centered on how they might reach each child in Room 205.

What a productive time for all of us, there in Room 205 at Seymour School. I felt so good, at the end of our three-and-a-half months together there. Each of our trainees left knowing how to find out what a child needed in order to move ahead successfully at school. They had tried themselves as teachers with a small group. They had seen me work with the whole group. Most, too, had led the whole group in lessons. They all had taken their children ahead in ways so the children could sense proudly their achievement. And I was so proud of the giant jumps so many children made during these three-and-a-half-months on the informal reading inventories we used to check each child's reading level.

We had all worked together in Room 205 from the school's opening that fall up to Christmas. During the Christmas break it was with nostalgia that I took out all the partitions and built a wall down through the middle of Room 205, separating it into two classrooms for two partnership teams. A graduate student and I got high ladders from Seymour's janitor to reach the old building's eleven foot tall ceilings in order to build the temporary wall from floor to ceiling.

After Christmas I continued to supervise the four teachers who now were teaching the class in two halves—a partnership of teachers in each side of Room 205. Other Program trainees came in to observe how the children continued to grow—children who many of the observers knew intimately from their experience with them. The children's year-long gain in reading test scores was impressive—twice the national average. Then, too, only seldom was a child absent, in this school where absenteeism was a fact of life in so many other classes.

The assistant superintendent? In mid-October, when he finally paid attention to what was happening in Room 205 it was too late. School was underway. His assistant called me and with measured words, carefully set a date when he and his boss would come for a full morning to observe. We were told to expect them on a particular Thursday. But instead they came on the previous Tuesday. I always supposed that this calendar switch, unbeknownst to us, was to catch us out. But Thursday, Tuesday—it didn't matter. Life in Room 205 kept on its vital way whatever day anyone might come in to observe. There was nothing that the assistant superintendent saw to complain about. Maybe he was impressed despite what must have been his feelings of anger at Jack's not involving him in the planning. Then too later the local Syracuse newspaper's Sunday magazine carried three pages of pictures and text about this new training program that was helping each child succeed while it was preparing teachers to make a difference in the lives of children from the housing projects and the nearby neighborhood where transient poor people lived. [11] As it turned out, the assistant superintendent could take some credit for something that the newspaper reporter touted as perhaps beginning a new wave in one of his schools. He could take some of the credit; Jack had taken the risk.

That second school year was full for me. During the fall, as I have described, I had to stay in Room 205 at Seymour School for most of each day, except for the Wednesday morning each week when all of us in the Program had our meeting together at our Program rooms near the university. There, on Wednesdays I taught our usual full morning training session for all the Program people as a group. Then in the afternoon I conferenced with as many of our people as time permitted. On Wednesdays, when we were away from Seymour, Jack arranged to have his best substitute teacher take the class all day. Then too, I had to make time to work with the other fifteen or so people who worked with children in various ways in our other school located in the "middle class" fringe area near the city boundary. Eileen was the main person there and I was the support. She was able to help our people, who chose to work there, have fulfilling experiences. Along with all my other work during this hectic time I had to go on exchanging journals and went on with my one to one conferencing. Our journals and one to one conferencing were the lifeblood of the program.

It all worked out. I guess it did partly because we all were working together—those thirty-three trainees and me along with our magnificent secretary, Helen Andrews, and people like Eileen and Jack Murray. And it was due in some part to that step by step process approach I have talked so much about on these pages. I simply didn't have to live with initial miscalculations in previously set up detailed plans which later resulted in serious tensions. I moved ahead to each next stage, free to plan and carry out a next step that would fit the new situation.

What happened in the Program after that? In the fifth semester, I placed all of the students who had started four semesters before, in paying jobs that September—right on plan. More than half worked in elementary schools in paid partnerships. Jack Murray hired eight of the trainees who had worked with me in Room 205. About a quarter of our teachers-in-training became paid reading teachers in the local elementary schools. All of our people were qualified to be reading teachers. I had taught them to analyze children's status in reading and then how to help each child to take the next best step from there. Being a reading teacher, I realized, was so good for some of our people who wanted to relate to children individually—the way the reading teachers worked in the schools—and preferred this to teaching a whole class.

During this fifth semester, that September through December, I worked in the schools with those who were teaching there. We continued with our one-to-one conferences but sometimes we had to sandwich them in when the children were out of the classroom, to gym or working with the art teacher.

After the Program ended, six or seven of the thirty-three Program people decided not to continue teaching in the conventional schools. All but one of those who did not continue teaching in the schools, with whom I have kept in contact, ended up teaching in some sort of a situation within a few years. Three trainees worked in the experimental school I later directed and about which much more is written below. One woman became a key person in organizing and making our city's science museum work for local children; another worked with children at a hospital; another became an education professor who taught teachers to individualize their teaching of reading and writing. I continued to meet with several of these people who seemed to be seeking a kind of teaching which was in tune with what they wanted for themselves. The way people chose to work after going through the Program was a tribute to the Program. The Program's idea was for each person to move out in her working life doing what best suited her.

For the final report to the state department of education, I asked each of the students to write her own assessment of the changes that happened to her which could be attributed to the program. I also asked each to be critical too and express any dissatisfactions. What came out was an inch-and-a-half thick volume filled with plaudits for the Program. I later found out, also, that fifteen of the trainees had crowded into the office of the School of Education dean to give him their praise of the program. Trainees also evaluated their growth in the Program at the conclusion of a half-hour movie which was made of the Program. The students talked about how this was just right for them as they re-entered the working world after being at home with their children. With our individualized way, each one of them could simply pick up where she was in her life and begin comfortably to do things so many hadn't thought they would or could do. So many talked about what an exciting sense they had of what individualized learning for children might be like; they had done that for themselves, appropriate to their experience, too. None of the students had any fundamental criticism of the program. I think this reflects the fact that the program was set up to fit each person as that person grew. They all succeeded.

I had poured in the kind of energy and creativity that I didn't realize I had in me and felt there was a lot to show for it. The results for the trainee teachers and for the children they taught confirmed once again, my beliefs in an individualized schooling for all students, adults and children alike. I had also grown a great deal in these years. For example, I had the opportunity further to develop my ideas of individualization to fit what was considered a difficult situation—an inner city school.

In the end, I realized that these last three years had been the best teaching years of my life.

Putting It All Together

One evening after the MTPT Program ended, Susan Manes called. She was one of our trainees who had just finished a year-long partnership position in a city school. She soon came to the point, "There is a firehouse for sale on the North Side. What about starting that school we talked about in our Blue Sky Group?"

We had formed The Blue Sky Group in the Program because so many of our students wanted to talk of a new breed of schools—schools for children which might implement the vision which was guiding our MTPT program. After Susan's telephone call, however, I felt hesitant. I needed time to think about plunging into a project to start the kind of school our people and I, in The Blue Sky Group, dreamed about.

But three things prompted me to agree to begin work on a school that fitted our dream. The first was this felt like what I was waiting for: the next step ahead, after our Program, toward realizing my vision for children in our society. The second was my anger and helpless feeling, because of what was happening to my children at an experimental inner city school they were attending. After some initial success, the school's principal had left for another job and what could have been a long term success broke down. For example, just a few days before Susan's phone call my six-year-old daughter Val had been robbed of her lunch money at school, by an older girl who threatened to beat her up.

The third thing was the enthusiasm and planning I shared with Susan and the others in our Blue Sky Group during the MTPT Program. The Blue Sky Group meetings varied from six to ten of our people—people who were seriously talking and writing about what an ideal elementary schooling for children might actually be like. They talked of a school for children based on the principles behind their education in the Program—particularly a school which would fit the diversity of our city's population. Not only did these Blue Sky people have what was happening to them in the Program to instruct them as to what might happen if teachers listened to each of their students, they had the love of their own children to power their growing excitement for what could be. They talked about an education for their own children where what happened to each child grew out of a trusting one to one relationship with a teacher who listened; they wanted this kind of an education for other parents' children. So did I.

A year later, Susan and I established the school, based on the learning principles we both had lived during our two and a half years in the MTPT Program. We called our experimental school, The Syracuse Institute for Enabling Education—SIEE, for short. We named it an "institute" because our intention was to invite other schooling innovators to join us—to bring our own small school and theirs to a shared location. We then would operate adjacent to each other. We might, to illustrate, have our school alongside a Montessori School, a Waldorf School based on Rudolph Steiner's principles, plus one or two others located in different spots at our institute. Each school would educate children individually but with some different ways. The multi-school complex never did materialize. We were the only one.

We had high hopes that perhaps our experimental school might change at least some of what took place in the conventional urban and suburban schools in our community. We thought that maybe we could show the public school people what it would be like to have schools where each child felt secure in a one to one relationship with a teacher who made sure the child would succeed. Bit-by-bit the children would learn to plan their own learning. This would be a far cry from the conventional teaching-learning going on in the city schools and in the few private schools in Syracuse. In these conventional schools, the point—from kindergarten onward—was to come out ahead in the race to do school exercises better and faster than your fellow students; some rose to the top and others struggled or never made it.

If we were successful in influencing conventional school districts to change toward the kind of schooling we would develop as prototype, we already had a teacher training program to go with it. Waiting in the wings was our MTPT Program to train teachers for this new schooling. We knew how to train teachers who would fit this individualized kind of teaching-learning. If the local schools took on some of our key ideas, our new teachers could apply what they were trained to do.

We had our work cut out for us—Susan Manes, her husband Sidney who was a well-known attorney in town, about twelve others and me. We began with a series of meetings where we wrote a goals statement for our proposed school. During this time parents who might want their children in the school participated with us in discussing what the school might be like. These discussions became an extension of our Blue Sky Group. Then Sidney shaped our statement into a legally worded request for a charter as a private school. Being a private elementary school meant, in effect, that the state would let us do anything we wanted so long as things didn't get out of hand. It was so good to have Sidney working with us. I always felt secure that we were not vulnerable from the state department of education establishment or any other authority. We had a top flight lawyer in our corner.

Once our statement was drafted and Sidney was securing our charter as a private school, I began thinking about where we might set up our school. I began looking in the spring following the end of the Program a year before. We were planning to start that September, 1970.

As I look back on it, in a sense I picked up where I left off at the Laboratory School. I began, here in Syracuse, with the idea of a library-centered elementary school that was growing so well when I left the Lab School. Thus, when I thought about where to start looking for space I simply began walking in the area around the city's central public library. We found the space in the YWCA, just around the corner from the library, using the empty basement which ran the full length of the building across the front. All along the street side of the airy basement room, the size of an Olympic swimming pool, there were tall windows opening out to a spacious light well paralleling the outside sidewalk. When I looked up through the windows and through the wrought iron fence bordering the sidewalk, I could see people hustling by. On one side of the basement room was a snack bar and kitchen area with running water.

The Y's board of directors rented the basement space to us, with the condition that we share most of the space if the "Y" were to need it. We were to have full use of all the "Y" facilities including the gym and a twenty-yard-long swimming pool. We also could use the two-story high auditorium in the center of the building with a real stage and curtains, just waiting for the children to put on plays like we used to do at Alpine School. According to our agreement with the

"Y," at the end of each school day we had to collapse our school into one end of their large front basement, behind a folding wall. Thus the "Y" only rented us exclusive use of a forty by twenty foot space at one end of the big basement at a low rent. By pulling our school back behind the wall at the end of the school day, the "Y" could use the bulk of the basement space for an occasional scheduled after-school activity or could use it any evening or weekend. We agreed that the two or three school days during the year when the "Y" would probably schedule their part of the basement, we would take the children on a field trip or just hold our school in way that wouldn't disturb what was happening on their side of the folding wall.

During that summer I turned carpenter, along with one or two others. We built a "mezzanine" from a large old boardroom table the University was going to throw out. It was fun to put extensions on the legs of this twelve-foot-long table and a simple railing around the top plus a ladder at the end and presto! We had a mezzanine which doubled the usable space where it stood. This gave us extra space and allowed children to look down on all of us from their perch on top. Later, one of the children's fathers and I built a set of school cabinets all on casters, each with a four by four foot bulletin board attached behind. From a local rug cleaning establishment we bought thick used rugs which they had cleaned but had not been picked up by their owners. We could roll up these rugs to allow the accordion wall to be pulled across at the end of the day. We needed very few chairs because we decided to sit on the rugs with the children much of the time. This saved money and saved the space otherwise needed for chairs, too.

Susan Manes was the head teacher at our new SIEE school. I took the role of director. Seventeen children were enrolled that first year. Most of the six or so women who were our core staff people, all worked about half-time or less, had their children in the school and had either been through our MTPT Program or knew its basic philosophy from a friend who had been in the Program.

It was a Godsend that we had such a small group of children during that first year—seventeen children from five- to eleven-years-old. This gave us the flexibility to try this and try that; not only to fit the school to the children but fit it to the teachers, too. I popped down to our school at odd times when I freed myself from my university work.

Right away I saw the children feeling at home at our school—feeling safe and able to explore the world and themselves, openly. It made me feel so good to see children seeming to sense they were in a kind of ideal family where little ones could learn from the older ones, where each one of them felt a close trusting bond with at least one of the staff people. Each child worked on what the teacher and increasingly the child decided was the next job. It might be an autobiography; it might be the phonics workbook that was full of consonant-vowel-consonant training for a child who was at the place where this practice was needed. It might be this week's journal to the child's key teacher. It might be learning a list of spelling words that would help a particular child be more independent in writing. It might be working with interlocking blocks that helped a child understand the basic decimal system behind our arithmetic computation. Children would go with staff people to the library just five minutes away. They studied and read there and could bring back as many books as they wanted. Some children used the library's reference room with its extensive collection of maps, its fascinating archival sources such all the back issues of *Life Magazine* and complete microfilm files of local and national newspapers. The children's room at the library was a treasure house. Inviting fiction books were everywhere. Its non fiction collection led children into all sorts of detailed knowledge.

Around the walls at our end of the "Y's" basement, we built simple slanting racks to display books face up, as we had done at The Lab School's paperback book store. Thus in one corner of our room, nestled in big soft pillows, children could read under canyon walls of attractive children's books. Not all our children could read all of these library books, of course. For our fledgling readers, some of our slanting racks were full of high interest but low vocabulary-level books. Our staff people knew how to fit a book from these racks to each child who had the reading independence to read it. For others who didn't have this beginning independence, we arranged things so children could get immediate help if they didn't know a particular word as they read along in their books. Our goal for these just-beginning children was to have them read fast enough to enable the context of the story to clue them in how they might sound out unknown words. All this was only just a part of our individualized reading and writing program.

Another part was our daily Newstime like I led at Seymour School, where one of our staff people would write in front of the children as she interviewed the children who volunteered at these sessions. In this and other ways children who were not independent in reading and writing soon got the hang of how writing and reading were talk-written-down. Newstime also was a time when other children learned basic punctuation as the teacher used correct conventions to make what she or a child wanted to say, intelligible to others.

We also used the schools' neighborhood—downtown Syracuse—as prime learning space. As children became used to the neighborhood, we allowed certain ones to go out in pairs; some could go out alone. Deciding whether a child could go out without an adult along, was done in close collaboration with parents.

Just at the end of the block one way from the "Y" was Columbus Circle. In good weather, office workers ate lunch around the Circle's elaborate cascading fountain. At the end of the block the other way, across the street was a park with grass and shady maple trees which we often used in the fall and spring. The courthouse and police buildings were a block away to the east of us.

A few of our children enjoyed spending time watching court cases. One boy met the police chief on his own; just went up to the chief's office and asked to see him, as I remember. This resulted in the chief coming as a "mystery guest" one day. Susan Manes invented this interview-time idea. Adults who had interesting jobs would come and the children would ask them questions about what they did in their jobs, in order to try to figure out their line of work. Children could ask any sensible question other than what work the person did. When they interviewed the police chief, dressed in his civilian blue suit, one eight-year-old asked him if he had his gun with him. The chief opened his coat and there it was, ensconced under his arm.

For about four of the school's first nine months I was away on a sabbatical leave. My family and I went to England where my daughters were enrolled in a school in the Kew neighborhood, across the Thames River from London. I worked mornings, for three months, in a "working class" London primary school near the old London Docks area. The children who went to this school lived in high rise public housing built on the areas flattened during the wartime bombing.

I visited many other schools while I was in Britain, trying to find out more about "open education" which education writers in the U.S. were saying was flowering in British infant and primary schools. I didn't find schooling which nearly came up to the glowing descriptions I had been reading in the U.S.

But what I did find in so many British elementary schools was a great deal of creativity. Children were expressing themselves in all sorts of art-work that was as beautiful as it was simple to make. I remember one school in a drab inner city London area where most of the parents were recent immigrants from India and Pakistan. As I entered one classroom in the high ceilinged old building I suddenly felt transported into a gallery with beautifully displayed artwork. For example there was a nook with colorful paper mache masks displayed against a brilliant golden draped cloth background. I saw eight-year-old children make the masks. The children were ordinary people—people like me, who wouldn't be called "an artist"—making the masks in ways that drew from their emotions. Children built their masks' facial features on styrofoam wig stands which showed just a hint of the mouth, nose and so on to help them build up a mask that would express the personality which the child wanted to show. Children made the features with plasticene clay and then they coated the mask's face with Vaseline. On this was laid layers of paper mache. When it dried the child gently peeled the mask off and painted it with color to match the mood which had been created on the face. It was finished off to a brilliant shine with a coat of shellac. As I walked out of that school, I couldn't wait to go out and buy three wig stands and the other materials so that my daughters and I could begin our own masks at home that night.

From my sabbatical visiting schools in England, I brought home to our SIEE School all sorts of ideas, such as making those brilliant paper mache masks. The ideas enabled each of the children to express themselves non verbally. This was along with expression in writing which the children were doing every day.

I brought these expressive art ideas to local teachers, too. In my teacher training classes I taught teachers how they might combine expressive art with their teaching of writing and reading. In my late afternoon and evening classes for practicing teachers I lectured about individualizing teachers' reading and writing programs, as the teachers in the course sat at tables working quietly on one art or craft idea I brought from Britain. During my summer courses I added photographic darkroom work where teachers learned how to develop, print and enlarge their black and white photographs. Bit by bit my focus changed to summer courses in photography which could help teachers heighten their awareness.

In these courses teachers did expressive work and let their cameras lead them to see sensitively what was around them. My hope was that this would carry over to their relationships with children. Eventually my ten-year-old daughter Val taught several of these courses with me. She would teach teachers how to do the darkroom work. Along with Val, Cathy Benzel, a local school art teacher who lived across the street from my home, sometimes helped me teach these classes. Often we had to restrict the numbers who could attend because so many teachers wanted to be there.

We set up a self-service art center at our SIEE School which was popular. It was positioned in the middle of our SIEE schoolroom in the "Y's" basement. There we offered our children all of the expressive art and craft ideas I had collected in Britain. The center provided children with paint and materials to make the ideas come alive. All these materials were displayed on those cabinets-on-casters I mentioned making, earlier. It just took a few minutes, first thing every morning, to roll the cabinets out from our area behind the folding wall.

My memories are so vivid of children being drawn to the art center when they entered the basement room in the mornings. In my memory I see the warm sun streaming through the big windows on the street side of the room, bordering our self-service art center. Whether children saw themselves as "artists" or not didn't matter. Everyone who felt the urge could easily gather what they needed and begin something that would be satisfying both in the making and in the final product. Instructions were written on the bulletin boards back of the cabinets.

For example children could choose to make a sheet of "stained glass" by painting liquid starch over bits of colored tissue paper they had arranged in artful ways on a piece of waxed paper. As the starch flowed on, the colors in the tissue paper bled together to create lovely light moods when the dried piece was peeled from the waxed paper and held up to a light source. Other children might make delicate Japanese-style line designs simply by blowing a drop of black India ink with a straw to direct their breath, thus moving the black trail expressively, on a clean white paper. Some children used these designs to accompany short Haiku poems.

When I came to our school almost every day, often I, too, would join in the creative work that expressed my feelings. I remember making sunbursts with all sorts of materials and paint. They just seemed to happen so often when I was in our school. I tooled these symbols onto a leather watchband for myself and on luggage I gave to my daughters.

Joyce MacArthur joined our staff about that time. Joyce was an artist who used earthy materials to produce work that to me came right out of her soul. She would work in the art area for a couple of hours, two or three mornings each week. Each time, she'd bring a different idea to show children. It was Joyce who admired children's tissue paper "stained glass" and then brought bits of real stained glass and strips of channeled lead which children could wrap around the pieces and join them together with the heat from a soldering iron. That was about as difficult as Joyce's projects ever got. She preferred to keep things simple and use easily accessible materials such as clay she might have dug. One week children made simple baskets from reeds Joyce had cut.

A few years later we would take groups of children from our school out to Joyce's farm, regularly. She and her husband had bought an abandoned farm with a large dairy barn on it. They had cleaned out the barn, poured a concrete floor, and built simple rustic living quarters at one end. For some of our city children this was a new world. When it was cool, Joyce would cook on her big wood and coal range which kept the place warm too. Most of our children never had used things like a pit toilet nor had some ever slept on the floor in a sleeping bag. Some had not heard animals rustle along the rafters or outside in the dead quiet of night at the farm. The beaver colony on Joyce's pond seemed to welcome the young visitors, some of whom watched for hours to see the beavers come and go to their houses on the pond.

Then there was Betty Lise Anderson who was a fifteen-year-old who arranged her high school schedule to work at our school, afternoons each week. She lived next door to me. I watched how Betty Lise enjoyed the little children on our block. She was a Pied Piper. My daughters, along with other kids on the block were drawn to her and joined in the all the creative things she was doing whether it was making a six-foot-long paper mache shark or putting on plays. There was a lot of laughing and fun but I noticed how every child felt relaxed and taken seriously when Betty was running things.

Betty Lise turned her magic on in our school. It was Betty Lise who organized and put on our musical plays for holiday times in the "Y's" big auditorium. There she was just out of sight as the children sang their hearts out or played their parts with spontaneous abandon; but at the same time somehow she kept everyone to the script they had written together—well, most of the time.

Along with Betty Lise, Ana Stave taught our children to do dance numbers for these productions as well as regularly scheduled "movement" classes. Ana taught dance at the university as an adjunct instructor and later took a full-time job teaching dance at the local community college. I wanted her to offer our children a chance to express their feelings through their whole bodies as I had seen done so often and so well in Britain. "Movement" was as common in many British infant and primary schools as physical education was in our elementary schools.

I think people such as Ana, Joyce and Betty Lise enjoyed the atmosphere at our school and felt that inner lift and sense of well being which I usually did when I left after my short time at the school three or four days each week. I sensed that they felt a sense of fulfillment in giving their gifts to children who responded so openly.

Occasionally we had evening meetings of the staff. Because everyone worked part-time it was hard for all of us to get together during the school day. Many of the staff people had to be at home for their own children after school hours. At these meetings, I enjoyed listening to people say what needed to be said. The atmosphere of trust in our school extended to our staff meetings. There was plenty of laughing as well as other open expression of feeling. People would take stands when it came to something about which a person felt strongly. Only seldom did this result in serious tension but when it did, we faced it openly. Probably the hardest thing we had to do was to coordinate the comings and goings of each staff member with the needs of each child. We had to make detailed yet flexible plans which allowed all the various people who came and went at our school to give the best they had to give. At the same time each person needed to know what seemed to be highest priority for each child's learning.

Probably this constant attention to coordination was why, in the later years of the school when we had forty-plus children, we found ourselves moving to a staff where most people worked full-time. But on looking back, I feel those first years of all part-timers were our best, partly because of all the different contributions from such talented and creative people, all who listened to children. I realize now that we could have worked with forty-plus children and still could have coordinated the comings and goings of part-time people.

One reason we could have done this was that our child study process kept all of the teachers tuned into all of the children. Let me explain: once a month, on child study day, parents would keep their children home and the staff and I would meet to focus our attention on about three to five of our children; by the end of the school year each child had been "up" for discussion on child study day, at least once. [12]

The child study process helped each of our staff people to know every child well, whether the staff member had one to one responsibility for that child, or not. This helped all the staff people relate to every child sensitively while it aided the teacher with one to one responsibility, to gain more perspective on the child. On these meeting days also we took about two hours in the afternoon to discuss school business. These afternoon sessions could be used partly to handle the necessary coordination of part-time and full-time people, too.

The child study process helped me, too. I found myself directing our elementary school in tune with each of the children in it. It helped me, also, to understand some of the concerns teachers had. I spent quite a bit of my time helping some of our staff people with whatever each one needed as the next step in their growth as teachers who might respond sensitively to each child. Thus, as each of our children had with their teachers, each of our teachers had a one to one relationship with me that often meant the two of us would spend time talking during the school day. This usually was easy to arrange because so much of the time children were working independently.

For example, take Leah Horwitz, one of our parents who was working part-time at our school. She also had helped us during the school's planning phase. Leah had learned a great deal about teaching children to understand the basic system under the arithmetic computation and other mathematical thinking children were being asked to do. Leah had learned this from Bob Davis, a professor at the university's math department. Bob had worked out ways to help children understand what math was all about—it's basic system and logic. Bob's child went to our school for a couple of years before they moved away from Syracuse. [13]

So Leah knew a great deal which would help our children be grounded in math and she was brilliant in one to one teaching which she did mostly. But she found herself sometimes not being able to manage to her satisfaction, small group meetings where she might be showing children something on our chalkboard or where she helped children play some of the many math games she created. As I remember, sometimes she simply needed to be assured that it was OK to be a directive leader. Perhaps Leah, like so many caring people in the '60s and '70s, had picked up the conventional "free school" wisdom that schoolroom boundaries were suspect, that adult imposed order was only done because of the teacher's lack of leadership skill, and that responsibility might very seriously compromise freedom. Sometimes Leah and I would watch Susan lead a group and then Leah and I would talk about the leadership dynamics of what we had just seen. We could see in Susan's sure leadership how children could be helped to be free. They seemed to sense a basic order free of intimidation—a chance to release themselves within a safe-feeling world.

In our school, children soon learned that they weren't in a place where they had to contend against others for dignity. Children of all ages worked side by side. Each of the children had their own academic work; children worked at their own pace; some in quite unique ways. Children weren't learning who was better than whom. This simply was not in the scheme of things, not in the air of the school. So when a child entered our school having been a loser in a conventional school or having been under some other tension caused by the previous school situation, sometimes things would get better without our having to work hard to bring it about.

I remember a quiet seven-year-old girl, Laurie, whose parents sent her to our school because at the city school where she had gone before, she had become tense and fearful each morning at the prospect of going to school. Almost every day when she returned from school she had a headache. The school psychologist was baffled. Parents and Laurie's teacher and the principal had done everything they could think of, but things didn't change for Laurie. However when Laurie was at our school the headaches and tension simply faded away. Our school's atmosphere did what the psychologist and others in her former school couldn't.

Because we fitted schooling to the child rather than the reverse, we didn't find ourselves needing the conventional school psychologists, counselors and social workers. These people, I learned from my experience in the conventional schools, spent so much of their time trying to adjust children who weren't fitting-in to the school's system—trying to return children to teaching-learning situations that might not have been right for the child in the first place.

But we didn't need to label children, after interminable "diagnostic testing" and staff meetings with "experts," as having some sort of a medical-sounding problem such as "Attention Deficit Disorder." In my view, such psychological labels so often narrow school people's awareness as soon as they apply the labels. They tend to see the child as the label directs, not as the teachers' senses might inform them if they were to know the child as a person who, like the rest of us, needs to feel significant.

We could know children that way at our SIEE School. We had natural listener-type teachers who spent time with the children in trusting one to one relationships. Our teachers could observe their children in situations where the children were natural with others—where the children could feel themselves in an accepting safe place.

This reminds me of Barry who, on the first day he entered our SIEE School at five-years-old, was wherever you didn't want him to be, did whatever you didn't want him to do. I remember the first time I saw Barry was when he had climbed atop the "Y's" snack counter challenging the world to take him off. I lifted him off in a way that said that he simply couldn't do that. From the beginning Barry found out we made boundaries for him which were crystal clear. From the beginning, also, Barry would test our policy never to expel a child once enrolled at our school.

We never really figured out whatever it was that was causing Barry to resist us and other authorities in his world; we never tried, really. But we helped him to accept his ways and learn to keep them from interfering with others. We also stopped him from trying to goad other children into fighting with him or fighting with others at our school. Barry grudgingly seemed to go along with the clear boundaries we set for him—boundaries which became more detailed as we came to know him and he us—as we felt the specific boundaries were relevant to him. As Barry came to know our school and feel it's fairness and decency, I sensed that he wanted us to help him keep himself from being such a bother. Because of our school's atmosphere and the lack of a who's better than whom tension, Barry never could find a rebellious group to join; he never was able to incite others to join him in gaining satisfaction, apparently, by undermining our social scene; he never was able to exalt in becoming a victim. There weren't any victims because there wasn't any oppression. Everyone could see this, including Barry as time went on.

During his first year at our school, five-year-old Barry mellowed. Our atmosphere seemed to be getting through to him. I liked Barry from the beginning. I always respected his grit and so did others on our staff. Maybe, one reason I could tune in with Barry so easily was that we both were independent spirits. But I had learned to turn my independent streak to good use—what we wanted to help Barry do. I felt Barry easily trusted me. When I'd interview with him as part of our child study process, I sensed an openness that made it easy for us to talk about things that mattered. As he grew older he developed a fine-tuned sense of self-awareness. I also felt his razor-sharp ability to figure out interpersonal situations. After being at our school for a few months we saw signs that he was beginning to admit that here was a place where people weren't out to get him, where he didn't have to get them before they got him. This awareness seemed to help him to dampen his war with authorities in his life. Whatever the reason, when he left our school at twelve years old, he was able to cope with authority in junior and senior high school and, as all of our children who started at five-years-old, he did well academically. I saw him when he was back in town during his college years. He talked of his girlfriend in a warm way. After being at our school, Barry was open to accepting himself and therefore it seemed, accepting others in a close way.

Then there was Norman. He too started our school at five-years-old. But from that point there was no similarity to Barry. Norman was an amiable boy with a somewhat babyish charm. Often when I arrived at school it was Norman who first said "HI." But only rarely did he respond to subtle overtures from me or others. He didn't seem to pick up the usual interpersonal cues children learn early in life. When teachers would try to teach him something, often there would be no response, especially in the first or second, of his four years at our school. Sometimes Norman would launch into monologues with little sensitivity to his listeners. Most of the time he would go on about stars, meteors, our moon and other facts of astronomy. He was quite an authority, as compared with most children his age. Especially during his first couple of years, Norman usually only would join our groups on his own terms; typically he would join in ways so that others would not reach out to him, emotionally. For example in our daily Newstime he would sit on the sidelines of the group seemingly watching every word that the teacher would put on the chart page in response to what one or another of the children said. He watched too, as children played games that were so effective in teaching the basic phonic sounds, the most used words and the arithmetic combinations.

We all liked Norman. Early on we felt Norman needed to be the way he was, even though, as with Barry, we didn't try all that hard to figure out what had caused him to be the way he was. He was welcome to be himself in our school where each of us was himself or herself, so long as what Norman did was good for him and so long as he didn't unduly distract others. At our school we didn't try to put a psychological label on him. We simply saw him as one of us and that's what he needed. Norman needed to feel he belonged. He did, at our school.

Norman learned and usually he did it in a way which fitted his world. He apparently didn't want to show that he had learned to read on his own, probably during Newstime each day, but also by doing the occasional written exercise. But he blew his cover one day when a teacher aide, one of our parents, firmly asked him to clean up after his work in our self-service art workshop where often he could be seen working on his own. To the teacher aide, he uncharacteristically blurted out, "The sign says 'after you finish' and I'm not done!" Then he proceeded indignantly to read fluently every single word on the sign we had in the art area, laying out the rules with line after line of detailed directions regarding where things were to be put after use. After that we checked and found that he could read much better than the average child of his age in the conventional elementary schools.

Norman was not alone in the world, as I said, at our school—he was just being in our world on his terms. That was an important gift we gave to Norman. He seemed to have to be non-responsive often, but in our school he didn't have to pay the cost of creating emotional distance between oneself and others. He was living with us and finding satisfaction in ways that he could tolerate. For example, he enjoyed taking part in our dramatic productions. But rather than make him do what a script said, Betty Lise allowed him to be the way it felt right for him in a scene. So at first when the rehearsals were going on he simply would hang around. Then bit by bit he, with Betty Lise's help, found a place for himself in the show.

By the time Norman left our school, after four years, I sensed that increasingly his communication was a two-way street even though his steps in this direction sometimes seemed small. Norman gave every sign of accepting himself and felt others did him, at least at our school. He progressed well academically and graduated from college. Thank God Norman's parents had the foresight to start his schooling off at our school.

Dennis' story was different from the others in its particulars but not basically. Basically Dennis, like the others I have mentioned, needed a haven. Our school was a place where he could be who he was, where he might come to accept himself, where he could come to know there existed a school where people knew he mattered as a person and were going to make sure he grew in ways best suited to him.

Dennis' parents sent him to our school because he simply quit doing writing at his former school. In his second grade at the "best" suburban district on the fringe of Syracuse Dennis simply had stopped filling in the exercise papers. He wouldn't write the bits of "creative writing" the teacher requested. He didn't act out; but he rebelled in a non-obtrusive and very effective way. He just quit. The teacher knew that he could write and read perhaps better than any other child in his second grade class.

The psychologists were called in. They tested Dennis, had professional meetings with key people from several levels of the school's administration, wrote reports and came up with nothing. They couldn't get him to budge. Then Dennis' parents sent him to our school.

In the beginning, at our school, we simply allowed Dennis to explore, to sit in with our group lessons, to participate in the expressive art world at our school, to go out to the downtown area when we and his parents were assured he could handle this independence. It was Dennis, by the way, who got to know the police chief and invited him to come to our school, as I described above.

Susan Manes and I talked about how we might begin starting Dennis doing the written work which he needed in order to become more independent and fluent in writing and reading and to use the library with ease. We talked of a plan to help him feel a part of our community—not just one more pupil in an impersonal institution. One idea was that Susan might ask Dennis to sit next to her as much of the time as this was practical—close enough to feel a strong sense of her presence emotionally. We figured that we needed to build his feeling that teachers at our school related to him as an individual who mattered in a unique way. Why not try this non-verbal way? Susan did this and began to ask Dennis for a minimum of exercise and written work each day. First it was a few words in writing—just a sentence about anything he wanted to write. In spelling, at first it was just one word a day which hitherto he hadn't known how to spell. It didn't take long for Dennis to feel all right about writing a weekly journal to Susan as he saw the others doing who worked with her one to one. His journals were full of sharp observations, poetic impressions, sensitive questions. Susan's journals to him completed a beautiful dialogue. Dennis was on his way. His way eventually led him to graduate school. Now he is a professor of English at a university, teaching writing.

Each year of the ten years I directed the school, I felt so good about how our school was developing. Form followed function. As our school grew—at a rate of about five more children each year—we changed things to correspond to what would make most sense to enable each teacher to do the best job. For example, for one (or was it two?) years Susan and her children were tucked in a quiet room at a hotel for women across from the library, for her morning quiet study period each day. When a new teacher, David, joined our staff full-time, after returning from a couple of years volunteering at a hospital in India, we rented a room in a nearby church where he did some of his work with those children with whom he worked closely.

We began our school's fifth year at a new location—in what looked to us as spacious quarters in an underused city church near the university. The "Y's" board had needed the space they formerly rented to us to start a second-hand store to augment their dwindling finances because most young women who formerly used the Y's facilities now lived in the suburbs. [14]

We benefited being near the university. Many of our children learned to be skilled in black and white photography at the university's Community Darkrooms. We used the university swimming pool. There, for the first half of each swimming session, college students from the physical education methods courses taught swimming and diving to our children. Our children took the role of learners and gave good experience to university students. Some of our children were beginners, who needed to learn to feel safe in the water; others were at the point where they wanted to learn how to do fancy dives on the springboards.

Enrollment continued to grow, year-by-year. We eventually enrolled over forty children, as I mentioned, from about five- to twelve-years-old. Most of our children were from families who could pay our tuition, about half the per-pupil expenditure of the local public schools. During the last two or three years of my directorship, most of our five-year-olds came from low income homes with children's tuition paid by funds from the county welfare department.

If Our SIEE School Could Make Sure Every Child Succeeded with Dignity, Why Couldn't Conventional Schools Do the Same?

In answering this question I came to see how the conventional system damaged so many children's chances in life. During the years I directed our SIEE School I also went on with my work teaching university students who wanted to be elementary school teachers. In addition I taught late afternoon and evening classes for local in-service elementary teachers. I often demonstrated in these teachers' classes how they might get into each child's shoes and then help the children learn in a way which was consistent with the best of what each one was becoming. Teachers seemed appreciative and tried some of my ideas. But increasingly, over this ten-year period when our SIEE School was flourishing, I didn't feel I was changing, basically, what conventional teachers did with children.

I didn't see my vision for a schooling which would fit each child, taking root in the local conventional elementary schools. I came to realize why, as I compared what we were doing so successfully at SIEE with what I saw being done in the conventional schools where I worked each week. What we were doing—an education in tune with each child—meant a radical change at the heart of the conventional schooling. It meant changing its teaching-learning system. And that meant, in turn, changing the ways the system was entrenched in established school curriculum and instruction, organization, recruitment of teachers and, most important, how the conventional system was entrenched in school people's and many parents' minds. When that realization finally sunk in, I found myself unable to go on in my role as a trainer of teachers for the conventional system. Here is the story of this growing awareness that began as glowing optimism about how I might change the way children learned at school—a story which led to this book and its Urban Little Schools design.

As our SIEE School began to flourish, I often felt exhilarated and optimistic. I felt that what we were demonstrating might impress local school people and lead them to change. They might begin to do at least some of what we were doing to individualize the way children learned in elementary schools. I felt excited when I lectured to my teacher trainee students about how they might use some of our SIEE ideas and our philosophy in teaching. My students at the university seemed to be excited, so often, by what teaching might be for them.

I tried to emphasize, in my university classes, how teaching could be sensitive and responsive to each child—in contrast with what some of the students reported seeing in so many of the public and private school classes where they observed. In doing this I spelled out in step by step detail how my teachers-to-be might reach each child in their own classes, using examples from our SIEE School.

My students seemed appreciative of how, in my university teaching, I would practice some of what I advocated they do in their own teaching. They liked, for instance, how with each of them I would arrange an interview for informal sharing, where we both responded to the kinds of questions I used in our SIEE School's child study process to heighten my sensitivity toward each child. Many students left their interviews apparently better able to understand how, with this kind of listening they might tailor learning in ways that fit each child. In my teacher education classes, I saw so many nod with understanding and approval when I showed them other ways they could teach so children might develop self-direction grounded in self-awareness.

I invited my teacher education class students to come to SIEE and observe. I accompanied this invitation with color slide-pictures showing some ways we heightened our sensitivity toward each child; how this child and that child was responding in so many lovely and productive ways; how the children obviously were on their way to becoming people who knew what it meant to work closely with someone they trusted, step by step. I told them Barry's story, without, of course, using his real name or other identification. From my university students' comments in class and in their writing to me, I felt that almost every one had known at least one child who projected an inner anger onto others as Barry seemed to do when he first came to our school. Then I talked about Dennis. As I talked I saw every one of my students listening with full attention when I told how he simply had quit writing, in his elite suburban second grade classroom. Then when I talked about Norman, so many of my students seem to know exactly what I meant when I explained how important it was that he felt that he belonged, despite his apparent need to create emotional distance from his schoolmates. So often when I would leave my lectures, I felt proud of our SIEE school and thankful—thankful that children could be themselves there. Justifiably they could feel significant. I felt so proud that our school was a haven for people who were learning what it meant to accept themselves and others too.

I felt proud of us when I showed color slides and movies showing our SIEE children reading and writing in ways that suggested that they were learning to be excited about books and reading and using writing to have close relationships with their teachers. I showed pictures of our children learning to understand the basis of the number system as they were involved in fun games with Leah Horwitz which helped them memorize basic arithmetic combinations. The colorful pictures also showed our children playing games that taught the core elements of reading and spelling. So many of my university students seemed involved and intrigued as they viewed slides of my leading Newstime sessions showing Jack Murray's Seymour School children looking absorbed with it all. I talked of how so many of these inner city third graders took big strides when finally they connected with how writing, and reading were talk-written-down, when they finally understood intuitively how spelling, punctuation and other conventions made it all possible.

In my courses I didn't use any of the typical education course textbooks. I found them written to implement the conventional teaching-learning system. Instead, I supplemented my lectures by draft copies of books I was writing or material I had already published. I wrote *God Bless the Grass: Case Studies in Self-Esteem,* to help teachers expand their awareness of the essential person within each child sitting in their classes. [15] In this book I told story after story of my work with individual children, many of whom had come to our school damaged by their former schooling experience or in a few cases a difficult home life. Then I wrote, *Reading, Writing and Self-Esteem* to help teachers listen to each child and then help the child learn to write and read in tune with whom the child was as a person.[16] I also used a series of pamphlets I had begun to write when I was in my last year at the Lab School, *The Language Arts of Individual Inquiry*. [17]

Quite a few of my teacher trainees at the university came to our SIEE school and observed. A few experienced teachers did too when I could arrange it with their school districts. I felt good about this. Maybe, I thought, I was planting the seeds that would grow to be school classrooms where learning was in harmony with each child.

But the seeds didn't grow. When I would go out and visit teachers' classrooms, both in public and private schools, I didn't see my vision happening to any extent. Instead, I found teachers who had been in my pre-service and in-service classes, and who I enjoyed as people, doing what all the other teachers did; they were following the conventional teaching-learning system. They essentially were submerging the uniqueness and essence of children while they got on with pressing them to do today's exercises, to reach the year's curriculum goals. Even when I would demonstrate in their classrooms how they might fit schooling to each of their children, it usually seemed to result in very little change.

We encouraged people to visit our SIEE School. We employed one of our parents, part-time, to be the school's hostess to explain the school to visitors. Parents were interested. But leaders from the local conventional schools didn't seem to be. School administrators and influential teachers didn't come to observe and possibly learn from what we were doing. Neither did most of my colleagues at the School of Education.

If conventional school leaders were to pay attention to what we were doing, they probably would have sensed, as I was beginning to, that we simply were operating on a fundamentally different premise from their schools. Our school's basic way and the conventional way used radically different methods and philosophies to help children learn.

In our SIEE School's way, which is basically the same as the Urban Little Schools' way, each child had a serious personal working relationship with at least one teacher whom the child could trust—a person with whom the child could be open and when necessary show some vulnerability. This was a teacher who essentially did not judge the child. Children easily could sense that the teachers saw them as fundamentally OK—as lovable and capable people who mattered, even if at times some did what they might come to regret. As the teacher and the child listened to each other, they worked on the immediate problems of the child's learning and laid out the next steps. They discussed and shared in ways that helped children face the hurdles and challenges of growing with dignity and responsibility. In our school's way, a teacher was there for each of the children, all along their learning journeys. The teacher's role was to help children become independent sensitive people who could lead a life of integrity as they increasingly drew from maturing inner wisdom.

At our school, visitors could see our way in action. Teachers and children listened to each other. Our teachers successfully were learning to get into each child's shoes, so-to-speak, to sense where the child might be coming from. We became increasingly sensitive to how a child learned best, how each related to people and events, how the child mattered in special ways.

The school's hostess explained to visitors how, on our monthly child study day, the staff people and I focused on just three to five of our children. We might view an 8mm movie which I had taken, showing one of the children during their day. We read interviews with the child which I wrote and anecdotes which each teacher wrote. Visitors could see how this process helped us to heighten our awareness of children. Each teacher came to know a child from many perspectives. In addition, parents were shown how our teachers tailored basic skills learning to individual children. Our teachers didn't have to let a sequentially organized curriculum do the teaching; a child didn't have to follow pre-set curriculum exercises if it made better sense to learn in another way.

In contrast, the conventional teacher's job was to teach the uniform curriculum—to press children through the sequentially organized exercises designed both to teach and also to sort out which children were better than which others in doing the curriculum tasks. Thus there were children at the bottom and an elite at the top—a pool of losers and an honored group of winners. The just-ordinary lackluster ones were spread out between.

Each day as I worked in the conventional schools with our student teachers, I'd be painfully aware of the children who saw themselves in or near the loser pool at the bottom of the rank order. Judging from such evidence as the number of children in the remedial reading classes, I estimated the loser pool to be about ten to fifteen percent of the children in "middle class" elementary schools where I worked and a much higher percentage in inner city schools located in poorer neighborhoods, where I sometimes worked. These estimates need to be increased if one adds in the children at the margin between the just-average ones and the loser pool at the bottom of the school's rank order. My impression was that most of the children who found themselves at the bottom, were from the poorer families, families where usually the parents were not considered winners when they went to school.

These were some of the children who at five-years-old, when they began kindergarten, probably had trusted the school's implied promise that if you did what the teacher asked, things would work out well for you. By about eight- to ten-years-old, I'd see these children feeling they didn't measure up, at least at school. Many had given up. Underneath perhaps an air of indifference and sometimes open resentment I'd sense how so many of these children seemed to feel seriously flawed and helpless to do anything about it. Three to five thousand hours of being seen as a loser at school is quite a force for conditioning.

Then too, as I found myself contrasting our SIEE School's way with the conventional system, I saw more clearly than before how, in the conventional school's rank ordered system, the teacher's most important and basic job was "control." The teacher's basic job was to keep their classes of children pressing onward through the curriculum, even though more than half of the class often persisted without enthusiasm, apparently seeing themselves as lackluster, "average" or loser students, while the "top" children typically did the work dutifully. New teachers, with whom I worked, quickly saw that "control"—keeping the class moving smoothly through the curriculum—was the key skill teachers needed in order to secure a teaching job and to stay employed. The new teacher's success in smoothly pressing children onward, was often called "having good classroom discipline," or "being good at classroom management."

The uniform curriculum, with its methods, textbooks and other learning materials which all the teachers were asked to use, tended to be dull. Some succeeded in spicing up the lessons a bit, but generally speaking the curriculum lessons were unexciting because the methods and materials were geared to what could be made to work by the least skilled and imaginative teachers.

Teachers were not allowed to individualize; they didn't have to know their subject well enough to come at it from a way other than the teaching methods embedded in the school's textbooks and other learning materials. Teachers also didn't have to know how to have different children learning in different ways in their classroom, side by side. [18]

Thus, except for teachers' making minor adjustments, they were not encouraged to try alternative ways so that a child who wasn't succeeding might do so. Therefore teachers didn't need to know how to analyze what a child needed to know and then how best to teach that to the child. Instead, all children in a particular group were given the same exercises to do. Then the children who regularly "weren't keeping up"—especially in reading—usually were sent to the remedial teacher and typically were labeled "remedial children." Often the remedial teachers used the same curriculum materials but at a slower pace and with one to one support.

"Remedial" was an official designation used in order to qualify for federal remedial funding. The effect on "remedial" children so often was to further deepen their stigma of being a loser which they already felt in the classroom. Ironically, many failing children liked to go to the remedial teacher each day. I knew the reason why: seeing the remedial teacher each day allowed the children to leave the classroom—it allowed them a bit of relief, to be out of the place at school where they felt most acutely the disgrace of not measuring up.

Then too, the teaching-learning system made it hard for teachers to get close to a child and discover some of the emotional reasons behind why the child wasn't learning. Defeated children tended to shy away from the teacher who gave out the low marks which these children routinely received.

Because of their system, school administrators didn't need to go out of their way to find and hire teachers who were good listeners to children. Why do that? Teachers who were natural listeners couldn't use their ability effectively to make learning responsive to each child. Instead, hiring priority was placed on securing teachers who could make the system work—teachers who would be good classroom managers, who smoothly could keep their classes pressing onward with "good discipline" and "control."

Finally, it struck me so clearly, that if maverick teachers were to individualize, were to plan and carry out special ways of learning for children, those teachers did it at their peril. The teachers were not only vulnerable to reprimand by the principal for departing from the uniform curriculum, but they risked severe and often telling criticism by dissatisfied parents. This was because if the child didn't succeed with the teacher's new way, it could be seen as the teacher's fault; the teacher's alternative way had failed. However if the child hadn't succeeded in the regular curriculum with its methods which were sanctified by the validity of tradition and presumably devised and tested by experts, it was easy for the school to say to the parents that it was the child's not the teacher's fault. After all, weren't many of the other children succeeding?

And this wasn't all that made me feel increasingly sad as I worked in the schools while I directed our SIEE School at the same time. As I worked with student teachers I became increasingly aware of how, despite what I did to help them be responsive to individual children, once out in the schools the new teachers were learning to draw power over children from a system which was in place to make children feel uneasy unless they felt approval from teachers and other school personnel. As children went through the grades they came to realize school was to be seen as a game where you easily could lose out—and many did—unless you pleased the teachers.

Under the facade of its being like a game, the system used a time tested way of controlling people—you stimulate their lurking fear, particularly in those who stray from doing your bidding; then you offer them surcease from that heightened fear when they do what you want.

The teaching-learning system heightened feelings of fear and self-diminishment in most of the non winners, particularly. Most were made to feel that their difficulties in handling the exercises with ease was their own fault. They were taught to blame themselves. If these children—the majority in "middle class" and inner city schools alike—didn't measure up to what the school asked of them, they risked uneasy feelings of being less than worthwhile—"I'm bad and it's all my fault." These children—particularly those in the lower fifty percent of the rank order—often faced the strong chance of feeling the fearful pangs of failure, shame and other self-rejection without recourse, without the support of anyone at school who, they knew, felt they were OK. So many of them from inner city schools, dropped out as failures. Often they ended on the streets as unemployed young people acting as if, more than anything else, they wanted to feel significant.

The winners in this system—the perhaps twenty percent or so at or near the top—also risked the undermining of their sense of self-reliance by the air of subtle fear in the school. Rather than learning to think for themselves, "top" children were pressed to look to teachers, their judges, for approval.

Some days, as I drove from schools where I was working with new teachers, I would find myself reflecting on other ways the fear-driven system of control might be seriously damaging children. I wondered to what extent the system was responsible for many children surrendering their own sense of individual self-direction to follow unquestioningly leaders in peer cliques or street gangs.

Then too, I wondered to what extent the system was causing so many of the children not only to find fault with themselves but to do it with others. I suspected that the system was responsible for much of the put-down atmosphere I so often sensed on conventional school playgrounds and school busses where children who probably felt a sense of inadequacy inside, picked on their more vulnerable schoolmates. Some of these vulnerable children retreated to the world of the outcasts where they got some satisfaction seeing themselves as victims. At our SIEE School we were bedeviled by the put-down atmosphere on the school district's busses filled with children from local schools, which took our children home. We could influence what happened to children all through the school day but we were helpless to do anything to lessen the hurting that surfaced in the busses. I asked myself, to what extent did this mirror children's ever present struggle to feel significant within a conventional schooling system that constantly reminded more than two-thirds of them that they were not quite measuring up, or they were failing, or they were just ordinary?

At SIEE it was so easy for me to see that at our school it wasn't "control" given power through heightened fear, rationalized as a game, that kept it all going; it was listening. We worked with a fundamentally different system and with teachers who had learned how to make it work. In our school every one of the children knew they mattered to at least one teacher who could be counted on. That relationship was the key reason why many things that seemed so difficult to accomplish within the conventional system worked out easily for us.

Our smoothly functioning businesslike atmosphere didn't result from the threat of fearful consequences if children didn't please the teachers; it came about largely because students were helped to take responsibility increasingly for the realities and frustrations of their lives. They were supported by that open listening relationship with a teacher who, children knew, was there for each of them. In our SIEE School, the teacher and a child, working together, easily could tailor specific working rules and boundaries to what the child needed. This was grounded in our assumption that the teacher took the ultimate responsibility and therefore held the final authority. Consequently, from time to time a few of our SIEE children, such as Barry, worked within relatively narrow behavior boundaries as compared with others who didn't need such restrictions. There was no stigma attached to a particular child working with special behavior rules. Children had grown to accept differences at school as being the norm; what you did as a result of working with your teacher wouldn't be necessarily what I might do with my teacher. Diversity was all around, in this school where those needing more or less structure in their lives, often worked side by side with children of differing ages on widely differing tasks.

Within this context of diversity in our school, I saw children taking each next step ahead in their lives from a maturing self-awareness. I saw this often as mirroring their teachers' increasing self-knowledge. Children seemed to feel themselves growing in what one might call inner dignity—growing in a sense of significance and worth as people who were supported by the assurance that they were OK. Life at our SIEE school wasn't set up as a perilous game which seriously might damage your chances later. Your being a winner or a loser, being someplace on a hierarchy extending from the "top" children down to the bottom children—that simply wasn't a part of our school. In our school's system, learning wasn't a contest where the ever-present risk was losing in the status race. Nor was learning done in order to lessen any school-implanted uneasiness. Learning was growing, together with a person who was there for you and who was growing too.

I think too, another fundamental reason lay behind my increasing frustration with the conventional schools' system was I finally began to sense that my goal of children's self-direction grounded in their increasing self-awareness—their listening to themselves—was just unthinkable to establishment-minded school people. It was OK to talk about helping children to listen to themselves, to come to know themselves and then to be true to the best in themselves by the way they lived. This was often extolled as a virtue. Speeches were given and articles and books were written, about how important it was to help children acknowledge and accept themselves. But to set about doing it—really listen to children in ways whereby they learned to listen to themselves, and then help them grow as self-directed learners and skillful independent thinkers in light of that—was too radical. It just wasn't done.

Twenty years ago, conventional urban school people didn't seem to realize the beneficial power in self-awareness. They didn't seem to see that children's rootless behavior, indifference to others, violence, all seemed to go hand in hand with children's lack of self-awareness. These school people didn't seem to understand how without being close to themselves children had no basis for piloting their own ships, individually, according to what was strong and good inside—how without strong self-awareness children had little sense of their own inner direction. Thus children were left to grow up as sheep, to follow without question whatever force had hold over them. These powerful influences might be the peer group, the gang, the pull of greed or hate, the yearning for drug-induced highs or the drumbeat of artificial sensation.

It took shock and outside help in these last twenty years, since 1980, to make at least some city school people realize the connection between children's responsible inner self-direction and their self-awareness. It took shootings in schools, estimates of ten percent of American school children coming to school each day with loaded guns, sharply rising children's alcohol and drug use plus youth gang killings.[19] It took Quakers and other outside groups coming into schools with programs such as "Alternatives to Violence" and conflict resolution programs where, along with other learning, the door was opened for children to experience themselves with heightened awareness and in this accepting process to come to know and accept others with empathy. [20] Then, finally, some of the same kinds of establishment-oriented urban school people who had shied away from helping children come closer to themselves, became proud of their schools' programs aimed, in part, at doing just that.

Thus, back in the 1970s, our SIEE school was ahead of the times as it helped children come closer to themselves. Our children were learning to reject that which was self-destructive even if many other kids were following a path which led to violence, casual teenage sex and so much other behavior which might feel good in the short run but which in the long run destroyed so many children's chances.

What we were doing at our school with such naturalness and which seemed to result in our children learning and living so responsibly, flew in the face of what, at that time, so many of my university colleagues and the conventional school administrators felt schools should not do. In those days they seemed to feel that schools should avoid dealing with children's fear and their awareness of themselves unless a child were in emotional crisis. The prevailing opinion among school people was that opening oneself to oneself was something normally to be avoided, something from which to distract oneself, or from which to flee in some other way.

At our SIEE School, on the other hand, I was helping teachers to be there, one to one, for children as the young people faced the realities of their lives with more and more self-awareness and acceptance. Then children wouldn't have to flee from fearful moods, to run from themselves. They wouldn't become freaked out, as a young person might put it, when those moody "I'm bad and it's all my fault" or other occasional heavy emotions that were often full of self-rejection, descended upon them. They wouldn't end up doing what so many other young people did. They wouldn't end up following the crowd to the quick-fix ways to feel good that ranged from mood altering drugs to alcohol, methamphetamine and on to crack cocaine and heroin. I didn't want our children to grow to be adults who risked the dampening of their will and their compassion, the undermining of their self-reliance along with erosion of their sense of dignity—never mind the obvious risk of addiction.

In contrast, I wanted our children to become adults who could accept occasional fearful self-rejection and other despairing feelings without becoming debilitated in the process. I wanted them to become people who might come to understand and change some of the ways they were living which caused or triggered their dark moods. I wanted them to understand themselves well enough to know when it made sense to let themselves experience these dark feelings, as well as to know when one had to withdraw from difficult feelings and perhaps deal with them later. I wanted them to be able to deal with the heavy parts of their lives in ways that worked, for them. One such way might be to find and teach trusted friends to listen without judgment, as teachers in our SIEE School did as a matter of course.

In these and other ways I wanted our young people to have the chance to be open to a meaningful relationship with their deeper individuality. I wanted them increasingly to be able to acknowledge and accept who they were, including any lurking destructive predispositions. Thus they would be in a position to accept themselves, to live true to the best of their innermost identity while not letting destructive urges gain control. These children wouldn't have to resort to suppression of disturbing feelings as a matter of course in their lives.

I had learned that too often when children habitually suppressed fearful feelings, they grew to be adults who had set the stage for violence—when those sometimes angry and at times almost demonic forces below could burst forth, uncontrolled, in destruction. This destructiveness was a latent invisible power which could and sometimes did rise up and possess individuals, gangs, or whole nations to do what, later, many look back upon with distaste or horror. I wanted each child to have a chance to face the deeply fearful, the vulnerable self-diminishment, as well as to be present to their loving and sensitive nurturing wellsprings. In our SIEE School, children learned how to do that, from those adults they trusted. They learned how to live with their inner worlds, to be with all they were while they were guided by what was good and increasingly strong inside.

As I have been saying, the contrast between our school's way and the conventional school's became more and more obvious to me. I saw clearly the damage done by the conventional schooling system to so many children. This awareness and my consequent frustration mounted—why did this have to be? People simply had to move their steering wheels a few turns and come to a place in our city where not only weren't children damaged, they were growing to be people of skill and dignity. Why didn't people pay serious attention to what we were doing? Why was it they seemed not to see what I was seeing being done to children out there in the schools using the conventional teaching-learning system? More and more I found myself the odd man out among my school of education colleagues, my teacher friends, and others who saw the conventional system in cities like ours having flaws maybe, but the best we could do—basically OK.

At the same time, I could understand why it was that so many of my friends and colleagues accepted failing urban schools as OK, even though they knew the statistics which showed losers and other discouraged children dropping out in droves or showed additional alarming signs such as how failing city schools were not preparing children adequately for college. [21] These adults were looking through the lens of their own experience. They had graduated from college; most had been in the winner groups in elementary and high school; their children too had learned from them how to play the conventional school game so that most of them ended up winners or near-winners. If their children didn't succeed, popular psychology doctrine taught parents the fault lay with them not the schooling system.

Sometimes these colleagues and friends said things like, "What's wrong with a system that helped me and the people I work with get where we are? You work hard and it pays off. Look at me. I made it. I went to college. I'm not doing so badly." They often argued that those who were losers in school ended up that way because they weren't naturally intelligent enough or they didn't work hard enough—they didn't have it in them or they couldn't cut the mustard. Along with inadequate parenting, they blamed children's school failure on the "I want something for nothing mentality of so many kids nowadays."

But for me these kinds of arguments were beside the point. Maybe some children were spoiled rotten by the culture and their parents; maybe some were genetically more able to handle intellectual tasks. Certainly some children's will was undermined by coming from what are called dysfunctional and child-abusive homes. But the point for me was our SIEE School's record and my other experience related in this memoir showed me that all children could succeed as independent learners and do it with self-respect. My experience working in conventional schools showed me why this didn't happen for most children in those schools.

Children who started our SIEE School at five-years-old succeeded. I knew that was happening because I was there and a part of it. I knew how teachers made sure that all the children who started at five-years-old and continued at our elementary school would be independent in using the basic skills, would be fluent readers and writers, most probably would be excited about books and reading, would know how to learn in ways that fitted themselves. I knew that children who left our school after years of sharing openly one to one with a teacher they trusted had every chance to become people who accepted themselves and others; most likely they would leave as people who followed their own drummer instead of blindly following the peer group. I knew that, on the contrary, most children in the elementary schools where I worked, risked seeing themselves as lackluster at least, as a result of their elementary schooling. And that was only one of the ways they risked becoming seriously damaged.

I found myself more and more often sick at heart. I believed in public schooling, along with so many other Americans. Now I was increasingly seeing my dream, our dream of equal opportunity for all, being lost by the one institution in America which was supposed to make the dream a reality—our schools.

My despondency led me to stop directing our SIEE School after ten years. A seemingly irreconcilable dispute between a teacher and myself over a relatively minor matter, made me ask myself if I hadn't done this job for long enough. We weren't changing what was happening in conventional classrooms. I knew I was more than a bit weary of the demanding unending work to maintain a flourishing innovative school on an uncertain financial shoestring.[22]

After I stopped directing our SIEE School I felt I had to get away. I took a semester's leave from my university job in order to study one and two room rural schools in New Zealand. There I spent seven weeks in rural areas visiting outstanding one and two room schools. I enjoyed meeting so many of the teachers and seeing how children responded to the accepting family atmosphere in almost all of the schools. As was the case at Alpine School, the schools provided a community center where rural families could relate to their neighbors.

One highlight of my trip to New Zealand was learning how children who lived on remote sheep ranches learned independently. These were children who lived even beyond the reach of one-room schools. There must have been quite a few of these children in New Zealand because the distance learning facility to serve them, located near Wellington, was housed in a new block-long building. I learned at the distance learning facility how teachers kept in close communication with the families and helped them educate their young children. To support parents, perhaps once during the year a teacher might fly in to spend time with children and parents at their ranch. As soon as a child became easy with reading and writing, the young people were educated by written instructions in mailed lessons. This was augmented by a two-week residential summer session where the students worked intensively with their tutors from the distance learning facility. Then students would return for the next year's learning at home, guided by the same tutor with whom they had worked in the summer. This was before television, videotapes, personal computers, e-mail and other ways by which students nowadays might learn independently by self-directed learning. Distance learning tutors at the center sometimes used audio tapes to direct students in how they should use the books and other print materials supplied by the distance learning faculty. Talking with distance learning faculty members left me with no doubts that secondary-age young people might be educated well in an independent learning center assisted by subject matter tutors. From my own experience I knew that this kind of independent learning needed to draw upon good preparation of younger children. They had to learn to be independent in reading and writing. Also I knew how important it was for each young person to be guided by a strong one to one relationship with a teacher. All that eventually did take shape in the Urban Little Schools idea.

Shortly after returning from New Zealand I quit my job at the university training teachers to work in conventional schools. I found my heart simply wasn't in it, particularly now that I didn't have my daily connection with our SIEE School to immerse me in what good schooling was. I simply couldn't go on being part of the education establishment leadership which I saw subverting the promise in public education without even being aware they were doing so. I found myself not wanting to have anything more to do with organized schooling—ever! Syracuse University made me an emeritus professor. I left, to begin a new chapter in my life.

But I couldn't stay away from trying to make schooling responsive to each child. After a complete break, lasting a few years, I found myself once again writing about schooling in harmony with each child. Based on the ideas and experiences I have described in this book so far, I designed the Urban Little Schools program—a radical change in the way children are helped to learn in schools.

In Chapter Three, I bring together the complete elementary and secondary Urban Little Schools design, specify its academic and character goals, and how these goals will be realized in the lives of young people growing up in the proposed schools.

Notes

1   For their privacy, most children's names have been changed. For the same reason, occasionally nonessential details about a child have been changed.

2   For more about individualization of reading and writing during this second grade year see: Newman, Robert E. (1960, May). Building each child's desire to read—A year-long language arts experience in the second grade. *Elementary English*, pp. 310-16.

3   Newman, Robert E. (1961). *History of a civic education project implementing the social problems technique of instruction.* Unpublished doctoral dissertation, Stanford University. (L.C. Card Microfilms No. 61-1209)

4   I explain how to make books and reading vital in a library-centered elementary Urban Little School, in Supplemental Article #3, under the subheadings "Stage Three: Building one's fluency in writing and reading through practice," and "Stage Four: Using and enjoying skillful reading, effective writing and library research in self-directed learning."

5   Dewey, John. (1916). *Democracy and Education*. New York, The Macmillan Co.

6   Dewey, John. (1933) *How We Think*. (Revised edition). Boston: D.C. Heath and Company. (original edition, 1910.)

7   *The Saturday Review*, under Norman Cousins' editorship was ideal for my purpose. It was a place where new ideas for schooling were being shared; it was read by teachers who wanted children to learn to love books, reading and writing.

8   After receiving her doctorate from Syracuse University, Eileen got a job as a professor at Miami University, at Oxford, Ohio. She trained teachers at Miami's demonstration school and directed the University's language arts center.

9   See "Stage One" and "Stage Two," in Supplemental Article #3 for a discussion of how Newstime fits into the wider picture of guiding each child toward independence in reading and writing.

10 Again, for more on this individualized way to help each child learn to write and to read, see Supplemental Article #3.

11 Empire Section. (1969, October 16). *The Syracuse Herald American*, pp. 31-33.

12 See Chapter Five for a detailed description and analysis of the child study process. The process is now built into the design for Urban Little Schools.

13   Bob's ideas influenced us to incorporate children's understanding of the logic of the number system into our math curriculum which generally speaking followed the texts used in the local public schools. Bob's methods emphasized children learning with hands on activities. Leah led most of these sessions based on Bob Davis' ideas. For more on Bob's ideas, see: Davis, Robert B. (1964). *Discovery in Mathematics: A Text for Teachers*. Reading, MA: Addison Wesley Publishing Co.

14   The "Y" closed it's downtown operation two or three years later. The building was demolished. The site is now a parking lot.

15   Newman, Robert E. (1980). *God Bless the Grass: Case Studies in Self Esteem*. Palo Alto, CA: R. & E. Research Publishers.

16   Newman, Robert E. (1980). *Reading, Writing and Self-Esteem*. Englewood Cliffs, NJ: Prentice-Hall.

17   Newman, Robert E. (1965, 1966). *The Language Arts of Individual Inquiry*. Chicago, IL: Science Research Associates.

18   Earlier in the memoir, I explained how I had learn on my own to individualize the teaching of reading when I began teaching.

19   President Clinton cited these figures in his "Safe Schools Summit" speech, as reported in *The Christian Science Monitor*, April 10, 1995, p 2.

20   Nowadays Educators for Social Responsibility maintains a widespread and burgeoning program for schools. Workshops and materials emphasize "...the development of cooperation, caring, communication, appreciation of diversity, expression of feelings, responsible decision-making and conflict resolution." (Educators for Social Responsibility, 23 Garden Street Cambridge, MA 02138.)

21   Forty percent of Washington, DC's high school students drop out before graduation. *Action for Better Schools*, (1998, Spring-Summer) newsletter of The National Coalition of Education Activists, p. 2.

22   After I announced my decision to leave the directorship of our school, I helped the new director learn the ropes but in a few years the school closed. Increasingly, instead of attracting parents who believed in its vision, the school became a rescue operation for children having difficult problems at home and in conventional schools. Too many of their parents wanted a quick-fix that the school couldn't provide. I learned from these events, how much a pioneering and financially vulnerable small school like SIEE needed the support of a backup organization firmly grounded in the school's vision and possessing effective power and finances. Such a backup organization is described in Chapter Nine.

3

Overview and Logic

A Context Within Which the Reader Can Fit
the Specifics of the Urban Little Schools Design,
Which are Explained in the Rest of the Book

After the overview of the Urban Little Schools design, immediately below, I list the goals implicit in the design. Then I discuss why we should expect these goals to be realized: How the academic and job-related goals will be achieved in the elementary and in the secondary Urban Little Schools; why we should expect the Urban Little Schools' character goals to be realized; and how through individualization the Urban Little Schools design enables teachers to achieve the goals in each child's case. In subsequent chapters I shall discuss individual elements of the design further.

An Overview of The Urban Little Schools Idea

At its heart, The Urban Little Schools idea is as simple as it is beautiful: teachers listen to each child. Teachers listen one to one as children talk, write and express themselves in other ways. It is a trusting relationship where both the teacher and increasingly the child, over the years plan step by step. Learning is tuned to each child so every single one is prepared for college or more suitable training, so children learn to think for themselves not blindly follow the crowd.

Urban Little Schools are proposed as parent-choice schools located within a short walking distance from where the children live—perhaps in a refitted old house, a few rooms in an underutilized school, or in unused space in an urban church. These close-by schools can bring children's parents and nearby residents together to provide stability, order, and vitality in declining neighborhoods. Urban Little Schools teachers each have a one to one relationship with twelve children or fewer.

Urban Little Schools can be parent-choice schools within a public school district or they can be private schools. Charter School status can be used to finance and facilitate pilot Urban Little Schools, in states which have the necessary enabling legislation in place. It costs a host school district about the same in per diem costs as the average district now pays per child. Outside financial support will be needed to help fund the ULS backup organization, described at the end of this overview.

In an Urban Little School just down the block or around the corner, children start at five years of age, learning step by step the skills of independent learning and how to take responsibility for their own learning. Entry to Urban Little Schools is limited to neighborhood five-year-olds and children, who might transfer from another Urban Little School. Thus the Urban Little Schools won't become a rescue operation to rehabilitate children, who have had damaging experience in conventional schools. In addition, by only admitting five-year-olds and ULS transfer students, most entering children will be of the age where they have not already been hardened by the urban street culture; nor will they have been molded by the conventional schools' largely impersonal passive learning system. In the Urban Little Schools way, there is no learning game to see who is ahead of whom—there are no losers and winning is beside the point. The point is to learn how to learn by doing it, as you plan one to one with your teacher, step by step in an open listening way. By working in this fashion with their teachers, ULS children increasingly learn to evaluate and to set new goals for themselves, in light of what has been done so far.

Thus Urban Little Schools children are guided to develop the skills and independent judgment needed to qualify each child for college or more suitable further learning. A young person works for 1200 or more hours on jobs alongside community people of integrity. Young people learn how to learn and adapt, to be self-reliant in the ever changing new market economy where workers often need to master new technologies, to learn new jobs and to start new careers.

Character development isn't taught in the Urban Little Schools; it's lived. Each child lives honestly with his or her teacher and works with principled community people the child can trust. From young people's experience learning to plan and carry out their own learning, they can find their own way guided by their tested inner wisdom and the examples set by teachers and on-the-job mentors. They are growing up in an environment which fosters being your own person—not blindly following the peer group or the street ways.

Urban Little Schools are not indulgent "free schools" where children choose what they want to do. Teachers and children work closely in a planning relationship, but it is only gradually over the years that the teacher passes more and more responsibility for planning to the child. Thus the children take independent responsibility for their own learning progressively, and always under the teacher's guidance.

Each Urban Little School child and teacher work together usually for longer than one year where children of differing ages learn side by side, sometimes in unique ways and always at a pace, which fits each learner. [1] Consequently this schooling can and does fit every one of the children. In the same vein, some children might take longer than others to reach academic independence or to be ready for college. They can, because learning is one to one and an individual matter between the students and their teachers. In these and other ways, readers of this book will discover how Urban Little Schools are individualized—how teachers fit learning to each child.

Teachers are trained to be skillful in helping every child learn efficiently and in self-directed ways. These teachers are selected from strong people, who by nature listen to children. Further, teachers are helped to know each child well. An example is the ULS child study process. Out of this awareness of each child, teachers help children develop the ability to follow their own inner strength and sound wisdom, step by step. Furthermore, teachers are chosen to be models of people, who, like the children under their care, are coming to take responsibility for their lives.

Elementary ULS teachers work in teams of four full-time people or more part-time teachers, in their small neighborhood schools, which each enroll about forty-four children, five through twelve years of age. Life in these elementary schools, just a few doors from children's homes, is similar in many ways to what home life in a nurturing extended family might be like. There is a special place for each child, as older and younger live and work together with acceptance.

The academic priority, during the ULS elementary years, is for each of the students to use reading and writing to help them learn independently. To a lessor but still important sense students need to be skilled in solving arithmetic problems accurately and learn the fundamentals of geometry and algebra. Students need to learn how to use their independent reading, writing and arithmetic skill as they use the library, computers and other resources independently. They learn content as individually they pursue library research during the last stage of their reading and writing training. At graduation, elementary students need to be able to write a clear essay explaining what they found out about a subject new to them.

In the elementary years, subjects such as science, history, and geography are introduced in meaningful ways so students will become fascinated and excited by what it might mean to learn more in these areas. As children become independent readers they are encouraged to explore the library's non-fiction collection, learning intriguing facts and ideas in colorful books, which emphasize overviews of the various subject fields. At the school's Friday afternoon "Events Time," knowledge comes alive: visiting scholars tell about what makes their work central in their lives; foreign nationals show slides of what it means to grow up in other countries; an auto repair technician might help students take apart a simple engine; a "mystery guest" answers questions until students discover what the guest does for a living.

Elementary students don't move to secondary Urban Little Schools until they can work productively on community jobs, frame and answer penetrating questions, and are prepared to learn on their own what they need to prepare for their community jobs. In addition, students don't move to secondary Urban Little Schools until they are able to learn traditional high school academic content systematically in the secondary Self-directed Learning Centers.

Most elementary children move to a secondary Urban Little School at twelve years of age. Other elementary ULS children might move at a younger or an older age; it depends on the child's ability to handle academic learning independently and to do secondary jobs well. There is no stigma to move to a secondary Urban Little School at an age older than twelve, because there are no rigid age-grade distinctions. As mentioned, older and younger work side by side in their Urban Little Schools. Also one's learning is a matter between each child and that child's teacher.

Because secondary Urban Little Schools young people are working in the community at least a third of their time and because they do their academic studying mainly independently, secondary schools have a different feel from the elementary Urban Little Schools. Each of these secondary Urban Little Schools enrolls about twelve young people from around twelve- to about eighteen-years-old. Each secondary teacher (or two "partnership" teachers sharing a full-time position) has his or her own schooling place situated in varied locations throughout the community.

These secondary schools are designed to be more like a learning headquarters than the kind of self-contained teaching and learning environment the young people have had in their elementary Urban Little Schools. For example, the twelve young people might have their own partitioned office adjacent to their teacher's. From this headquarters, the young people range out to jobs, to the centrally located Self-directed Learning Center or to make use of libraries, swimming pools and other community resources. In the Self-directed Learning Centers the young people master the high school basics largely through independent learning, done with videotaped high school courses, courses on computers and occasional small laboratory classes. Students also are helped, when needed, by tutors. As they continue their one to one work with their secondary teacher, each of them is helped to decide the right next steps in academic learning and on jobs. Students work at paid and unpaid jobs alongside community people whose lives are good examples of the values the Urban Little Schools stand for. Before they graduate secondary students must qualify for college or other more suitable training of their choice.

Adolescent young people in the Urban Little Schools are helped to grow as strong individuals in a schooling, which values diversity—where young people of differing ages, ethnic and/or racial backgrounds, economic privilege and values all are learning in school side by side. The secondary ULS teacher's group of twelve meets weekly to exchange thoughts and anecdotes. For special events they often meet with young people from other secondary ULS groups.

Secondary young people relate to several different adults every year, who are good role models—in school and in the wider world of work. This is one more way this high school education doesn't accentuate the adolescent's trying to be like all the others. Also the secondary schooling doesn't press young people into an artificial age-alike peer group and teenage culture whose ways and mannerisms often have grown to be apart from the values, which make sense in the wider world.

In addition, the Urban Little Schools students, both during adolescent years as well as in the elementary school years, are helped by their teachers to chronicle their growth as unique and self-reliant persons, in the student's record portfolio. It reflects the student's growth from the first year in the Urban Little Schools. The portfolio is shared with parents periodically. In words, test scores, sample schoolwork, Urban Little Schools' work references, and in pictures, each portfolio also interprets the student's growth to people who might provide subsequent learning opportunities to the student. These might be teachers, prospective Urban Little Schools' community employers or college admissions officers.

Teachers make it a point to work together closely with their children's parents. If parents ask for it, teachers can act as the children's advocate in securing special services that will help the children take full advantage of their Urban Little School. These close neighborhood ties can enable Urban Little Schools to back up parents, who might want to help vitalize the adjacent community.

This can be particularly important in declining city neighborhoods where many parents and others simply don't know where to turn to uplift neighborhood spirit while trying to rebuild dissolving community infrastructure. Washington, DC, for example, is such a place. Several pilot Urban Little Schools might be established in at-risk neighborhoods, which were unstable but not yet completely without infrastructure. Subsequently, additional Urban Little Schools might be established on the declining inner city fringes of these areas—step by step edging renewed neighborhood spirit and structure toward the most neglected parts of the inner city.

In the Urban Little Schools, all children, underprivileged and privileged alike, can grow up with hope, dignity, and with a sense of one's individual significance. They will grow to be adults with an even chance of making a good and meaningful life whatever the circumstances in which they find themselves. Here are some of the reasons why:

- Each child has a teacher the child can be sure of—a teacher who knows emotionally and specifically how the child is one of a kind and can help the child grow step by step in harmony with that uniqueness. This is a teacher who will make sure a child has the basic skills of reading, writing and computing, which are necessary for independent learning.
- Each child has an elementary and secondary schooling which opens future education and job doors. Children are prepared to go on to college or to fit into more appropriate further learning. They learn to make sound decisions about fitting themselves into the right job and about retraining themselves for the next job or career. Much of this independent skill and wisdom comes from planning and solving problems in concert with the their teachers, one to one, step by step; it also comes from working with respected community people on paid and unpaid jobs for about one to two thousand hours during secondary Urban Little School years.
- Each Urban Little Schools child can resist the cynical no-hope-for-the-future message from the streets of many declining city neighborhoods. This is because at school the ULS children are living a life of expectation and fulfillment—connected to a wider world beyond the hopelessness of the streets. One to one with trusted adults at school and in the community, ULS children learn to face each problem as it presents itself. Out of this, children learn to think and act according to their own values, well-honed in honest dialogue with a teacher whose life is an example of integrity. With this background, a child's inner rudder can keep the young person from falling prey to such manifestations of the street culture's hopelessness as drugs, crime and violence.

The proposed Urban Little Schools can be started as Charter Schools, independent private schools, or as an autonomous school system within a city school district. The Urban Little Schools explained in this book are assumed to have such autonomous status as part of a school district, contractually defined according to how administration is to be handled and how the ULS component will be evaluated regularly. Further, the Urban

Little Schools are assumed to be under the authority of a strong backup organization, which is described in Chapter Nine. This backup group maintains a continuing presence and control of the Urban Little Schools within the school district, in ways such as these: it leases and outfits the small school buildings and the self-directed learning centers, to the district (or from the district, if buildings belonging to the district are used), plus funds start-up; it directs the selection and training of teachers who receive the same pay as other teachers in the host school district; it secures some of its funding from donations and through the sale of self-directed learning materials it develops for the Urban Little Schools; it helps others to replicate the pilot schools, assuming that prototype schools live up to expectations; it coordinates the annual or every two-year evaluation whereby each Urban Little School is assessed thoroughly by outside judges according to specific goals clearly defined in the contract between the backup organization and the school district.

The Urban Little School's Goals: How They are Realized

The Urban Little School's Academic and Job-related Goals

- Each student who leaves the Urban Little Schools will be equipped to succeed with self-reliant skill at college or at other more appropriate training; this success will enable the young person to have an even chance in the job market's competition.
- Students will be adept at using the skills of independent learning such as reading and writing fluently, using arithmetic to estimate and compute easily, knowing the library like the back of one's hand and knowing how to use computers and other tools for self-directed learning and expression.
- We can expect that by the time they graduate they will show in many ways that they hold books, reading and writing to be vital personal experience.

- Finally they will be able to chart their own course of job success in the sometimes ruthless market economy; this includes training themselves for the next job, the next career.

The Urban Little Schools' Character Goals

- On their ULS jobs, young people will be able to make openness and listening facilitate efficient and successful work. They will be able to work well in teams or to carry out individual assignments successfully. They will be able to do this partly because they will be seen as people others can trust—responsible people who others can count on.
- We can expect ULS children to leave their schooling years with a sense of earned self-respect. This includes accepting themselves as they are, while at the same time working to improve themselves. Their self-respect should be evident in how they know and judge themselves accurately and how they plan their own learning realistically.
- Young people will show many signs of being strong and self-reliant—people who have a clear sense of themselves and can guide their own lives without blindly following others. Thus they should be expected to be able to live within a street culture, which encourages such things as drug taking, violence, gangs, rampant teenage sex, while at the same time they won't be swept up in such a way of life.

How Elementary Urban Little Schools are Designed to Realize Academic and Job-related Goals

The basic academic and job-related goal of the Urban Little Schools is that children learn how to succeed independently, first during their Urban Little Schools years, then at college or in further training and finally on jobs which fit them. To reach this goal, the Urban Little Schools are designed specifically so that before moving to the secondary schools, each elementary child will work independently in writing, reading, and arithmetic plus computer and library use. Children must be able to use these skills functionally on their first secondary ULS community jobs. When children leave their elementary Urban Little School, they have to be able to learn high school basic subjects independently at a secondary ULS Self-directed Learning Center. There, typically they will learn from televised traditional-format courses and courses taught on computers, which involve the learner interactively. These elementary ULS minimum exit requirements are spelled out in detail, in Supplemental Article #2.

Meeting these exit requirements doesn't mean elementary ULS children will be subjected to undue pressure or stigma if they don't move to the secondary school at age twelve. This is because each child's academic program is individualized. Seldom are two programs alike in terms of sequence or pacing.

Mastering reading, writing, and using these skills in libraries and on computers is given the highest academic priority in elementary Urban Little Schools because these abilities are fundamental to independent learning. To this end, in elementary Urban Little Schools, learning to write and read is not an exercise but an integral part of communicating. Important rote learning such as memorizing the basic reading words and phonics practice is given priority too. Often memorizing and practice is aided by doing it as part of games and in other ways which heighten a child's motivation to learn.

In regular journals with their teacher, elementary children use their reading and writing to communicate seriously all through their elementary years. At about the time children need lots of meaningful practice to become fluent in writing—about seven or eight years old for most ULS children—they get much of it through writing journals. During this period the children will be exchanging with their teachers, probably at least thirty-five substantial journal entries each year. In this communication the child and teacher write about what is important to each of them and they plan for the child's learning. In addition, the two also conference regularly.

The library is offered to the child as an intriguing and beautiful place where one's life is extended and made richer. Many older elementary ULS children will work in the library, shelving books and doing other tasks which help librarians. This also is preparation for community jobs in children's secondary Urban Little Schools years. As secondary students, they might spend mornings for several months doing such library work as handling the charging desk at the children's room or assisting the reference librarian in helping patrons secure information or books.

Children use computers as a part of their daily individualized learning in elementary Urban Little Schools. For example, most children from five- or six-years-old write the journals we have been discussing, on computers. If they are not independent in writing, they dictate their journals to a person who writes what the child says on a computer. Then, bit by bit, typically, young children take over and write on their own. Children learn handwriting as their hand and arm muscles allow them to write with ease.

As a part of children's learning to be independent, their math program in the elementary Urban Little Schools is grounded in an understanding of the number system. Children learn to estimate the answer to arithmetic problems as a guide to make sure they have made the right moves to reach their answers. Also, early-on, arithmetic is made functional. For example, as mentioned, children might work in libraries where they need to know how to use the decimal system that is the basis for the library's shelf organization. Then later, on their secondary ULS jobs, from about twelve-years old upwards, they need to use their skill with number relationships to handle the work requirements in most job placements.

How Secondary Urban Little Schools will Realize Their Academic and Job-related Goals

We should expect that ULS young people's ability to plan and reflect on what they are learning and becoming will mature as they go through their secondary Urban Little Schools. One reason for this is that they will be building on the academic self-reliance they learned in their elementary school years—seven years of independently progressing step by step in a planning partnership with a teacher they trust. In the secondary Urban Little Schools the teacher will build on this independent ability, guiding students to learn the high school academic basics taught in the Self-directed Learning Centers. The student and secondary teacher plan how best to do this self-directed learning as they share in regularly scheduled one to one conferences and journals.

We should expect that secondary Urban Little Schools students should learn to be job-wise—the last on the list of academic and job-related goals—as they work at each of their community jobs. Because of their practical on-the-job training, ULS young people will learn how to decide for themselves what work is right for them; they will be helped to figure out how they can train themselves to be competent on a new job; they will learn how to decide for themselves what further training they might need to upgrade their skills once they are working, and then do it. Later, as an adult with this kind of education, they should be able to decide when it might be time to learn a new job or to start a major new chapter in their work life. They should be able to do this because they practice all of these challenges in concert with their secondary ULS teacher for about five years during one to two thousand hours of on-the-job experience.

Finally, secondary students will not be graduated until they are able to succeed in college or further specialized training. As was the case in the elementary Urban Little Schools program, secondary young people can remain without stigma in their Urban Little School until they are capable of succeeding at college or in further post-secondary training. Specific minimum requirements for graduation from secondary Urban Little Schools, are listed in Supplemental Article #2.

How Both Elementary and Secondary Urban Little Schools Should be Expected to Help Children Realize Character Trait Goals

When I talk of character traits, I am speaking of such characteristics as self-respect, respect for others, responsible independent thinking and consequent self-direction—all leading to a life of integrity at work and in personal relationships. This includes developing realistic understanding of yourself, which means such things as coming to know and accept one's feelings of self-diminishment without fleeing from often concomitant fearful dark emotions. Here are some of the ways these character traits will be learned in the Urban Little Schools:

Children can be expected to leave their Urban Little Schools at about seventeen-years-old feeling a keen sense of their own worth and ability. They will have earned this belief in themselves. Over and over again, for twelve years or more, they have seen themselves defining challenges and meeting them. For example, they have seen themselves increasingly plan their own learning effectively in ways from which one can draw satisfaction about one's accomplishments. They have seen themselves learn how to figure out what they needed to succeed in a new job, and then learn that self-reliantly. All this has become undeniable evidence of their capabilities. Also, every one of the ULS young people can see increasingly how they are mastering the tools needed for success such as their knowing the library, knowing how to use computers to learn, to write and to communicate with others. Then too, the young people can see themselves in the mirror provided by their teacher's positive regard for them as individuals. Their teacher is a person who the young person can count on to give accurate feedback enabling the most suitable next steps to be taken. The teacher and the child are partners in keeping track of the young person's development.

Also, in their teachers, the young people have a model for self-respect. By coming to know and value their teachers—as ULS young people do in their journal exchange with teachers, for example—young people can sense what self-respect is all about. Inner city young people can see in their ULS teachers, people whose values are different from some of the street values many central city children are offered. For example, teachers' lives demonstrate how honesty makes sense, how it's OK to be open and show vulnerability in certain situations, how compassion can be basic to satisfying relationships, how there is a future in one's life toward which to look.

Working one to one with their natural listener teachers, it shouldn't be surprising if ULS young people come to stand out because they too are good listeners. It just stands to reason that young people will come to be good at listening in ways that enhance communication and that helps to bring about good working and personal relationships. In their one to one relationships, the children increasingly learn to take the other person seriously, to ask questions and to pay attention to what the other says. In their one to one relationships the teacher and the child listen and find out the other person's point of view. Listening is functional. Good solid work gets done as the child and teacher listen to each other with respect.

Acceptance just doesn't happen by chance. It is embedded in how students and teachers live and work together. ULS children grow up in a school environment where they are accepted and where they learn, because of this, to accept themselves and to relate to others with acceptance. Thus acceptance enables the kinds of relationships which allow each person to grow and to be the best one can be.

Interpersonal trust and straightforwardness are character traits, which ULS children have learned to make work between people. It pays to be open with your teacher and yourself in your planning relationship. You and your teacher are partners guiding your path, step by step, with you taking more and more responsibility for your own learning. Both of you need relevant emotional data to do this job. You can't move ahead unless you both know what's going on—know how you feel about what you are doing at the moment, know what tensions you feel which might get in your way. With your teacher, it helps to sit back, so-to-speak, and with candor reflect accurately and incisively on your learning up to this point and then figure out what's next to be done.

All this adds up to schools which help young people to be strong and come to have a clear sense of themselves—to be persons who are developing solid self-direction. These young people should have the ability to figure out the next steps and then to take them independently or in concert with others. They have been doing that for years, guided by their teachers.

Finally, all this helps these young people to know what it means to feel they are valued, and have a sense of belonging in their group, which is characterized by acceptance, trust and caring. That, as opposed to the urban street culture where in cliques and gangs, fear and sometimes violence presses group members to conform to their group's codes.

Ten Reasons Why Urban Little Schools Enable Teachers to Individualize Education for Each Student

The Urban Little Schools program is specifically designed to allow teachers to work closely and sensitively with each of their twelve students, ensuring all students succeed at school and have an even chance to have a good life.

1. Urban Little Schools teachers can individualize because they are listening people who have shown they are responsive to how a child might best learn. For example, most pilot teachers may be ex-preschool teachers who have been observed to be natural listeners in how they related to each child under their care. Additional teachers would be selected,

primarily, from people who have shown themselves to be sensitive toward children as they worked as assistants or volunteers in Urban Little Schools.

2. These new teachers will know what it means to take responsibility for one's own learning in an individualized education. They will have tried out independent learning in their own teacher training, guided by an experienced Urban Little Schools teacher. This kind of enabling relationship between teacher and teacher-trainer is designed to be similar to the relationship the new ULS teachers will have with their students.

3. Teachers are helped to raise their awareness of each child with whom they work. This helps teachers to tune each child's learning both to emotional as well as academic needs. In addition, as part of this awareness process, the children are helped to become more and more in tune with themselves as worthwhile unique people. By helping teachers to become aware sensitively of each of their children, any mismatch between teacher and child who are expected to work together one to one, can be corrected. In elementary Urban Little Schools this process is called the child study process, which is explained in Chapter Five.

4. Elementary ULS teachers are trained to fit basic academic learning to each child. A prime example is how teachers are taught to fit reading and writing learning to each child. Teachers learn how to analyze a child's status and how to determine the next steps, which will be needed to enable the child to master the fundamental literacy skills so vital to independent learning. Thus teachers are able to help each child learn to read and write with independent fluency and then can guide the child to apply this learning in using libraries, using computers and in communication with others. How to do this is taught to new ULS teachers in Supplemental Article #3.

5. Elementary teachers are enabled to take the necessary time to work closely with their children who are not yet academically independent, while at the same time effectively guide others in their groups of twelve, who are independent. For example, the Urban Little Schools elementary teacher leans heavily on the periodic conferences and journals to guide the more academically independent children in the teacher's multi-age group. These more self-directed children have worked with the teacher long enough to be able to plan ahead and then carry out their plans on their

own. That leaves time for the teacher to work one to one several times each day with the two to four children who are not yet independent in reading and writing—the key skills for academic independence. These more academically dependent children typically need guiding attention at intervals during the day in order to help them carry out the learning which best fits each of them. In addition, teachers can call upon some of their more independent students to help the academically dependent ones. If the budget permits, the teacher can also have help from a part-time assistant teacher.

6. Teachers will have enough time to focus on helping each child because of the Urban Little Schools entry policy. The entry policy stipulates that only neighborhood five-year-olds and transfer students from other Urban Little Schools will be admitted. Because of this policy, an undue amount of teachers' time will not be consumed, by the following: (a) spending time rehabilitating incoming children who have been seriously damaged by prior schooling experiences; (b) taking time from other children to help older transferring students learn how to learn independently in a trusting one to one relationship with the teacher; (c) taking precious time to help incoming children unlearn any conventional school conditioning such as "the name of the game is to find out what the teacher wants and then do just that"—as opposed to the ULS way which is that children are active in planning their next learning steps under guidance from a teacher. [2]

   In addition, because of this entry policy teachers can help inner city children learn the ULS way before the hold of the street culture has become a vice-grip on them—a street culture, which teaches that openness and honesty with school people is to be ridiculed, brands the child who succeeds at school as a lackey of authority, and pressures children to look to the peer culture and its clique or gang leaders for direction.

   Finally, teachers can help five-year-olds recover more easily from damaging prior relationships, or other bad previous out-of-school experiences than if the children were older.

7. Starting a school with five-year-olds also allows teachers to keep their eyes on the long haul, to plan and work with the idea of a full Urban Little Schools education ahead for children—an education which could

help children to build their own strong inner resources, step by step over the years, in ways which are tuned to each child as a learner and as a person.

8. The backup organization provides support, which gives secondary ULS teachers time for their three vital time-consuming counseling roles with each secondary young person: (a) academic planning, (b) job-related guidance, and (c) listening to each young person. The backup organization runs the Self-directed Learning Centers and does much of the ground work in establishing job contacts for subsequent follow-up by teachers, for instance.

9. Also, during the children's secondary years the teachers have time to fit each child to the right community jobs. This often will entail being with employers and in spending time at their workplaces. To allow secondary teachers more time, they work and are paid for 185 days instead of the 175 days teachers usually work each year. (Two partnership secondary teachers can share one year-long position thus allowing each teacher time off if that is desired.)

10. Finally, the Urban Little Schools backup organization helps teachers to individualize by supplying self-directed academic learning materials from which the teacher can tailor each child's academic learning whether the children learn in an elementary school or work in the secondary Self-directed Learning Centers. These learning materials can range from the very basic computerized games, which help children learn arithmetic times tables, to computer programs that teach topics such as cell structure, membranes and cell motility. [3]

Now let's move to the next chapter where we shall see how an elementary Urban Little School works.

Notes

1   New Urban Little Schools are begun with a few five-year-olds per teacher while the new teacher learns the ropes. Then the next year more five-year-olds are added to increase the size of the group and to compensate for attrition, and so on. Thus the multi-age span emerges in six years following initial start-up of the school.

2   For more on the difference between the Urban Little Schools way of learning and the conventional schools' teaching-learning system see pp. 67-78.

3   A two-part biology program, which teaches this content is "Cell Biology," Parts I and II, on computer compact disks. The two CD disks sell for $139.95 from Learning Services Company, PO Box 10636, Eugene, OR 97440-2636.

4

An Elementary
Urban Little School

I have drawn the elementary Urban Little School in this chapter's illustration as a composite of the best features of the Syracuse Institute for Enabling Education school—the experimental forerunner of the Urban Little Schools. We developed and changed the SIEE school year by year, during the ten years I directed it. This was partly because we grew from seventeen children to more than forty children. But the continuous modification of our school was intentional; it was integral to our experimental process. We aimed at developing an individualized elementary schooling which was practical and worked for each child as well as for every teacher. I wanted our gradual development to inform us, to teach us what should be done to make what we were doing ever more responsive to each child. We tried one way and then adjusted the rest of the school to that. Then we changed again. Each time, each step of the way, we put our accumulating wisdom into the new features.

In this chapter, I describe how a school with the best qualities of SIEE can meet the challenges of an urban neighborhood that shows the results of neglect and poverty. The Fircroft School in Twin Rivers is the setting for this illustration.

Twin Rivers is drawn as a Midwestern US City of 650,000 people. Its city school district enrolls 93,500 children. The city's economy now offers mostly low paying service jobs to workers who used to find good employment in its now gone manufacturing sector. Twin Rivers is located in an urban area which is called The Point, bounded by the confluence of two rivers which then flow into one of the Great Lakes, two miles downstream. The largest single employer in the city is the Twin Rivers campus of the state university, enrolling 14,300 students, located at the tip of The Point. Suburbs containing 300,000 more people are situated across the two rivers from the city proper.

The story takes place fifteen years after the pilot elementary and secondary Urban Little Schools were established in Twin Rivers as autonomous components of the Twin Rivers School District. The board delegated authority to the ULS backup group, called the Urban Little Schools Foundation, subject to a biennial evaluation of the ULS component submitted to the board. The district pays, on a per-pupil basis, what it normally pays to educate the average child in its district, less costs incurred for the thorough biennial evaluation of each of the Urban Little Schools and payment for the ULS share of the district's special education program for severely handicapped children.

The Fircroft Urban Little School is one of the first two pilot elementary Urban Little Schools established by the ULS Foundation in Twin Rivers. It now enrolls children from age five to about twelve years old. The school is situated in what was a turn-of-the-century luxury three story brick house with an ample basement and attic. Forty-one children attend The Fircroft School. Their building faces Prospect Park, a thirty-acre wooded and grass covered area containing a playscape with slides, climbing gyms and other apparatus for children. One of the city's branch libraries is around the corner and a block away from the park.

The building was picked to house an elementary ULS for its location and because it was large enough—five bedrooms and ample other space which could easily be turned into study and conferencing alcoves. Because the building was in need of repair, the owner readily agreed to the alterations the Urban Little Schools Foundation proposed to make. The Foundation's offer of a five-year lease made the owner even more receptive. [1]

Downstairs in the three high-ceilinged main rooms, four-foot-wide mezzanine balconies extend out from walls. They are simple in design, made from construction-grade two-by-fours and plywood. Children can work up there at child-sized desks in private-feeling "offices" as they sit on the thick carpet, separated from the next child by sound absorbing semi-walls. Below the mezzanine are alcoves for one to one conferences and small group meetings. In front of the big bay window, which looks out on the back yard, are the art tables near the school's readily accessible self-service creative materials center. The art area and the mezzanines also double as extra seating space for the daily meeting of the whole school, which is held in the large open space in the middle of downstairs. These meetings sometimes have fifty or sixty attending because, along with the children and teachers, there usually are visitors, volunteers, and parents who are encouraged to drop in on this neighborhood school just a few minutes from their homes.

Because of the space arrangement, several small groups can meet simultaneously without distracting each other, while at the same time individuals can have privacy to use the self-study equipment and materials. In out-of-the-way places there are computers and video playback equipment for children to view self-study tape recordings and work with interactive multimedia computer software. Children and staff also use computers for word processing. The computers are almost always busy. Children use them for writing, study and reference as well as for self-directed learning exercises (such as the basic math program's interactive learning lessons, which are self-paced with simulated problem situations).

The building's plentiful corners and alcoves are used, too, for teachers' office niches, where often one can see individual children and their teachers conferencing. Each of the youngest children and their key teachers usually have several private contacts every day. Older and more independent children have longer and less frequent conference times. They each usually exchange written journals weekly or more often with their key teachers.

Almost always, during the day, there are visitors circulating unobtrusively at Fircroft, many from out of town. Children seem happy to answer visitors' questions. Any distraction arising from this questioning seems balanced by the children's sense of significance as they realize what they are doing seems important to the visitors. Visitors are helped by Maude Mapstone, this pilot school's hostess, to blend in quietly with an attitude of respect for the children and the teachers. One reason this unobtrusiveness is possible is that visitors, ahead of time, understand what to expect at Fircroft. Maude sends them written material; she often meets one to one with them the day before they observe and she meets in the morning with the day's group of visitors before school begins. She is available also, to talk with visitors during the morning in her office next to the front door. Her office used to be part of the old house's dining room.

Maude is a Fircroft parent who works for the Urban Little Schools Foundation. Because of the way her work is organized, Maude can leave Fircroft when her child leaves at the end of the day. Her husband gets their boy off to Fircroft in the morning because Maude meets with the visitors at 7:30 for coffee and food in the kitchen. Then the visitors move to an alcove in the main downstairs room, to hear Maude talk about what they are likely to see during the day. The school's basic daily time sequence is on a poster in this area:

BASIC DAILY ACTIVITY RHYTHM
(Except for Friday Afternoon)

8:30	Arrival, settle-in and conference time
9:30	News and Goods and Newstime Groups
10:00	Snacks
10:15	School-wide meeting
10:30	Quiet study time and conferencing
11:30	Silent Sustained Reading, Ask for a Word, and Book Time groups
12:00	Lunch
1:00	Storytime
1:30	Quiet Study Time and conferencing
2:30	Cleanup
3:00	Time to leave

At about 7:45, Maude goes over the posted sequence of events that typically happens each day. She points out how the simple daily schedule allows most children to move freely throughout the school to avail themselves of the best space, tools and supplies to carry out plans they individually have made with their key teachers. The youngest children, however, often work in a designated area so that one of their key teachers or an assistant teacher always can be nearby to help them. Also, some older children who seem to need more defined behavior boundaries, work in certain designated areas. Maude sometimes contrasts this with conventional schools. There, all children are restricted to classrooms, to their desks and to designated playground space. Then when children move to work with special teachers, such as the school's art teacher, they usually go in groups.

She explains to the visitors that the only exception each week to this posted sequence of events is Friday afternoon, when the school's program becomes like a cafeteria, offering children different classes and meetings from which to choose. This is called Events Time, when typically there are five to seven different small classes or seminars varying from art and music to perhaps a hands-on session studying the human skeleton, or a workshop in how to draw cartoon faces, or a demonstration of how to throw clay mugs on the school's ceramic wheel. These workshops can be led by community people, children, teachers or parents. Often these events are samples of a planned series of meetings, such as when a group might form to rehearse chorus singing for special concerts at a department store over the holiday season.

Maude explains that the children move in and out of the school's program rhythm according to the individual plans which they make one to one with their key teachers. Each teacher has responsibility to guide twelve of Fircroft's children. (There are also two part-time teachers, who take one full-time key teacher position, in partnership.) Maude touches on how all the teachers help each other to ensure that there is the best possible one to one psychological fit between teachers and the children under their care. Maude talks about the teachers' balance of work each day. She explains that Fircroft key teachers typically do about ninety minutes of group teaching and the rest is one to one work. That, as opposed to conventional elementary school teachers, who typically do group teaching almost exclusively.

Maude points to the 9:30 schedule item, "News and Goods" and "Newstime" groups. She explains the difference between the two groups: Newstime serves children who are not yet independent in writing. The teacher writes on a large pad of newsprint in front of the young people, as they share in the group. Teachers write about their thoughts and reactions that come from what children share or perhaps simply summarize what a child offers. Often Newstime extends a bit longer than the allotted half hour because it is important to make time for every child to speak if he or she wants to.

For these fledgling readers and writers, Newstime is one of the most important lessons each day, in addition to their journal exchange with their key teachers. In their journal exchange, children who can't yet write dictate their journals, which are then passed to the child's key teacher. The next morning a reply is in the child's mailbox. Beginning children soon get the idea: in journals and Newstime what comes out on paper is talk-written-down that is worth reading. From this point children can learn the fundamentals of spelling, punctuation, grammar and usage from the example set by the teachers' writing in journals and Newstime each day.

"News and Goods" is a group time for children who no longer need to learn from the writing modeled for them by the teacher, as is done in Newstime. In the News and Goods group, each child has an opportunity to speak and share something that feels at least a bit good. Children share unpleasant things at this time, too, but usually they share their distress and things that don't feel good, in their journals and during private conferences with their key teachers. Maude emphasizes that it is important for the ULS day to begin with each child having an opportunity to share.

Maude continues explaining the schedule. She discusses how the time period from 11:30–12:00 is used for most children to read, either on their own if they are independent or to read with teachers' help. Three different kinds of activities are set up to help children do this, depending on the child's degree of reading independence: "Booktime" is for those who are not independent, where teachers have cozy groups of not more than ten children. They often immerse themselves in a pile of large soft pillows, where the teacher starts things off by reading a picture book to the children. Then in the remaining fifteen minutes or so children look at their own books which the young students usually have been helped to select from the library. Often children will begin to read words in their books. Teachers help them with unknown words, if they are asked to.

For children who are almost independent in reading, there are "Ask For a Word" groups. Here children who are beginning to be on their own in books, typically read in individually chosen books, which have colorful and interesting stories but low difficulty levels. With just a pointing gesture, a child can ask for an unknown word to be spoken softly by the teacher. Teachers who lead these groups position themselves so every book's writing is in view, albeit upside down in most cases. Next to the teacher often is a child who is reading quietly into the teacher's ear. The idea behind the teacher's giving out unknown words when asked, is to keep the story moving fast enough for the beginning reader so that it can sustain the child's interest. Thus the child can use the story context and phonetic clues to help figure out unknown words. [2]

The third kind of reading activity is for those who are independent in reading but who need practice to become fluent or for those children completely independent in reading, who are exploring literature and ideas in books from the library. It is called "Silent Sustained Reading Time." Children disperse to quiet spots in the building to read on their own. Subsequently during their regular conference times or in their journals they share with their key teachers about the books they have been reading and the writing they have been doing.

Often Maude uses her six-year-old son Pete as an example of the rich language learning at Fircroft. He's beginning to recognize many words and to know the sounds of letters. He learned many of the basic phonic elements and the most common reading words by playing group games, usually with not more than four children and often an adult who plays, too. An example is an adaptation of the old familiar parlor game Fish.

Pete's experience with written language helps him to understand how reading and writing are talk-written-down. Twice each day he is in a warm and inviting group where a teacher reads a story. One of those times is with the whole school community after lunch. Then another time Pete is in a Booktime group where he hears a story read. There he is beginning to read high interest but low vocabulary load books (called "easy to read books" in libraries) on his own with the teacher telling him an unknown word occasionally if he asks. He's at the point where he could be in an Ask For a Word group but he and his key teacher decided that he stay in his Booktime group a bit longer because he didn't want to leave his best friend, also in the group. Once each week he is helped to select books at the neighborhood branch library.

Pete writes each day. He dictates a journal to his key teacher. Other teachers or assistants take his dictation on a computer word processor. Sometimes he writes brief journals and other pieces on his own. Usually there is a teacher nearby who can help him spell a special word. If he chooses to spell the word phonetically, that's okay at this stage of his learning. He is beginning to write on the computer word processor because writing with a pencil or pen is still slowed for him by his immature finger-muscle coordination—normal for boys of his age. He shares his independently-written pieces with his key teacher at their conference times. At this stage he conferences with his key teacher every day. All this is augmented by his participating in the daily Newstime Group, where he is usually involved with the emotion and mechanics of what the teacher, who leads the group, writes on the large chart in front of the children. Pete, and most of the beginners at Fircroft, typically learn to be on their own in writing ahead of their independence in reading.

While using writing to share his feelings and thoughts, Pete learns more advanced reading and writing skills on the computer—in games and in self-directed exercises. Because some of the computers have small keyboards, which can be used by the younger children, Pete and others can learn to touch-type on the computer keyboard usually as soon as they show the requisite small muscle coordination. These touch typing lessons and practice continue periodically over the years, keeping pace with the physical growth of children's hands—as their fingers can span more and more of the keyboard.

Maude explains that computer learning provides an important way for Pete and the other children to study math. In order to play computer games successfully, children need to be able to use their math skill and knowledge. The interactive multimedia computer games help children individually to learn elements which they will need in order to meet the challenge of each game with satisfaction. In addition they learn and practice basic math combinations by playing games in small groups of children, often led by an adult.

Finally, at the end of this morning's orientation time, Maude usually shows a minute or so of a videotape which is always at the ready for visitors. She encourages visitors to come back and with earphones to play the full fifty minute tape whenever they can take the time. They can buy copies of this videotape and others, to take with them. The tape shows teachers conferencing with children; it offers a view of teachers and others in their monthly child study meeting, discussing four or five children.

The videotape contains an interview with Alan Wu, the school's lead teacher. In the interview, Alan, a man of about forty, discusses how the school helps children and teachers come to have a clear sense of themselves and how teachers help each other to respond to and nurture each child. This process is illustrated by a videotape sequence showing Alan having lunch with a child. On the videotape, the child and Alan are deep into an interview where each looks to be involved in what they are discussing. The interview is part of the child study program which Alan leads. [3]

When Alan Wu joins the group of visitors at the end of their morning orientation, often they feel they have already been introduced to him. One day a visitor asks Alan how and why he became an ULS teacher. Here is his reply:

"I got hooked on Urban Little School children when I was a children's librarian. I worked at the branch near the University Urban Little School. So often it felt like ULS children and I tuned in with each other so easily about a good book. Sometimes I felt I got more out of sharing with some of them than perhaps they did in talking with me. Sometimes, right away I'd find myself sharing little bits of how the book made me feel, before I asked them for their reaction. That sort of thing.

"It was so easy to help most of these children choose books that might speak to them. They seemed to *relate* to books, not just to read them for sensation or diversion. I later learned more about this. Urban Little Schools children learn to read and write as a part of their thinking, their communicating, their feelings, their wanting to understand. It's all a part of each child's learning to be independent. Learning to read and write as exercises to please the teacher just doesn't have any place in this kind of being with books and reading and writing.

"My wife and I wanted a ULS education for our son and daughter who were two and three years old then. That's why later we moved into the University Urban Little Schools' neighborhood. The University ULS was the other, with Fircroft, of the first two pilot schools established in Twin Rivers. One day at the library, shortly after we moved into the neighborhood, a five-year-old Urban Little Schooler, who reminded me of one of my children, asked me why I couldn't teach at her school. I felt like giving her the biggest hug ever. That decided it."

Usually this short time with Alan is the last part of the visitors' orientation before they begin to circulate and observe in the school. Here is a description of what they might see one morning:

Children arrive at different times between eight-fifteen and nine-thirty. Almost all the children have arrived by eight-thirty. Because they live close by, they don't have to wait for the school bus to take them. They seem to want to be at school.

The sound of singing accompanied by rhythm instruments can be heard from the music room upstairs. Maude explained that a man from the neighborhood stops by most mornings on his way to work to play the piano for those who want to make music.

Some children are seen playing board games—down on the carpeted floor shaking dice and moving their counters. Others work with various kinds of construction materials: Legos, and other kinds of interlocking blocks, wooden boxes and pieces used for large construction. Some children are in the dress-up corner playing house. The assistant teacher is on the rug with a small group of younger children playing Consonant Bingo. A few children are reading in little hideaway nooks. One boy is at a computer writing his journal.

Several children are in the kitchen drinking hot cocoa. They can eat all the fresh stone ground bread and apples they wish. There are two bags of fresh vegetables on the counter waiting for Maxine. Maxine, Maude had explained, is Sammy's grandmother. She comes in about 10:00 these chilly days and makes two or three pots of vegetable soup for visitors and school people. Other parents often drop in to help and chat. Maude mentioned that the large cooking kettles Maxine uses and most of the other kitchenware came from garage sales. ULS teachers use their petty cash accounts to buy garage sale items and whatever other incidental items they wish to purchase for use at the school. Many of the tables, bookshelves and some interesting art supplies also came from garage sales or other recycling sources.

Outside the kitchen, other children are seen at the art tables occasionally chatting while painting, gluing toothpick sculptures, continuing with a stained glass project. A teacher is circulating, spending time with this child or that one.

At nine-thirty all come together in groups of about ten. Three of these groups of children are having Newstime. Children and teachers are doing this in such a way that each of them can feel taken seriously as a special person, in the reality of their Urban Little School, each morning.

Nine children and Joseph, their teacher, are in one Newstime group. It is meeting in Maude's office near the front door. The children are sitting on the rug facing an easel holding a large pad of chart paper. Children, when it is their turn, may share something which is on their minds. Usually these are bits of news from the children's lives or something they have heard. Joseph usually asks questions which help children to elaborate. He acknowledges each child's sharing with a sentence or more on the chart paper.

At this point, Joseph, is on one knee, next to seven-year-old George, who is standing at his side. Joseph listens and often asks questions that grow from his interest, such as: "Where were you standing when you first smelled the smoke from the burning roast?" "What did your mother say when she opened the oven?" "Who else came down to the kitchen?" "What did you have for dinner then?" When Joseph seems to feel the urge to write on the large chart paper behind him, he does so. In this case he turns and puts down the following:

"Wow, there was smoke, screams, and a cold dinner at George's house."

At the end of Newstime, in unison all read over the words Joseph has written on the large sheets; there are three sheets covered with writing. On this day, as is often the case, Joseph leads all the children to act out the emotion in some of what they read. This means some good reading practice—a few trials and several rereads to get ready. Writing merges with emotion. When they come to the sentence above, they scream out the word "screams."

Another small group is sharing News and Goods in the ceramic alcove, just off the main art area. Ten children are sitting in a circle with a teacher, Gina, on an extra-thick soft rug rolled out for this occasion. The children are from about seven to twelve years old. In News and Goods the children begin the day also having a chance to be seen as the special person each is. Here's some of what happens:

Gina begins News and Goods. She pauses to think; then her face lights up as she tells how good it feels to have written a letter to the editor last night. She mailed it just a few minutes ago. It is on behalf of a friend, whom some people in town don't seem to like. Gina explains that her sticking up for her friend feels good, but the particularly good feeling is that she wrote the letter. So often it feels as if she puts off things like that and never does them.

Across the circle a boy raises his hand, "The lady upstairs' dog just had five pups; *and* we're going to get one."

"Thanks, Calvin," Gina says, and waits for the next New and Good.

Sarah tells hers: "I'm going to my dad's house this weekend."

"What's one thing you do at your dad's that you like, Sarah?" Gina asks.

"Sometimes Dad and I put pennies on the train track. Then the next day we go back and see how many squished ones we can find."

"It makes me feel good, when I hear you talk about times with your dad," Gina remarks with a warm smile. "Anyone else like to share a New and Good?"

All share who want to. Today each child does.

At about 10:15 all the people, and rabbits (there are two who have had free rein in this house during the last few days) come together for a fifteen minute meeting. There are forty children and seventeen adults. The big people are teachers, assistant teachers, volunteers, parents, neighbors, and visitors. A teacher begins to make announcements and firms up special plans for the day.

"David and eleven people in his group will be interviewing a 'mystery guest' at lunch time. If you want to help question this woman, to find out what kind of work she does, meet with them in the story corner. Trisha and Richard will be spending the afternoon with their friend Bill. You might remember Bill. He was a 'mystery guest' some time back—lives in that gray house on Locust Street, near the corner. He just retired from his little bakery on the boulevard. I was told that Trisha and Richard are going to make donuts. Maybe they'll bring some back.

"Here are the lists and times of those groups going to the library and swimming today." She points to papers taped to the wall. "If you want to go to the library, be sure to put your name on that list. Jorge and Janet are working at the library, this month. They'll take the lists over when they go to work. Maybe if the list is long they'll suggest two groups—like yesterday. Oh, and swimmers, don't forget your towels.

"Some of the people won't be in their quiet work places because Charlotte will be here, working with those who are writing their play. They'll be in Maude's office. We haven't been able to learn what the play's about; but I heard there is some good dancing and singing in it. I guess it's mostly a secret. They're making the costumes at Charlotte's house on Temple Street.

"Consuela is working individually with those children who are writing autobiographies. She'll be at the computers under the mezzanine from ten-thirty to twelve o'clock.

"The quiet study time will be at the usual 10:30–11:30 and 1:30–2:30. Let's try to keep from talking except when we absolutely have to. Like Mario suggested yesterday, one way we can tell if it is really quiet is when we can hear the furnace blower going.

"Carolyn, Tammie's mother, will be in the art area all day. She wants to be there for those people who are making paper mache masks. If you are working on a mask and still have to paint or shellac yours, see if you can work out a time today to do that. The bank on the boulevard wants some sort of a display from us. Maybe the masks will be it? We can talk about this again."

Dan's hand goes up, "During Events Time on Friday, Sam, Shawna and I will be offering a session for people to plant flower and vegetable seeds in boxes filled with new dirt from our compost pile. We're working now to get the boxes and seeds ready. Then in about a month, when it's warmer outside, we'll offer another Events Time for people who might like to join us. By then there's no chance of frost. We'll set the little plants out in the vegetable garden and on the sunny side of the school."

One of the teachers sitting in the art area raises his hand and speaks. "That reminds me," he says, "As I announced a while back, on Thursday of next week I'm going to take a group to Bridget's farm for the spring cleanup. Most of you know the farm from our trips there last year. We'll stay overnight and come back the next day. Let me know if you'd like to go. We need about ten children. I think six have spoken to me already about going. I'm talking with their parents about this now. Most of the cleanup is in the house, which has been closed for the winter. Probably we'll start regular school trips to the farm after the cleanup. I like the farm in the spring; especially the quiet out there. So good in the evening around the wood stove when people read bits from favorite books. Bridget usually has cocoa on the stove. Some parents will come along too.

Gina raises her hand and says, "Speaking of parents, some of them along with their neighbors are planning another lot cleanup; this time on Hawkins Street—you know where that old wreck of a car is at the back. The City will move the car. It sounds as if it'll be the same as they did with the lot on Fircroft—make it into a little park with plots of grass and all. Breakfast for the workers will be here at the school on Saturday morning, I'm told, in two weeks, that's the 23rd; and then people will go to work cleaning and digging. The folks living on the side of the lot with the big oak tree told the parents planning this event that they will keep the grass mowed. Even if your parents can't make it this time, you can come. That's Saturday the 23rd. Breakfast's at ten o'clock. Let me know if you'd like me to talk with your parents so you could take part."

Several others make announcements before the meeting adjourns.

The announcements mainly alert people to upcoming events and some of the non-routine things that will be happening. That way the school's life will have a predictable character. People will better understand why some children might leave the school and where they have been. Everyone will know what each person is doing outside the school or inside. It all will fit into the daily pattern where children and adults are purposefully engaged, where children are working individually from plans they have worked out with their key teachers.

Visitors often sense, however, that what they see—people at work, the mechanics, and the school's organization—doesn't fully explain what they feel is in the air. That's true. It doesn't nearly explain how it happens that both teachers and children appear to be aware and open with each other; how the teachers were selected and trained to work individually with children so each of the children not only would learn how to think for themselves but to live as if each person mattered.

It's not possible either, for the visitor, to know the innumerable little ways that Fircroft is a haven for children and teachers alike in coming to draw from what is essential and right in themselves as they take each step ahead. What visitors see only begins to explain why comfortable sensitivity and trust seems to exist between people, how it seems to influence so many people's developing self-acceptance. Visitors aren't a part of the respectful listening which goes on between key teachers and the children with whom they work closely.

Visitors aren't involved in the school's child study process, which focuses on four or five children each month. The child study process is led by the lead teacher who comes to know each child sensitively, and who makes sure every single child is succeeding and that the school is aligned with each child's deeper world.

The next chapter discusses this child study process in detail.

Notes

1   As part of the preliminary negotiations between the Foundation and Twin Rivers' Board of Education, it was established that the city council would look kindly on petitions to rezone any property needed for an Urban Little School if that property were in an area reserved for residential use only.

2   For much more about how children learn to read and write in these kinds of ways, see Supplemental Article #3.

3   The child study program is designed to heighten teachers' awareness of each child. It is described in the next chapter.

5

The Child Study Process

Basing an Elementary School on Teachers' Heightened Awareness of Each Child

In this chapter I shall explain one of the most important and unique features of the elementary ULS design: the child study process. In Chapter Two's "Professional Journey" memoir, I mentioned how I led the child study process during most of the ten years I directed our SIEE Elementary School, the forerunner of the Urban Little Schools. In this chapter I shall explain and reflect on the process which the staff and I developed at SIEE.

The child study process enabled us to ground our school in a new mentality far from what guides the schooling of children in conventional schools. This way of thinking put each child's needs absolutely first—first before teacher welfare issues, first before the methods of learning we usually used, first before our categories or preconceptions into which a child might be fitted. [1]

At SIEE, the child study process was our concentrated yearly focus on each child and that child's world. In this process we strove to know every child close to her or his essence—as the special individuals they all were. In the child study process, each child's development was followed closely by me, the school's director, and was reviewed by all of our staff people and of course by the child's key teacher. Out of this sensitivity emerged the child's schooling, guided by the key teacher and increasingly involving the child in planning what to do next. [2]

Here's how our SIEE child study process worked: As the school's director, I led the teachers in the process which culminated each month in our child study meeting. In that all-day meeting we focused on four or five of our forty or so children. Thus over the year we focused on every one of our students. All the school's key teachers were there, plus any regular assistant teachers. [3]

All our staff people, along with the child, the parents and often others who knew a child who was "up" for child study that month, were asked to contribute to the process. But only staff people attended the monthly all-day child study meetings. This was done in order to create a safe feeling atmosphere during the meetings where teachers could feel free to explore their emotions and the possible motivation present in their relationships with children.

The child study meetings were designed to help teachers connect psychologically and emotionally with the children being studied. Teachers helped each other develop a special sense of themselves in relationship to those children with whom they worked one to one. Teachers gained perspective not only on their relationships with children under their care, but learned what it meant to have a productive responsive fit, psychologically speaking, with any child.

The child study process thus was designed to bring about the deepest possible richness in what took place between teachers and children in our school. Sharing this kind of sensitive awareness at our child study meetings helped teachers be more articulate, too, as they communicated about their relationships with children.

In my role as the child study leader at our SIEE Elementary School, I observed every child who was "up" that month, from as many different angles and perspectives as I could. I did this in ways that might set the example for teachers—ways which might encourage them to come to know their children perhaps even more than they might have done otherwise.

I observed the child in our school life. Because ours was an activity-centered, hands-on kind of school, as illustrated by the Fircroft School in Chapter Four, children could be seen doing what came naturally to them. Thus during the first hour of the school day, for example, it was fruitful for me to follow a child, perhaps taking notes systematically—like jotting down at five or ten minute intervals what a child did. Also I could watch and note the ways others related to the children I was observing. I enjoyed and often was intrigued by how the children seemed to see things, the ways they expressed who they were, by their actions. Also filming the child with my 8mm home movie camera was another way which helped me to record the child's behavior, which I could later show to the staff at our meeting. Filming also focused my attention on the children I observed. Then too, later in the month, in my interview with the child, I raised my sensitivity to the child further as I enjoyed sharing my humanness with the child—my ways of looking at the world, my sense of humor, some little stories from my life, perhaps.

I saw my job as child study leader to bring to the teachers my sense of heightened awareness arising from my focused attention on each child being studied that month. In my writeups to the teachers on each child or when I led our child study meetings I never put children into some psychological category such as "hyper-aggressive" or "autistic." Early on I learned that those who categorize children that way almost always assume more than they really know about the complex and changing emotional world of a child. My job was to help teachers tune in with this dynamic world of the child, not oversimplify it with judgments, which could color the way they and others related to the child. I found these kinds of categorical judgments from the psychological literature often would stop teachers from continuing to listen, or to continue to try to refine their understanding of a child. When I did come up with hunches as to why particular children seemed to act as they did in particular circumstances, I tried to express these cause-effect ideas tentatively, to be explored further by the teachers who worked with the children. In this way and the other ways I shall discuss, I tried to be a catalyst to help teachers raise their sensitivity toward every child. Now, more details of how I did this.

During the first two weeks of the new child study month I would make a point of noticing the children we had chosen. I usually would tell the children who were "up" that month, that this was their turn. Children came to know that their being "up" meant something special for them. Not only did it mean being given attention more than usual; it meant going out to lunch with me, for our interview, if the child wanted to do that. At lunches, most children chose hamburgers with all the trimmings, along with a rich dessert.

As a part of preparing the children for my gathering information about them, I sometimes asked if I might call their parents to arrange a home visit so I could see some of their special things there. Usually I didn't have to make a point of asking for permission to film them with my home movie camera. I did that all the time at school so children were used to being filmed. [4]

I ended up going to most of the children's homes at least once every two or three years. I knew all of the parents at our school because I was the person who first explained the school to prospective parents. Because of this, I knew which parents might be receptive to my coming for a home visit. If parents would prefer to come to school to talk about their child, fine. A child study visit by me was in addition to the annual reporting to parents done by their child's key teacher and to the teacher's innumerable other contacts with the parents.

At the children's homes, often I would ask them to take me for a tour, showing me some of their things. Usually children would need some prompting for talking about what, for them, was commonplace. One way I did this was to ask children what they would pick up and take with them if someone smelled smoke and said maybe there was a fire in the house. I remember one boy turned and picked up a book which was in a drawer where his clothes were kept. It was his personal journal which he kept at home. He offered to let me look at it. I don't remember specifically what was there but I remember my emotions. I felt honored, closer to the boy than ever before.

On home visits I enjoyed talking with the parents. I felt, from almost all of the parents, an appreciation for our child study concern for their children, which buoyed me up. I felt parents saw my visit as one more example of how we put their child into individual focus at our school. So often parents would relax and talk about little things which added up to some of what counted in their lives. I felt, too, after our discussing their child, that my visit had helped some parents to see their child a bit more appreciatively, maybe from a perspective they didn't usually use.

When the child and I went for our luncheon interview, I gave myself another perspective on each youngster as a person. We usually had lunch together in the dining room of a motel near our school. Almost always we would sit at one of the rear window tables. Usually we had the same waitress. I smile now when I remember her. Here's an example, recreated from my memory, of a luncheon interview I had with seven-year-old Sonja one day in May:

Over sandwiches and french fries Sonja and I both answered some of the questions I have found are good to help share one's thoughts and feelings. At one point, I asked my favorite question I call The Giant Memory Machine Question: "Let's pretend that a giant machine were wired to this table. It will take all of our memories away for a while except those which we tell it we don't want to be without, even for a few minutes. What would be one of those special memories? The machine will let us keep the memories we tell it here."

I went first, telling something that I had never shared this way before. It was something touching, that had just happened the day before.

Sonja then told about how special it was to climb high up to her secret place among the leaves in a tree behind her apartment house. She talked about how she knew every limb of the tree. "I think I could climb up to my special spot where I think, even though it was pitch dark." This prompted me to ask, "Like, for example, what is one of the little things that you might think about up there among all those leaves?" And we began—questioning, reflecting, sharing. I kept sketchy notes as the two of us talked.

After our interview, I read my write-up to Sonja. Knowing this was just a first draft, Sonja had the opportunity to change whatever was not accurate or to leave out anything she wanted deleted.[5] The teachers then read the final draft at the next child study meeting.

When Sonja heard the writeup, she wanted to add things she thought of as she revisited the interview. These new additions were noted in the final copy. Of course, there were some things that never got into the interview writeup sheets. It was important to me to be sensitive to special childhood secrets that the world shouldn't know.

As in the example above, I almost always used the Giant Memory Machine prompting question during these interviews. With the children's permission, I almost always would answer the question first, after telling the children they could then answer the question after I did. The question prompted me to think of a memory which was important, a pleasant memory I didn't want to have the imaginary machine take away, even for a little while. This felt good. It prompted me to reflect for a moment on little things which had happened recently that I enjoyed because I made it a point only to share fresh memories I hadn't used before in one of these interviews. My major memories from the past had all been used up in previous interviews.

My answering first, tended to set the tone of our luncheon interview, too. It helped remind children that this was a time when we could talk about things which were important to us even though they were minor things, not all that earth shaking.

So often when a child would answer a question, like the Giant Memory Machine one, I would find something in the child's response, to ask about, further. Asking questions I cared about was important; I wanted to make my questions engaging for me. Then I would find myself immersed fully in what we were doing and my follow-up questions would come spontaneously.

I remember the time a ten-year-old boy answered the Giant Memory Machine question by telling me he didn't want to forget the memory of the cake at his father's birthday celebration. The way he talked about this prompted me to ask him about his father. His love and respect for his father came out so naturally in what he said. I told the boy I'd like to get to know his dad. After that, I called his father and asked him if we could have lunch and told him why. "You must be a great guy," I told him, "from your son's description." His son had it right. I have kept up this friendship with the boy's father. We often have lunches now, even though his son is grown and lives in a distant city.

Thus usually from my example of first answering one of my prompting questions the interview would center itself on things both of us found interesting. Occasionally I had to use an additional prompting question to get things moving. A favorite was my "Magic Shoes" question: "If you had on a pair of magic shoes which could take you anyplace, could do anything for you, what is one thing you would ask them to do for you?" Then, sometimes I would ask, "What's one little thing you like about yourself?" Another prompting question that sometimes was appropriate was "What's one little known fact about yourself?" Again, almost always I answered each question myself before asking children if they wanted to do so. I remember one time answering the "What's a little known fact..." question by telling the child how I cut my own hair.

It was important to phrase my questions, as I did above, to ask for one instance, one memory, one little thing, rather than "the most important time...," or some reference to a peak experience. The point of my questioning was to help us experience our feelings usually in the context of our everyday lives and not to analyze or compare them. I could do this simply by asking "what's one time" instead of "what is the best time."

If children tended to talk too generally rather than from the specifics of experience, usually I could move their answers to be less abstract by asking for examples: "What's one time that you felt angry at Johnny down the street? You know—what did he do? How did it make you feel? That sort of thing."

This gets at one reason why it seems to me our children almost invariably seemed to look forward to the annual interviews I conducted with them. Together we made the everyday, special; made the stuff of their lives more interesting and significant. For instance, as mentioned, I only asked children to elaborate when I was genuinely interested in something which I sensed was relevant to what the child was saying. I was responding to my curiosity, to what intrigued me, to what seemed unusual to me, to what I suspected I would enjoy hearing more about.

Also, we were both enjoying a new set of relationship rules. We weren't sitting there primarily to be friends. We were there to leave the interview with a greater sense of who we were, what we cared about, how he saw our worlds.

In my writeup for the teachers I tried to reconstruct our interview, using the child's words as much as I could, from the scribbled notes I took during the interview. Often, at the conclusion of my interview writeup, I added thoughts of mine which arose as I revisited our interview. Also sometimes I would add further thoughts from the child, if the two of us had gone over some or all of the interview writeup.

I usually finished my writeups during the last week of each child study month. It was a culmination for me. All the data and impressions coalesced. As I wrote, I usually experienced a sense of specialness about the young person. Often this hit me with immediacy as I sat there, by myself, at my typewriter. I recommend the procedure for anyone who leads a school like ours.

Because I came to our once-a-month child study day session having just written my piece about each child, I felt close to the children we were studying and to their worlds. Consequently I could lead these meetings so teachers also might find themselves present to the essential aspects of each child.

We began our child study meetings quietly, by reading the writeups all of us on the staff did on each of the four or five children who were "up" that month. We passed the stapled sheets from person to person around the table which was loaded with food we had all brought, pot-luck. So as we read we could snack. Typically a teacher's writeup on each child filled two or three sheets of paper unless the child's key teacher did the writeup. Then it was longer. Mine usually were longer still, but teachers had received advanced copies of my writeups a day or so before the meeting.

After about a half hour, someone would suggest starting to discuss one of the children. From there we moved through the day discussing each of the four or five children individually. This was sometimes interspersed with my home movie film clips about the child, or with still photos I had taken at school or at the child's home.

Usually during the last hour or two of our child study day meeting, we discussed school business. We didn't have any other regularly scheduled staff meetings. Part of the reason we didn't need more business time together was that I had discussed any problems or issues with teachers during the preceding month when each teacher and I had our regular lunch-time conference. Thus most of the school's problems were defined and well on their way to solution by the time we met as staff group.

But I am convinced that the main reason we got so much business done in such a small period of time was that, after our child study session, the petty tensions which sometimes arise from making a school work smoothly simply weren't all-consuming to us. We just had been through four or five hours discussing what was of most importance. We almost always felt so good about how we seemed to be keeping our school in tune with every single child. We all seemed to feel we belonged, in this school which made sense to us. Every one of us was doing vital work, was a person whose ideas and concerns were recognized.

Reflections on Why the Child Study Process Works for Both Students and Their Teachers

The child study process bases the whole concept of schooling on the staff people's sensitive awareness of each child. It enables the trained teacher to do what makes sense for each student, step by step, instead of necessarily following prescribed or traditional educational practice and offering essentially only one learning path and pacing for all students.

It opens the door for teaching children with highly diverse needs and backgrounds. To do this, the process helps teachers to understand and to identify with the world of each child under their care whether that world might be harsh or ideal, privileged or underprivileged; whether children might have a keen sense of their own significance as a worthwhile person or see themselves as lackluster at best; or whether some children might have strong and continual parent support at home or might come from homes where parents were hard put just to keep their own lives going.

This child study process, developed at our SIEE elementary school, is built solidly into the design of the elementary Urban Little Schools. The ULS lead teacher's most important role is to tune in to each child and to help the other teachers do so, too. That is why the lead teacher acts as the key teacher with only eight children and the other three teachers each work with twelve.

This process also helps make the one to one match-up between children and their key teachers the very best fit possible. Perhaps another teacher might fit better with a particular child? In the child study context, switches are not seen as failures for teachers but as one more thing the school does to fit learning to every child—in this case fitting the child to the teacher and vice versa.

In addition, the child study process can make it OK for teachers to be openly enthusiastic about their work, at school. In my experience in conventional schools, openly expressing excitement about one's work with children is almost forbidden between most teachers. In places such as the typical school's teacher room you can feel the taboo at work. It's OK to talk about "difficult children" or other frustrations or smile at children's antics; but it isn't OK to express a sense of passion about one's work with children.

Perhaps one reason it seems taboo is because teachers—urban teachers particularly—are doing a job fraught with deep conflict. Most teachers hold the abstract value that each child matters. Yet many of the best teachers know in their hearts that the conventional system they are using limits the chances in life and on jobs of the system's academic losers and "just ordinary" learners—despite the hard work teachers do.

At SIEE we didn't work in that kind of fundamental conflict. We shared all the time about this child or that one in ways that suggested we were intrigued and caught up in our job. We knew from our experience that every single child who started young enough and stayed long enough would have at least an even chance on jobs and a self-respecting life. This was a fundamental reason our school was such an fulfilling place in which to work. We inspired each other. It was heady stuff to share such things as how our children were coming to feel their own power and direction. Our child study process helped children to do this. It worked.

As I visit with our school's graduates nowadays I am struck by how so many have turned out to be strong effective and sensitive individuals who seem to draw from the best within. They listen to you in conversation, for instance. I am convinced that their taking others seriously is at least in part a reflection of how we listened to them individually at school and through our child study process—how this resulted in learning which fit them. And it was contagious. Because children were listened to and given sensitive attention, they learned to do the same for people with whom they lived and worked at school and then beyond.

Notes

1   It was in addition to our reporting to parents, to traditional achievement tests we might give, plus any overall evaluation of the school we might do for the state department of education.

2   In the ULS design the lead teacher takes the role I took at SIEE. The staffing pattern makes this manageable. The lead teacher, such as Alan Wu in Chapter Four's illustration, is the key teacher for eight children while each of the other three teachers is the key teacher for about twelve children.

3   These meetings were in lieu of the usual teacher meeting days taken in conventional schools. Our parents knew the value of our child study process so they pitched in helping to provide childcare for children from homes where both parents worked.

4   Nowadays I would use a video camera, which makes the process easier and less expensive.

5   Nowadays this editing process is easy. With the computer's word processing capability, changes in a report on a child can be made in moments.

6

A Secondary Urban Little School

The idea for a secondary Urban Little Schools component, grew as a natural extension of what I had learned from my ten years as director at our experimental SIEE elementary school. Children who had come up through SIEE didn't have a complementary secondary schooling to complete their elementary education. They didn't have a high school where they might have used their independent academic skills to the fullest and where they might have developed further their ability to take responsibility for their own learning and for their own lives. Instead they had to go to conventional junior and senior high schools. For many of them, this conventional secondary schooling turned out to be a kind of holding period between our SIEE School and college or other further education.

How might it have been if the children could have had five more years—a secondary education—of schooling which would have complemented and extended what we developed at our experimental SIEE School? In this chapter I present what this secondary education might be like—which could be added to the ULS elementary education we have been discussing. Students who graduate from an elementary ULS would receive a secondary schooling which could build on and extend what they had done.

They would get a secondary schooling where they could feel they belonged in a group of self-reliant clear thinking individuals who listened to each other. Also they would be working alongside community people of integrity, learning to be job-wise during their high school years. All this and they would continue to be guided in a close trusting relationship with their teachers. In this one to one relationship they could bring together their independent learning and thinking skills, with their ability to succeed as self-reliant decent people working in what sometimes seems a heartless market economy.

Thus, elementary Urban Little Schools children wouldn't be asked to go to a typical high school where young people find themselves in age-alike groups which devalue individual self-direction, where they are pressed to conform to what others do or risk the stigma of "not being one of us"—an outsider. They wouldn't be asked to go to a high school where teachers and young people almost never listen seriously to each other, one to one. They wouldn't be in classroom learning situations which seldom touched their ingenuity, humane passions and intellectual curiosity. Also they wouldn't feel pressed to accept the typical secondary school student's value code: you are significant in the high school world if you are "cool" and belong to a status clique or gang; it helps if you are an athlete, a trendy girl out of the teen magazines or a guy who others don't dare to cross.

As an alternative to this the ULS design draws on what I knew. I knew the power of a strong teacher-child relationship to help young people succeed in tasks which fitted and fully challenged them. I knew too, how in this relationship children could talk openly and be listened to by someone they trusted. I also knew how this relationship could be supportive in helping young people to work on community jobs where they could enter the wider world, learn from some of the best people out there, while reflecting on their experience, one to one, with their teacher.

I had tried out work-study during my own schooling. When I was fourteen years old, I worked as a regular in our junior high school's library, doing simple book maintenance, shelving books and working at the charging desk. That job opened me to the world of books and reading. Also, I had tried out work-study education at Antioch College. There, for three years I alternated campus study with jobs which opened my eyes to the job world, to the person I was and wanted to be. For example, on one semester away from Antioch, I worked as the assistant to the executive secretary of the Overseas Press Club. My desk was right above the electrically printed moving stream of news which girdled the Times Building on New York's Times Square. In Pittsburgh, as an Antioch work-study student, I read and excerpted all the books on salesmanship extant for US Steel

Corporation's sales training department. On this job I found out the kind of work I didn't want to do. In my case I didn't want to be a sales executive as my father was and as I had intended to be.

Other jobs, both at Antioch and after, allowed me to find the direction I did want to take. Bit by bit I came to understand myself and the job world well enough to seek employment that was right for me. After I took a few days off one job to observe in an elementary school, I knew that teaching was for me. I remember so clearly, talking with a boy at that school. Something happened to me in that conversation. When I walked out of that school that day, I knew I not only wanted to teach, but I knew also that my relationships with children had to have the kind of open listening quality which seemed to be in the air between that boy and me.

I learned from my jobs how it was quite possible and practical for young people to participate as workers in the world while they trained to make a place in it for themselves. I coupled this understanding with my knowledge of the power within a trusting relationship between young people and their teachers.

In the next section, again set in the fictional city of Twin Rivers, I describe the design for secondary schooling for young people who had come from elementary Urban Little Schools. In their elementary Urban Little Schools they had learned a lot about who they were as people; they also were academically independent and were experienced in working with their teachers, one to one. They were ready for the kind of secondary Urban Little Schooling you can read about next.

Portrait of a ULS Secondary School

Jeremy, the thirty-four-year-old teacher of the Oaktree Little Schools Group, works principally one to one with each of his twelve secondary young people. All of the young people have moved to this secondary ULS group from Twin Rivers' elementary Urban Little Schools, like the Fircroft School.

Jeremy works out of three rooms on the second floor at the back of a church which had unused space to rent. The church is located on a corner in the still vital fringe of a deteriorating inner city neighborhood. Most of the congregation is now older. The younger members largely have gone—

across the nearby river to the suburbs. Along with Jeremy's office, the ULS rooms contains fourteen other offices which Jeremy built with the help of his wife, who works as an assistant at the University Urban Little School. Jeremy and his wife have two daughters, who both attend the University Urban Little School, too.

Jeremy's office is large enough to hold all twelve of the students when they have group meetings. The students' offices are four-by-five-foot partitioned spaces, each with a built-in desk and bookcase, a study lamp and tackboards on the walls. Telephone extensions in each office are connected with two lines that are listed as "Oaktree Urban Little Schools Group." Centrally located are two personal computers and one printer. Windows in the three rooms look out over the nearby houses and stores.

When you come into the office space you seldom find more than four or five young people there. About a third of their time is spent working with people in the town and surrounding areas. When they are not working with these community people, they spend quite a bit of time in the library, both in the center of town and in the branch libraries. In addition, most study at the ULS Self-directed Learning Center. At the Center, tutors are available to help young people to learn traditional high school subjects and advanced-placement college courses through self-study done with the aid of computers. They also learn from videotapes and written material, which is individualized and self-paced. Most of the young people study in late afternoons and in the evenings when they are not working on community jobs. Two of the young people are working primarily out of their homes this year. This is a matter which each person decides with Jeremy and with the parents.

Jeremy maintains at least one weekly private exchange with each young person in the Oaktree Group. Typically, they exchange a written journal one week and have a one hour conference the next.

The every-other-week journals quite often are free association pieces. All of the young people have had a lot of practice; they began exchanging journals while attending an elementary Urban Little School. Jeremy writes about six journals each week to those whom he doesn't see in a one to one conference. He finds his journals help him to grow, to see himself from a step away so to speak, to address feelings and thoughts that otherwise might get washed away in the hustle of his day. Jeremy doesn't have to teach his students how to write journals because his journals to each young person are examples which suggest how it might be done. Here is one example:

• • •

To: *Rashida*
From: *Jeremy*
Date: *March 15, 2000*

I'm here in my office looking out the window as I type. It makes me feel good that I know how to type without looking at the keyboard. I'm looking at the workmen putting up an addition on the building across the alley. They are people in their twenties, I'd guess. Two young men. One is working putting up a brick wall. I see the other one pop up on the scaffolding every now and again but I'm not sure what he's doing. Oh, I see him now. He's bashing bricks in the house wall, making a hole in the building where, I guess, they will attach one wall of the addition they're building.

I'm glad you contacted Mr. Saunders at the swimming pool. Your being on the staff there on Thursday evenings makes sense. Good you got your Red Cross lifesaving ticket last summer.

Makes good sense too that you've enrolled in the auto repair class. I encouraged Miguel's group when they discussed starting this as a Special Event. Makes me feel good that I had a part in doing this. I think one reason the used cars Anna and I buy last so long is because we treat them gently. I feel that much of this comes from sensing what is going on down inside, in the car's working parts. I feel I'm sort of in tune with the car. It's easy for me to relate to it, sort of personally.

I read the second chapter of your biography of Margery Sharpe. Such a moving piece—all her eighty-seven years worth of life. I feel so good that you are talking with Mrs. Sharpe every Tuesday morning. What a good idea of yours, to do that. Sounds like Joe Bannister will be a good editor for you. As far as your concern about this costing Oaktree too much, keep in mind how much you are learning from working with Joe. Not only is Joe a super editor, I find him a person with a kind of special wisdom. I'm so glad you can learn about editing from Joe and perhaps get to know his slant on life, too. We can talk about it more later when you have had a few more sessions with Joe.

I agree that I too have sometimes found it unnecessary to tape record interviews so long as I take good notes. But often I find that the act of tape recording them sort of sets the tone that this is a kind of business session, not just a social chat. However, usually I find myself not listening to the tapes. Just takes too much time—two interviews worth of time. But tapes can come in handy. You can always refer back to the tape if you need specific information.

You talk of Mrs. Sharpe meeting her husband when they both worked in a factory, where she worked at a machine putting handles on aluminum teapots. Have you ever been in a factory where people do that kind of repetitive work? I'd like to talk with you about the pros and cons of working for a few weeks or so in such a job. I think I could arrange it if we feel it is a high enough priority.

Now that you have learned how to develop and enlarge your own prints, what about making part of your biography into a black and white photo essay of Mrs. Sharpe going about her day along with photos taken earlier in her life? Current photos could show her gardening, talking with you about her life, other things she is doing these days. We have enough money in the revolving fund to cover your work in The Community Darkrooms if you do this.[1] You can put copies of photos right into an essay you write by using the scanner over at the Self-directed Learning Center. Then if you want to desktop publish it, in a few copies or more, they can help you do that, too. Maybe you already know about that kind of service they do? I wonder how Mrs. Sharpe might feel to see it all in a book, permanently bound. Let's talk about it. I realize that this will mean a lot more time on this work. If you're like me perhaps at this point you need to finish what you started and get on to the next project. I find I have trouble, often, extending a project of this sort once my questions have been answered to my satisfaction.

But, having said that, I remember how satisfying it was for me to do a photo essay based on the old relics at Suburban Park—what remains of that fun center out in Hoopertown. For some reason, after it was closed, no one tore it down. It just sort of fell down, piece by piece. I went out there with my niece Alison and we shot about a hundred black and white pictures. Just took pictures of everything. This led us to interview some people who used to go there on the trolley car and roller skate or ride the roller coaster. One older lady told us how it was to dance to the big bands when they came there during World War II. I had such a stimulating time making that photo essay.

That reminds me of the Margaret Bourke-White's black and white photographs. She was about the best photo-essayist that *Life Magazine* had in its heyday, I guess. People she photographed trusted her. You can see that in their faces. She did a series of photo essays during the Depression years and after, in the US and elsewhere.

Remember *The Family of Man* book of pictures of people, that we all looked at last year? The man who put that together, Edward Steichen, shows such a sensitivity to people. His life story is in the downtown library. It's titled, *A Life in Photography: Edward Steichen.*

You mention your feelings about Paul's crying openly at last week's sharing session at the beginning of the Thursday meeting. I too feel good about what happened. Makes me feel proud that in our group people can "let it out," whether in words or in non-verbal ways like Paul used.

Almost every day I am in touch with emotions that make me feel sad, feel helpless, self-doubting, and not quite good enough—sometimes downright unworthy. This includes those angry self-diminishing emotions. I find almost all of those emotions cry out for me to experience them, to face them, to accept them. Then when I do, usually, they sort of don't get in my way, don't scare me all that much. Also, so often when I really experience my dark feelings, really accept what's there, emotionally, it seems to result in a kind of clearness. I guess another way to say this is then some inner doors seem to open for me, that otherwise have been closed—doors behind which lay perhaps the deepest wisdom and guidance. It took me a long time to be able to be with my feelings. I grew up with the idea that it wasn't cool to feel anything but self-confident emotions. Crying was babyish. All that. It felt so good to see Paul dealing with his emotions so ably, at thirteen, during our Think and Listen Time last Thursday evening.

Cheers, Jeremy

• • •

Every Thursday evening the members of the Oaktree Group have a meeting. There the twelve young people, Jeremy and usually either Marilyn or Miguel, who are other secondary ULS teachers, meet in Jeremy's office. At the meeting Jeremy or a guest might teach students about a new study technique or explain a new job opportunity. Students also might learn about what the others are doing on their jobs and find out about such things as new software at the Self-directed Learning Center and upcoming Special Events, which are open to all the young people in the city's secondary Urban Little Schools.

As the prelude to the Think and Listen Time, people can share if they are moved to do so. In this sharing time the young people and their teacher use a "listen-and-accept" format. The idea is for each of the young people to speak from heart and mind—not to draw on others' words, such as the writings of some author. It's fine to use outside sources, such as a book or a TV documentary, but the import of what is said should be one's own thinking and feeling about it, not primarily a report of the feeling or thinking of another. At Think and Listen Time, each person (either a teacher or a young person) speaks after a period of silence which follows the preceding person's words. No one speaks twice until all have had a chance to speak once.

In Think and Listen Time, listeners don't give advice or critical comment on others' statements—just acceptance. It is not the role of the others present to set the speaker right. One reason for this is that sometimes what is said by a person contains prejudice, formerly repressed emotion and other only semi-sorted-out remnants of each person's experience and struggles growing up so far. The sorting-out is best handled by the person involved, perhaps with Jeremy in their journal exchange or at one of their one to one conferences.

Typically the one to one conferences usually take from forty minutes to an hour, at least every other week. Usually Jeremy and the young person confer in Jeremy's office. Here is a bit from a one to one conference between Jeremy and Kadeem, age fourteen:

Kadeem begins by speaking with Jeremy about several things which are on his mind. When he finishes, Jeremy says, "Let's see. I have to think now what I wanted to talk with you about. Let me look at my notes here in your folder. Oh yes, it's about your Spanish and your algebra self-study courses.

"So how's the new Spanish course going? When I get the time I'll take it myself. Maybe I can't squeeze it in, though. The people over at the Self-directed Learning Lab think it's great. Tell me what you think about it."

"I like it a lot," Kadeem began. "It's mostly games. You begin like I've done before—just put the CD into the player next to the computer. It follows the same pattern as the other interactive learning games we play. You know, first you prepare a little until you think you know enough to play and then you try playing. You learn more when you start playing the games. One of the simpler Spanish course games is like the game 'concentration' my brother and I used to play when I was little. It's where cards are turned face down on a table and you have to remember where specific ones are. I learn the Spanish words and phrases I need in order to play a game like 'concentration' on the computer's screen. The speaker's voice tells me what to do and corrects me, all in Spanish. Lots of good helps for learning. It makes me think. And it's kind of fun most of the time; time goes by fast.

"The part of the program I'm on now uses cartoons in comic strips. I can just point the arrow on the computer screen to things in the cartoon pictures and the cartoon speaker tells me what they are called in Spanish, while that word comes up on the screen.

"The setting in the comic strip I'm working on this week is a restaurant. When I'm ready to understand what the cartoon people are saying at the tables or at other places in this restaurant—that is, when I have learned most of the vocabulary and phrases—I point to a talk balloon over a person who's talking Spanish with another person. Then I hear what the speaker says, in the conversation. Next I can hear the reply of the other person. I can slow down the speaker's voice if I need to. Then the talk comes across one word at a time. By the time I'm finished with all this I can understand what all the cartoon characters are saying.

"It's like I was in Mexico. Like I'd be in this cafe; I'd ask what this and that was. I might ask someone who speaks English what's this or that word on the menu; then I could talk and explain the menu to someone else. I could tie in what Spanish I had learned before, with what I just had learned. I'd probably have to ask the speaker to slow down—*despacio, por favor*—but when they slowed and repeated and when I learned the words and phrases I needed, I'd catch on.

"The object of this week's work—the restaurant game—is to know enough Spanish to understand what's being said, when I'm told to point to a certain cartoon frame, say, where the waiter is telling a couple how good the chicken-with-rice dish is. I can play with six, nine or more frames on the screen depending how much Spanish I've learned up to that point. Next week the comic strip setting might be at the library, and so on." [2]

"How does that tie in," Jeremy asked, "with the Spanish conversation you and your tutor have?"

"Well," explained Kadeem, "after, say I've played the games in the restaurant sequence, Mrs. Martinez and I usually pretend we're at a restaurant. Like I said, each week I play games that have to do with a different kind of setting. Then we use that setting in our conversation. She never speaks English to me now. I'm getting pretty good so long as I can ask her to repeat and slow down—like I can do with the computer.

"Mrs. Martinez tells me that you get a better accent if you concentrate on listening and talking first. There are reading and grammar exercises I'm starting, too. I'm looking forward to learning to read and to write easily in Spanish. I'll be able really to explore ideas and things with Spanish speaking people. Then I can get on a Spanish language e-mail bulletin board and communicate with Spanish speakers all over the world. I've watched Margaret Ehrens do it. She has a person in Montevideo, Uruguay, who she talks to on e-mail. She has her own e-mail address. Got it from the school district. It's really simple. In a matter of minutes what she has to say is in her Uruguayan friend's dad's computer.

"Tell me more," Jeremy asked, "about how are you learning to read and write in Spanish."

"I work in a computerized exercise sequence. Now I'm beginning to write. At first it was just teaching me about vocabulary and phrases. At this point it tells me what to do and gives me feedback each step of the way. I mean, it points out my mistakes and tells me if I'm right. One really good thing is the 'spell check' in Spanish. I do my writing on the computer—you know just like we use it for word processing in English. When I'm through with a part of my writing, I click the pointer on the 'spell check' symbol at the top of the computer screen. A window comes on the screen and in it the computer shows me each word that isn't spelled according to the computer program's Spanish dictionary. The window's small enough so I can see the portion of the page where the word is that probably is misspelled. A couple of times my words weren't in the computer's dictionary but I had gotten the spelling from Mrs. Martinez so I guessed they were OK. I just clicked on 'ignore' and went on. In the 'spell check' window, the computer offers me suggestions about what is the correct spelling of the word it thinks I misspelled. Usually I get about three or four choices.

"Mrs. Martinez reads my work. We discuss my writing together. I like the way she seems to try to see things my way. She asks me a lot of questions about what I'm writing; all in Spanish, of course. I don't feel I'm writing for her—but for me."

"Thanks, Kadeem," said Jeremy. "Now what about your algebra course? I'm glad Mrs. Carrington is your tutor on that. I like her. She told me how much she's enjoying working with you. I wanted to check with you. How are things there?"

"Well," responded Kadeem, "it's OK. I like how she listens when I have a question on the textbook we are using. It's an advanced textbook. Builds on the fundamentals in algebra I had in elementary school. I call her sometimes. Or the evenings when she works at the Center I can just ask her directly.

"That's just it. The only problem I have is I need to go to Mrs. Carrington too often. It sort of slows me down. Just need to be more on my own. I've learned how to approach a textbook pretty independently once I know the big ideas, but sometimes I need to find more background about particular topics than I have. Mrs. Carrington always will give me what I need but that takes too much of her and my time, often. I wonder if there isn't some on-line computer source I could turn to for a bit more specific background when I need it?"

Jeremy replied, "Ask Mrs. Carrington about the IBM K-12 algebra course software. As I remember, the course is broken into two parts; covers the basic ideas, concepts and skills of algebra—all interactive on the computer. [3] Maybe give it a try. When you need more specific background you might get it quickly if the course is user-friendly. I haven't taken it but others have and liked it. You might turn to the computer program if that seems better for you—to give you more background, like you say.

But I'd like you to stay with the textbook in the main, unless using the textbook is just not worth the effort. As we've talked about before, the state exams in algebra ask you to do things just like you are asked to do in the textbooks. Learning from that algebra textbook should help you use what you know, on the exams."

"I'll try that Jeremy. Thanks.

"You know," Kadeem continued, "I really feel good about working with Mr. Fleck building that little sloop. I never thought of myself getting so excited about sailboats; but I sure am now. I hope I can spend more time with him than just two days a week. We're steaming some ceiling supports now. Wow. That oak smell when we open the steam chest. We went sailing out into the lake, past the islands, last weekend in his yawl. I did all the sailing for quite a bit. I'm getting so that tacking up the river is pretty easy unless the wind's dead against us.

"I call him Ralph," Kadeem said. "He wants me to do that. He's going over to Currytown to select some birch boards at the mill there. Wants me to go. I'll have to reschedule a meeting with Mrs. Carrington but I think it will be OK. We're going to stay overnight at his sister's. OK?"

"Yeah," replied Jeremy, "that makes sense to me if it's OK with your parents. What about making working with Mr. Fleck the centerpiece of your job program? Like you mentioned in your journal, he'll be finishing the fiberglass work on the boat's deck and then it won't be too long until he's doing the cabinetwork. I'd like you to learn from him about fitting hardwood. I just like to run my fingers over his work after it's joined. Your work with Ralph Fleck seems to be at such a good stage."

"I'd like to think about that," responded Kadeem, "and I'll talk with Ralph about putting in more time."

"Good," said Jeremy. "Be sure to set a definite ending date with him so you will be able to move on to the next part of your job program. When you talk with him perhaps you might mention again your need for a flexible work commitment so you can go out and sample other jobs from time to time. You know, like you did on your last job—you kind of sampled two new jobs and then eased into the one with Ralph Fleck. Let's talk again about this."

"Oh Jeremy," said Kadeem, "before I forget, I want to set up my home-school conference time. My dad and mother can make it Wednesday night. OK with you?"

"Yes," Jeremy answered, "at 7:30."

Kadeem asked, "Do we need to do any more preparation for this parent conference? We've brought my portfolio up to date. I guess we'll show my parents the portfolio summary like we usually do each year."

Wednesday evening's meeting with Kadeem's parents came fast for Jeremy. He knocked on their door. Georgia, Kadeem's mother, let him in. Mack, the big tan dog wagged at the door. Jeremy knew Mack from the other times he had visited. Georgia and Todd, Steve's father, both worked away from home during the day.

After a time for sharing, Jeremy, Georgia, Todd and Kadeem settled around the table in the front room. Jeremy laid the summary sheets of Kadeem's record portfolio on the table. The portfolio's supporting materials were in his record box. The box neatly fitted into Jeremy's briefcase which was open on the side table. He laid out Kadeem's timeline which was on nine typewriter sized sheets, all scotch taped together, accordion like. Each sheet represented a year—from the time Kadeem had entered the Urban Little Schools at five-years-old. Kadeem's life in his elementary Urban Little School and his continuation in the secondary Oaktree Group was shown on the sheets—one for each year—with symbols and summary statements. The symbols and notes referred to the papers and photographs in Kadeem's record box. [4] In the record box, sheets showed Kadeem's progress in learning to read and to write, his coming to know and use the library, dated samples of his creative and expository writing. Other record box sheets contained notes about his coming to know the logic and conventions of mathematics, notes about his jobs, his interview writeups by earlier ULS lead teachers and photos of Kadeem at different ages. A pocket in the box contained certificates awarded at the successful completion of each high school basic course he passed at the Self-directed Learning Center. All was in order, with index tabs for quick reference. If Kadeem chose to apply for college, the portfolio was designed to explain his ULS education to an admissions officer. If Kadeem transferred to a conventional school, his parents could use the portfolio to explain to the teachers, there, what Kadeem had done in the Urban Little Schools.

Jeremy went over the contents of Kadeem's portfolio briefly, for Kadeem's parents. They had seen it before, except for the latest fold-out page on which Jeremy and Kadeem had summarized what had happened with Kadeem since the last conference with his parents.

After the four of them had talked about what was on their minds, they each paused and looked over copies of the Urban Little Schools expectations handbook.[5] This was the usual routine. Often one or more of the goals listed there brought up questions and thoughts from parents, the young person or Jeremy.

Notes

1   Students who work for wages have their earnings put in this revolving fund; it is used for the facilitation of student learning and to pay for tools, uniforms, transportation, etc. Some students contribute more than they might use, during a particular year; others might draw more than they put in. Any surplus is transferred electronically to students' savings accounts next year, as a dividend.

2   Kadeem is describing the pattern used in some of the interactive multi-media learning games produced by Syracuse Language Systems, Inc., 5790 Widewaters Parkway, Dewitt, New York 13214.

3   For more on this algebra course, see "K-12 Educational Solutions," (IBM K-12 Education, 4111 Northside Parkway, Atlanta, GA 30327).

4   Urban Little Schools secondary young people take pictures of what they do on their outside jobs. Each Little School has cameras and film for them to use. Many young people develop and print their own photographs in the Community Darkroom. The Urban Little Schools pay an annual fee in support of The Twin Rivers Community Darkroom.

5   See sample expectations in Chapter Ten.

7

The Secondary Urban Little School Teacher's Basic Job

The secondary teacher has a many faceted job, as shown in the last chapter's illustration.[1] Along with guiding each young person, a teacher like Jeremy has to relate to parents and other community people. He also has to be a school administrator who deals with everything from liaison with the host school district and the local library system, to making sure a dripping faucet is fixed. Then too, he teaches in the traditional sense, giving short presentations in his group's weekly Thursday evening sessions. Along with all this, he has to be a public relations person who is sensitive to the "image" his secondary Urban Little School is developing within the community.

That list could go on and on. But as I see it, counseling is the pivotal work of a secondary Urban Little Schools teacher—academic counseling, job counseling, and listening counseling. As academic counselor, the teacher helps the young people in his group of twelve to use effectively the Self-directed Learning Center and other independent learning resources they might utilize to learn the traditional secondary school subjects. As job counselor the teacher helps each young person learn to prepare for and to succeed in jobs which fit.

Listening counseling permeates the previous two roles. The teacher, as a listening counselor, can help students come to be more aware of themselves as independent people in a world where some might need every bit of their strength to make it. This is true particularly of children born into poverty in our cities. Not only will these young people have to succeed, eventually, in the adult world outside the urban inner cities but also in many cases, they will have to prepare for this shift while at the same time living in neighborhoods where guns, gangs, and drugs are commonplace. Now to explain these three counseling roles in more detail.

The Secondary Teacher's Role as Academic Counselor: Helping Each Student Study Independently at the Self-directed Learning Center

As we saw Jeremy and Kadeem doing in the illustration above, the secondary ULS teacher and each young person plan together how the young person might best learn high school basics. Most of this learning will be done at the centrally located Self-directed Learning Center and it will be coordinated when possible with what the young people are learning on their jobs. One way the teacher can do this is to understand the content and the independent learning process used at the Self-directed Learning Center. Both in the teacher's initial training and in continual upgrading, the teacher needs to keep abreast of new developments at the Center. These could include new technology, new academic content and new personnel. With this in mind let's discuss the Center.

The ULS Self-directed Learning Center will be the place where the secondary young people will spend perhaps a third of their school time. The students will be learning high school content in ways tailored to fit each of them, to prepare them to succeed at college or other further training. The Center will be developed and maintained by the ULS backup organization. The Center will feature televised high school courses and multi-media interactive computer programs as well as other individualized learning materials such as programmed textbooks. Young people will be helped to use traditional textbooks in independent ways, too. They also will learn how to take traditional high school and college tests in connection with their courses. Should they need aid, young people studying in the Centers will be able to call on tutors familiar with the various disciplines as Kadeem did with

Mrs. Martinez. Tutors will be chosen from the community, from industry, from colleges and from local high schools.

In helping their students to use the Centers, secondary ULS teachers will be able to secure study option lists provided by the backup organization. These will detail resources available for young people at the Self-directed Learning Centers.

Let's take, for example, a study list for a ULS young person learning English composition and literature. With this list, the student and teacher, step by step, can put together the best English program for the young person from the array of possibilities at a Self-directed Learning Center. Here is the list of options available:

- a capsule course on TV emphasizing the logic, basic ideas and vocabulary in the field of English;
- a televised course of traditional high school English lectures taught by a teacher nominated by her students for national recognition, accompanied by textbook study with periodic tests;
- an interactive multi-media computer-based English grammar and usage course where the learner is directed to solve problems, often meeting challenges in games;
- a programmed textbook in the mechanics of English composition; short courses on TV, each based on key books, such as Strunk's *The Elements of Style*. [2]
- a computer-based course in expository writing keyed to resources typically available in local libraries;
- brief introductions to books, short stories, articles and poems which feature interviews with authors talking about how they had begun their writing and how they do it now;
- a writer's workshop which meets periodically at the Self-directed Learning Center;
- evening tutorial one to one sessions with an outstanding high school teacher who discusses and monitors each student's independent written work, similar to how in British universities tutors follow students' work in preparation for their culmination projects that integrate what they have learned.

To continue our example, a young person's self-directed English program can be synchronized with jobs and community learning opportunities. For example, the young person might have a job working in the publications office of a local business, or a job helping out in the editorial offices of the local newspaper. Then too, the young person might attend a night school course in autobiographical writing where students write stories from their lives. In these ways the secondary young person could study deeply in the field of English or could learn the minimum in that subject area—a minimum that would be necessary to pass the standard college entry tests and to succeed in college level courses.

Thus in academics as in all aspects of each young person's growth, the teacher and the young person will be able to tie students' secondary learning to the individual student's growth as a person. Because academic learning will be organized to fit each of the students, young people will be enabled to move out from where they are, in a given subject, rather than to follow a lead that might be far in advance or far behind their experience or readiness.

The Secondary Teacher's Role as a Job Counselor

Young people in secondary Urban Little Schools work on paid and unpaid jobs, with community people of integrity. One of the teacher's priorities, then, is to find employers whom the teacher feels will set good examples for young people.

From the beginning, the teacher will be provided with sufficient time and support to set up jobs for students. This kind of facilitation is explained in Chapter Twelve where startup of pilot secondary units is described.

The teacher's startup plan, detailed there, will be as follows: the teacher will begin by working with just a few young people during the first pilot school year. Because all the students will have come up through the elementary Urban Little Schools from five-years-old, they will be prepared to learn independently, will be old hands at conferencing and exchanging journals, and so on. The teacher, too, will be a former elementary ULS teacher and therefore will be familiar with the potential in the new secondary students.

Because the new secondary teacher will have come from the elementary Urban Little Schools, with several years' experience in the community, we can assume the teacher will be acquainted with possible community employers—employers of integrity who might be interested in the Urban Little Schools and what they could do for young people. Using these employers as the core group, the teacher should be able to place the first few young people on jobs with employers whose lives express the values of the Urban Little Schools.

Then as word spreads, grounded in the successes of ULS young people on these first jobs, more employers can be expected to be open to considering ULS young persons for short-time employment. If a possible new employer has practical questions that person simply can call one of the previous employers of the student in question.

When I think of possible employers, I think of the partners in a worker-owned bakery which until recently operated in Syracuse where I live. The partners were people who not only cared about good bread, they cared about their customers and each other. To secure extra help and to introduce the bakery to community people, they encouraged outsiders to come in to work on a part-time basis. They paid the extra people in bread and other baked goods. The work wasn't easy, especially in the summer when outdoor heat and the heat generated by the big ovens made even routine jobs real tasks. A ULS young man could start in that bakery doing the never-ending job of washing pans and utensils; he might then graduate to kneading and panning the dough and possibly could wait on customers, after he demonstrated he was genuinely amiable and could handle the cash register.

As I envisage it, the teacher should not stop with a good placement. The teacher shouldn't be an outsider but should be a presence, in appropriate ways, on the young person's job as much as possible. For example, from time to time the teacher might bring a video camera and take close-up shots of the young person working, say, at an auto repair shop. There, the teacher might take shots of the student changing a car's radiator. This kind of involvement might lead to the teacher's learning some of the repair operations. It might be enjoyable for all, too, when the people in the shop viewed a videotape, edited appreciatively. Videotapes and still pictures too, also could be shown to prospective employers and to owners of businesses who might be attending weekly service club meetings (Kiwanis or Lions Clubs are examples). [3]

The backup organization could help the teacher to secure jobs which suited each young person's needs. Contact people from the backup organization could talk with persons in the community with whom ULS young people might work. These contact people then could prepare a continually up-to-date list for secondary ULS teachers. Teachers could use the list to contact community people who had said they would be open to bringing in a ULS young person to work with them on a paid or an unpaid job. Such a talk might lead to the teacher's spending part of a morning in the employer's workplace. After getting to know the teacher, the employer should know the teacher could be counted on to support any forthcoming employment. This might assure a prospective employer that if there were to be a problem, a phone call could fix things.

From my experience (I placed some of our SIEE children on occasional jobs), the best way to interest prospective employers, is to help young people succeed well working with employers who had students previously. If teachers have done their homework—if they know the jobs and what they require of a short-term employee—then the teacher can help the young person prepare for the job in ways which lead to success.

Another way the young person could be prepared to make a success of each job, would be to listen to the experiences of the other students. Once each week all the young people and their teacher Jeremy met together and often shared about their jobs. Because of his one to one relationship with each young worker, Jeremy knew appropriate questions to ask. He might ask the young person to recount one or two little things about the job which seemed satisfying. Boredom? What were lunch times like? If you could do it all over again, what preparation would you give yourself?

Then, in the regular one to one conferences and journals, the teacher would be able help the new workers reflect on their experience. Young people could learn to sort out emotions, perceptions and possibly be helped to return to their jobs with a clearer head.

A kind of job which ULS young people should be uniquely qualified is working as conflict mediators in schools and teen centers. They could help young people to resolve conflicts and also to teach other young people how to bring two disputing people into a place where they could listen to each other to resolve a problem between them.

In my mind I can see ULS young people in Jeremy's secondary group taking to this kind of mediation like ducks take to water. Their ULS years would have been perfect training for being conflict mediators. During those years they learned how to listen to another person seriously by doing it themselves as they conferenced and wrote journals to their teachers, and as they grew up in the school's atmosphere of listening seriously to the other person. [4]

I learned about how I might help people mediate conflict, when I went through a long weekend workshop (Friday afternoon through Sunday). The workshop was designed to teach us how we might mediate conflict between people who initially weren't listening to each other. The workshop worked. I found it a marvelous introduction to conflict resolution through mediation. As participants in role plays, we learned by experience a process of teaching people to resolve their own conflicts, initially by the two of them genuinely hearing each other—maybe for the first time. Then we learned how to help the disputants draw upon their own resources and figure out how both of them might leave the session having at least the minimum each needed in order to resolve the conflict.

The Secondary Teacher's Role as a Listening Counselor: Helping Young People Draw Direction and Strength from Inner Resources

If secondary young people are going to step out in life following their own drummer, taking direction from the best within them, it makes sense that they are learning to have a clear sense of themselves. This kind of understanding is basic to the self-reliance on which many urban young people need to draw if they are to be successful in lifting themselves from what might be an oppressive street culture. The culture I am speaking of challenges anyone who dares to leave its grip, anyone who dares to opt for a life other than no-hope-for-the-future cynicism and indifference toward those not in your clique or gang. Those ULS young people who live with this kind of culture literally at their doorsteps, have to accept who they are, and have a sense of direction. They simply have to, if they are going to be able to handle the emotions and vulnerabilities involved in holding their own against possible challenges from other young people who are being swept along in the street culture.

Secondary Urban Little Schools are designed to enable young people to grow in this kind of self-awareness, fundamental to self-reliance. Of course some of the young people also have valuable help outside their Urban Little Schools—their families, their churches, their close friends, and the examples they can find in good books. But other young people have precious little outside support to help them grow in the kind of clear sense of self which enables strong self-direction based on decency and responsibility. This is the kind of self-awareness on which the young people can draw as they move ahead step by step, into a life of success on the job, in relationships, and in doing what one might to help others in this world.

But whether young people have outside emotional support or not, at school every single secondary ULS young person can count on serious listening and acceptance from his or her teacher. The teacher will make the young people's school a place where their self-respect can grow. Their teacher will conference with them at least twice each month, will exchange journals regularly too. The teacher will lead the weekly evening Think and Listen group where the young people can feel accepted for the persons they are. This is the teacher who will arrange jobs for the young people where they will be able to use and further hone the elements of their self-respect as they work alongside community persons who show integrity on the job and in their lives.

Because it is so important to help each young person come to have a clear sense of self, I want to elaborate here on how a teacher might do this— how a teacher might help each of the young people to grow in self-awareness, in self-respecting ways which can be the foundation for them to step out in charge of their lives. This includes a key objective of the listening counselor: helping adolescents to grow in their ability to face fear while at the same time not losing their sense of direction and self-respect.

My assumption here is that each secondary teacher has to do such listening counseling her or his own way—a way which fits the teacher's own understanding of what it means to come to know oneself and is consistent with the teacher's own understanding of how fear and other pivotal emotions seem to work in the teacher's and most others' lives. Therefore I speak of how I might do listening counseling, in light of my own experience and understanding.

1. As a listening counselor I would help young people to get feelings out, so they could listen to themselves, see themselves, come to know and appreciate themselves better.

I would make sure that in our honest open relationship, the young people felt OK to speak with me of their frustrations, their "down" feelings, felt safe to express their love and caring emotions as well as other feelings such as anger. Our conferences and journals would be designed to enable this kind of learning. There the young people could talk and write about their frustrations, their satisfactions, their sense of significance, and such difficult emotions as fear, guilt and self-doubt. In our conferences and journals, they could talk and write about their values, their yearnings and perhaps their frustrations reconciling their own sense of direction with the realities of the workaday world—perhaps what hard work, openness and responsibility seem to mean for them as they deal with learning to be successful on jobs.

This one to one process between the teacher and each young person is not psychotherapy. It is an awareness process much like the interviewing I described doing with elementary children at our SIEE School, in Chapter Five. It is a time when the young people might hear themselves, during the years when adolescents tend to be grappling with their emerging identity. In their conferences and journals it's OK if the young people talk and write spontaneously, it's OK to express that which otherwise might evade expression. In this haven for young people, they are accepted. They can trust the person listening to them. Their teacher isn't there to judge their worth. The teacher is there to help them have a greater sense of who they are and how they perceive their world.

This kind of an awareness-giving exchange is particularly important for those young people going to Urban Little Schools who live in neighborhoods dominated by the urban street culture as I have mentioned. Many of these young people will need all the help they can get to relate to the two cultures in which they live simultaneously—an urban street culture perhaps characterized by gangs, indifference to others, violence and no-hope-for-the-future, as opposed to the culture of their Urban Little School which might be described in words such as listening, openness, responsibility, and caring.

2. As a listening counselor I would help young people to face fear while at the same time help them to follow their own drummer in a world where sometimes this is difficult.

Here I want to discuss how I might help young persons to come to know and accept two kinds of fear—first, the fear of doing a hard and perhaps perilous thing, something which is downright scary, which others might find too overwhelming or difficult to attempt; and second, the fear generated by dark unwarranted fearful emotions which can undermine your resolve, make you see yourself unjustifiably as "bad," "weak," "full of shame," simply not worth much.

As I see it, as a listening counselor helping ULS young persons face the first kind of fear—being afraid of something that is obviously scary—comes down to my own ability to know, tolerate and accept fear in my own life. I am speaking of knowing in my bones as well as my head that it is perfectly natural to feel fearful when facing danger, despite how this might be seen as not "cool," or be seen as "weak" by others. From my experience I know that fear, which might be so strong that it can numb your mind for a bit, is something you can accept. I have come to know that it is perfectly natural for one to be afraid sometimes—as it might be if you were an inner city adolescent following your own drummer, doing it your way in a world where most others feel helpless to resist following the crowd. It might be dangerous to go against what some other young people were doing; maybe you would have to proceed at your peril. In these situations it's perfectly natural to feel afraid.

But then, there are the second kind of fearful feelings—usually dark fears which are not grounded in reality. These are sometimes frightening emotions often full of guilt, self-diminishment and loneliness, which can rise up from within to bedevil a person. Often they are triggered by frightening real situations but are not warranted by the facts of the scary scenes. You simply are not that "bad," not completely without recourse, not abjectly alone, not to blame for it all, not "nuthin'."

I would see it as my job to help young people tolerate and accept these dark unwarranted fearful feelings which can and do arise and color their world, maybe undermine their resolve. To do this I would help young people to be present to those feelings, to be open to themselves, to acknowledge those lousy feeling states, not try to hide them from themselves or others, or to blame others for causing one's ungrounded fearful feelings. In our one to one conferences, I would make it safe for young people to get their feelings out, to experience these heavy moody parts of themselves without feeling "weak," embarrassed, or self-diminished because they might be feeling these scary unjustified emotions. I would help young people to live with heavy feelings matter-of-factly. A young person thus could acknowledge them, could accept them and in the process, get on with life.

3. As a listening counselor, I would help young people come to know and appreciate the ways each is significant and worthwhile.

Honest appreciation is one of the most important positive balances to the kinds of dark unwarranted self-diminishment I have just described—self-diminishment which in so many young people's teenage years seems to be lurking ready to emerge at any time.

When I speak of honest appreciation, I mean appreciation tied to evidence which is hard to deny. The way I propose reporting to parents is a good example of this. Jeremy spread out a series of sheets, each listing what Kadeem had accomplished in a particular year. Kadeem's pictures were on many of the sheets showing how he looked then. The portfolio spelled out how he had developed to be the young person he was at the moment when Jeremy and Kadeem were showing his record to his parents. The record was stuffed with facts, figures, and data which made it plain what Kadeem had learned in the key areas of reading, and mathematics. Also samples of Kadeem's writing illustrated his development in this key skill area. A summary of what Kadeem had learned at the Self-directed Learning Center appeared on his secondary report sheets. Certificates from completed Center courses were in a pocket of the portfolio. Messages from employers were there, attesting to how Kadeem was able to pull his own oar, on the job. It was pretty hard for any dark unwarranted self-diminishing feelings to counter all that. Those were the facts.

Then, too, at a more casual level, the same principle applies. When I express my appreciation to a teenager I often tie it to a fact the young person cannot deny. "Chester, your neat smile in this picture I took of you helping a customer on the bakery job gives me a lift."

One way I teach people to take honest validation is by my example—how I accept it myself. If young people tell me a thing they like about me, I often respond by saying something such as, "Thanks. That makes me feel good."

Validation isn't difficult for most very young children. They usually find it easy to validate themselves, with remarks such as "Look what I can do." It's only later that our way of life tells young people that it's bad openly to appreciate themselves or another.

Secondary Teachers are Offered Assistance and Support In Their Demanding Work

Here are some of the ways Urban Little Schools are designed to offer help and assistance to secondary teachers as they do their sensitive, time-consuming job:

- The backup organization manages and maintains the Self-directed Learning Centers.

The secondary teacher guides young people to draw upon the resources at the Self-directed Learning Center without having responsibility for the Center. The Center's independent learning materials are provided by the learning specialists in the backup group. The backup group hires tutors and arranges for laboratory classes, seminars and other activities when needed. Computers and other technology are maintained and upgraded by the backup group. All will be there for the young people to learn high school basic content on their own, with the help of tutors if need be, and under guidance from each young person's secondary ULS teacher.

- A Floating Teacher is provided to help the secondary teacher.

Every ten secondary teachers has the help and assistance of one Floating Teacher. The Floating Teachers are secondary ULS teachers who don't have direct responsibility for their own groups. Instead they spend time with each of the teachers who lead the ten groups which a Floating Teacher supports. They sometimes attend the weekly evening Think and Listen sessions and in other ways come to be acquainted with the young people in each of their ten groups. One important function of the Floating Teacher is to support teachers and young people in case of a mismatch. Sometimes a young person might better work with another teacher in another secondary ULS group. The Floating Teacher can handle such a switch smoothly. Then too, a Floating Teacher might step in if a teacher is out with an extended illness. Finally, Floating Teachers will be in a position to sense the pulse of the ten groups they facilitate. They can offer this understanding to assist the backup organization in how to help the secondary teachers even more.

- Two part-time teachers might handle one secondary Urban Little Schools group, in partnership.

There could be two part-time partnership teachers responsible for a secondary Urban Little School with its twelve children. Initially, when a secondary Urban Little School is started, it probably would be a good idea for only one teacher to set up the school. Then, once the group is functioning smoothly, this teacher might choose a person who would fit well as a partner. A candidate for this kind of partnership position might first try it out as an assistant working with just one or two young people.

Partnerships are often valuable for reasons such as these: the two teachers can dialogue about each of the students; it might provide a better chance for an ideal fit between a teacher and every single student because there would be two teacher possibilities for each student; in some cases, the secondary Urban Little School could be staffed with both a woman and a man which would have obvious advantages for those young people who might work better with a person of one sex or the other.

The advantages of a partnership would have to be balanced with the additional complexity introduced by two people working with the same group of twelve students. This could be minimized, of course, simply by dividing the students into two subgroups, one group being the special responsibility of one of the partnership teachers and the other being the responsibility of the second teacher. Both teachers, at the same time, could make sure they knew all twelve of the students well.

As far as the teachers' salaries are concerned, a secondary ULS teacher could job-share and receive a bit better than half the typical teacher's salary. This is because the salary allocated for each secondary Urban Little Schools teacher pays for an additional ten days of work over the 175 days teachers typically work. Each partnership teacher, therefore, could receive more than half a typical teacher's salary if the two were to split the salary evenly. [5]

- Teachers will be offered chances to listen to themselves, to be with themselves

Teachers who listen actively and constantly to young people, as secondary ULS teachers do, can become emotionally drained. Many might use chances to be listened to themselves. Also they might benefit from opportunities to express the parts of themselves that often aren't expressed. I have listed below some of the ways which I have found have helped me be more aware of my own emotions during the years I was working with children in responsive ways. The ULS teacher training program might provide these and other ways teachers could listen to themselves.

1. Being Quiet with Oneself and Journal Writing
2. Autobiographic Writing
3. Taking Black-and-white Pictures Sensitively; Then Developing and Printing Them in Ways which Bring Out the Subtle Human Interest and Beauty of Your Work
4. Being Close to Oneself in Nature
5. Expressive Dance and Movement

6. Reading Memoirs of People Who are Honest with Themselves
7. Being with Oneself at Self-renewal and Retreat Centers [6]
8. Peer Counseling

Parents and Others Can Support Secondary Urban Little Schools Students and Their Teachers

Helping young people to succeed academically, to work on the jobs from which they can learn the most, and to help them come to understand themselves so they can face emotions such as fear, is a big job in the best of circumstances. And often the circumstances in an urban setting aren't the best. ULS teachers need to do all they can to work in concert with other adults who are significant in a young person's life—particularly, of course, the student's family members. But maybe, unfortunately, a teacher can't depend on significant support from one or more family members. Perhaps though, the teacher might bring out some family support which is latent. This support might come from a grandparent or from a grown brother or sister. The teacher might help others, whom the young person respects, to be the best models for the young person, such as a ULS community employer with whom the young person works or has worked.

When I think of a secondary teacher as a working partner with family members, I think back to Jeremy's home visit with Kadeem's parents. Jeremy had earned the respect of Kadeem's mother and father. He had been visiting with them for longer than just one year. They understood what Jeremy and the school were doing to help Kadeem make it, as a responsible person of decent character. They had come to trust Jeremy. What Jeremy and Kadeem did at school, his parents not only understood but supported.

One reason for this kind of close bond is Kadeem's parents choose to have their son go to an Urban Little School in the first place. If what the school stood for were not something they wanted, presumably they wouldn't have put their son's name on the waiting list.

Second, parents are given chances to size up their son's teacher. Again, Jeremy showed himself to be the person who was there to make sure Kadeem succeeded. In parent-teacher conferences Jeremy showed how he and Kadeem were working together to help Kadeem increasingly take responsibility for his own growth academically, job-wise, and in character development.

Kadeem's parents didn't have to worry that the school might alienate their son from them. They could see that the goal of the Urban Little Schools was to bring the family and the school together behind the child. For example, there never would be a serious worry that the teacher would encourage young people to dwell on blaming their parents for their problems. Also there never would be a serious question that the teacher intentionally would keep parents in the dark about a distressful topic which the teacher and the young person were discussing at school. In some circumstances the teacher would have to handle this communication with parents sensitively so essential confidentiality for the student was respected. In this vein, teachers might have to help young people come to be able to talk with their parents themselves about a particular challenge the young person is facing. School-parent communication in sensitive areas should be one of the topics which parents and school people discuss seriously when the parents are making up their minds whether to send their child to the school.

Along with the support of parents, the teacher has another group of allies in helping the secondary ULS young person—some of the adults with whom the young person works. It is obvious Kadeem admires and respects Ralph and likes him a lot. When Jeremy goes to lunch with Ralph or when the two of them meet in other ways both can help the other guide Kadeem.

Also sometimes ULS teachers need to bring in a person other than themselves if a young person might want or need to talk with a someone of the opposite sex from the teacher. This is an advantage of having a teaching partnership consisting of a man and a women, as I mentioned. This is where, also, a Floating Teacher might help. The Floating Teacher might arrange for the young person to work temporarily with another secondary ULS teacher of the opposite sex from the young person's teacher.

So in the Urban Little Schools design, there is an infrastructure of helping persons with whom secondary teachers can share their roles as listening counselor, job and academic counselor. It's important, of course, that the teacher keeps a coordinating position with this group of adults who, in different ways, are in the young person's corner.

That brings up a final point. Some ULS teachers might need to be helped to be easy with family members and others who could offer help for the young person. From my experience, I suspect some ULS teacher trainees will need help to overcome personal reluctance to venture beyond the security of the school building in order to make frequent and rewarding visits with family members and other people in the community, when such visits are appropriate.

Notes

1   The job of secondary teacher might be shared by two part-time partnership teachers. This possibility is discussed further, below.

2   Strunk, William Jr. (1959) *The Elements of Style*. (Edited and revised by E.B. White). New York: The Macmillan Company.

3   For a fascinating photojournalism view of what people do in varied city jobs see: Howells, Ron. (2000). *One Hundred Jobs: A Panorama of Work in an American City*. New York: New Press.

4   See ideas in the *Alternatives to Violence* training manuals. Write to: AVP Distribution Service, 844 John Foster Rd., Plainsfield, VT. Also write to Educators for Social Responsibility for their current resource catalogue: 23 Garden St., Cambridge, MA 02138.

5   See more about partnershipping in the section at the end of Chapter Twelve. The section is entitled "More on Startup."

6   A guidebook to these centers is: Kelley, Jack and Maria. (1996). *Sanctuaries: The Complete United States*. New York: Bell Tower Books.

8

How Might it All Add Up In a Young Person's Life?

For the past few chapters we've been discussing how teachers might guide ULS children as they grow from five years old to when they might leave a secondary unit, around seventeen years old. Now let's spend some time on how it all adds up—what a young person might be like who had grown up through the Urban Little Schools.

I suspect most readers of this book would respond by saying young graduates of the Urban Little Schools would show a great deal of uniqueness—would follow their own drummer in ways which grew from a good perspective both on themselves and on their world. I would expect them, in addition, to show some important characteristics in common which not only would benefit themselves, their families and those with whom they worked, but would benefit our world. Here are some of these commonalties:

- I would expect the graduating young people to show self-reliance and independence yet be sensitive toward others.
- Graduates should be able to handle their fearful emotions without resort to denial, delusion, self-deception or without fleeing from fearful feelings in some other ways—ways which might interfere with their ability to solve difficult and complex problems. These problems might be personal in nature or might be dilemmas which could impede sound group decisions.
- Graduates should judge themselves based on a sense of self-awareness. That, as opposed to relying on the judgment and approval of others in deciding on one's next best step.

- I would expect to be impressed by how skillful these young people had become in educating themselves, how job-wise they were in determining how to move ahead to the benefit of their employers and to themselves.
- Because they were self-reliant, they would be able to live on less and would be comfortable with modest lifestyles which freed them to make choices for their lives which were in tune with whom each was and with what each person could do best. Thus they would be freer than most to choose jobs which fascinated and intrigued them, not necessarily jobs which offered the highest pay.
- Then, too, I would expect to find many of the young people to be intriguing as conversationalists, especially if the conversation were grounded in questions that mattered in our lives. They would show a clear awareness of their world without a need to deny harsh reality. If I were talking with one of the graduates, I probably would feel relaxed and trusting in the young person's company. Also the young person should have things to say which would make someone reflect on what was said, for some time after.

These expectations are projections based on my ten years of experience at the SIEE elementary school, leading our child study program where my central role was to get to know and to follow each child with awareness. When I think of the children who stayed at our school long enough for their experience to be formative, I think of young people who were learning to see beyond shallowness, cynicism, TV role models, and peer groups. They knew how to listen and did it. They were taken seriously and took others that way. They could size up themselves accurately and clearly understand their world.

These were young people who showed the results of growing up in a school based on the awareness of each child as a person. Continually, these young people were asked to reflect on what they had done and what impinged upon their actions. They often did this kind of thinking in journals and in other close listening interactions their teachers and I had with each of them. The self-respect which emerged from these experiences was based on the solid evidence of their accomplishments and the respect shown to them by their teachers.

In writing the illustration below I combine my SIEE experience with how it might have been if our children had continued on with the kind of secondary schooling we have been discussing in the previous two chapters.

In this story we are with seventeen-year-old Chris as he talks with his teacher Jeremy about his ULS education and what it means to him. In four months Chris plans to leave Jeremy's Oaktree Group. Chris is seventeen now. He began at The Fircroft Urban Little School when he was five-years-old. That was three years after the school opened.

At this point in Chris's secondary Urban Little Schools education, he is working steadily, afternoons, in a jewelry store repairing watches, clocks and jewelry. He began this job at odd times about two years ago while still working every morning at Twin Rivers' daily newspaper, *The Independent.* He had worked at *The Independent* office for four months, delivering and picking up the interdepartmental mail and running office errands.

After working half-time for eleven months at the jewelry store, Chris has become quite adept at clock repairing. He checks his diagnosis of a clock's problem with Glenn, the twenty-seven-year-old man with whom he works and who is introducing him to the trade. Almost always, these days, Chris's diagnosis of a clock's problem works out to be right. He enjoys working with the jeweler's fine tools and the various metals. In this, he builds on a previous job working in an art and craft cooperative. There he tried his hand at various crafts while being available to do odd jobs for the various crafts people and artists. He found he liked to spend most of his time with a calligrapher there.

Not only does Chris share Glenn's fascination about working with jewelry and watches, Chris easily can be himself with Glenn. Often it just takes a slight nod or movement for them to communicate. Laughing comes easy, too.

For the final piece in Chris's portfolio he will write about himself at this point in his life, in light of his ULS education and other formative influences. Urban Little Schools people call the essay the "How it Was and Is Paper." In the story below we are with Chris and Jeremy, in Jeremy's office, as they discuss the paper and Chris's thoughts about what he might write.

• • •

Jeremy and Chris's "How it Was and Is" conference began by their discussing a few routine matters. Then Chris asked, "So, how shall we begin talking about my paper? I feel a bit uneasy about writing this."

"Uneasy?" asked Jeremy in a matter of fact way.

"Yes," explained Chris. "On one hand I want the paper to be me; sort of open and straightforward. Yet it's a public statement, really, even though I can decide who reads it. Any thoughts about that?"

"Well," Jeremy responded, "I've found that with others who have written the paper, one thing which helps is for them to begin, at this conference, by being as open as they can—not to worry about privacy. I mean just open up if you feel like it, and perhaps go into personal detail. Then after our conference here, go out on your own and settle into writing the paper in any way that seems to be comfortable for you."

"That makes sense to me," said Chris. "This conference, then, is an off the record kind of thing. I'll think of it as a kind of starter, not as my saying things that necessarily might later appear in the final paper."

"Yes," responded Jeremy, "that's the way I see it. I've found, too, if we tape record this conference, the tape later helps some people focus their thinking. I think of one person who did that. She took the tape home; then went through it and made note cards of significant items that might appear in her paper. So, what about taping it?"

"OK," agreed Chris. "You start. Ask me some questions."

Jeremy put on a ninety-minute cassette and started the machine. "OK. I'll sort of get myself into the shoes of a parent who's interested in the Urban Little Schools. Let's say the parent knows about the elementary part but needs to know more about the secondary ULS years.

"This parent's initial question is about how the Oaktree Group compares with the conventional high school. The parent might ask, 'How does a secondary Urban Little School compare with the regular high school as you see it? What's the difference?"

Chris settled back in his armchair quartered from Jeremy's, where they both could look out the window. "Well, I'll just talk as things hit me. Of course I can't speak for all secondary Urban Little Schools, just our Oaktree Group.

"I think of how sometimes over the last few years, I've felt like I was in another orbit from most high school kids. I'd see bunches of kids, from Metropolitan High on the streets; sometimes I wished I was one of them. But other times I was glad I wasn't. Like I was so glad I didn't have to sort of submerge myself in a clique of kids—have to wear certain clothes that seemed to fit in with what all the others were wearing. You know.

"Funny, all that looking at the Metro kids seems sort of like distant history now. After Carol and I began to go around together, I felt strongly what I was doing, being in our Oaktree Group, made so much sense. I really didn't have much of an idea of what high school was all about until Carol began to tell me what happened to her there.

"I'd hate to do what she does—have to sort of figure out what each teacher wants and give it back to the teachers on tests. It's not that way in all her classes. She really likes her biology teacher—kids around with him and all that. But so much of what she talks about just seems like another world to me.

"I guess, Jeremy, it made a really big difference when I found myself with the special friendship Carol and I have. I've come to know some of her friends and she has mine. We often spend time at Glenn's house, after work. He has the neatest little kid—Frankie. Wow, I hope that if I have a child it will be like Frankie. I mean he's really himself, yet he usually seems interested in what I have to say; it's just fun to be around him.

"Is this what you want to know?"

"Yes." Jeremy paused. Then he said, "Are we at a place where you could take another question from me or do you want to go on as you are?"

"Give me another."

"OK. Here's a question that almost all people ask who want to find out the impact an Urban Little Schools education has on a young person. The question has to do with how well you feel you are prepared to lead a life in which you will feel satisfied. I guess it's a kind of two part question: 'What about your ideas of what a good life for you seems to be; and to what extent do you feel ready to take the next steps into it?'"

"Wow. Jeremy, that seems like a big one."

"Yeah, it is. I just need the thoughts that might come to you—thoughts you might have—no more. Don't push it. I mean, just talk from how the question hits you."

"OK, let me think." Chris sat for two or three minutes looking out the window.

"You know Jeremy, it's good to watch those fellows over there building that building addition. The two I can see from here look about Glenn's age—in their late twenties. I guess something I've learned in our Group is that I could get a job building with bricks, like they are, and do it well. That time I worked with Johnny Sims on his house, I learned enough about masonry work to do that. Because he's retired he had time; he'd tell me to stop and then he'd take time to show me. I think I could wire a circuit for my own house addition, too; maybe not set up the wiring for a whole house but I could learn soon enough.

"I guess that's one thing that strikes me. I mean I feel I could go out and learn what I needed, now—like learning about wiring a house. I could get a few books and with what I know, I could do it. With all the stuff Glenn teaches me it wouldn't be much more for me to learn the next steps into several different kinds of work. Like now that I can fix clocks, I could move into fixing computers. Glenn fixes computers too.

"Glenn's thinking of starting a business fixing office machines including desktop computer systems. He tells me that there isn't much money to lay out at first—just your tools, which we already have, and a well equipped van which you can back right up to your customer's place. I know I could work with him and do a good job. Like I said, all I'm learning from him about clocks is super background for fixing computers. Also, from what I learn watching him fixing computers, that job is mostly just diagnosing. I mean once you figure out where the trouble is you just replace the part of the machine where the problem is. Working with Glenn has taught me a lot about diagnosing.

"I can use the library of course. I think I got hooked on the library when I worked there shelving books. I was eight when I began to follow a library person around, helping to shelve some of the books. Then when I assisted at the reference desk, it was great. I remember about three or four years ago how neat it was to work with Sally Pendergast at the reference desk. I've talked with you before about this—how people would ask Sally all sorts of questions and sometimes Sally would start me helping them. She'd keep an eye on me as she worked with other people. After I sort of got the hang of it, I knew I helped her handle a lot more people than she could otherwise.

"Like at lunch time when people would line up for help and most were in a hurry, I really felt I was helping. The library patrons and I knew that Sally was keeping a close watch so they would get good service. Like in a few days I really got fast at using the computer to tell patrons if we had a book on a subject they wanted to know more about and if the book was in; then I learned to do a search for books and send out interlibrary loan requests. Next, in just a little while I began to use some of the reference books that answered a lot of people's questions—like the current US statistical source documents.

"I estimated one day that there are less than fifty key reference books or computer resources Sally uses over and over again. Those are her first steps in helping people. Most of the time she doesn't need to go beyond that point. I got to know those books and computer resources. Funny, so many library patrons seemed surprised that a fourteen-year-old could handle all that. Maybe it was just that they had never gotten near that side of the library when they were kids.

"Working in the library doesn't seem like a job. It all seems to me like something I grew up with. Well, it was. Like, the other day, I taught Carol how to define a research question with key words and all those other ways my teacher taught me at Fircroft, so I could organize a topic to open up the indexes and reference collection in the library. Carol didn't know that *The New York Times* microfilm collection was in the library's holdings. Turned out what she needed was on *The Times* microfilm. She had a lot of fun finding out about some events in the '70s women's movement—that was her topic—once I showed her how to use the index and how to get her question set up so that she could use it easily. It was kind of exciting for her to read about history when it was hot news.

"Well, let's see," continued Chris, "what was the question, Jeremy? I got so carried away I forgot the question."

"It was," reiterated Jeremy, "about how well prepared do you feel you are. I mean prepared to go out and start to be what you...what makes sense to you—in terms of a doing a job or earning money, while still being the kind of person you want to be."

"Yeah," Chris answered, "so much of what I have done has helped me to.... Well, how will I put it? It's helped me to be the person I want to be—the person who sees things and then sort of sifts it all according to what really matters. It's a kind of discovery process. Sometimes it feels like I'm standing alone. Sometimes that feels a bit heavy; but at the same time it feels good not to be swept along in the tide. It never stops, this process. I expect I'll be doing it all my life and piling up a lot of knowing. I'll continue to do this— to think through what I know as I experience new things, as I get deeper and deeper into things. It's really helped me to do this, here in the Urban Little Schools, as I write and talk with you and the other teachers I've had and as I listen and think with the people like Glenn.

"But you know, there is another part of your question that I want to move to. I know how much parents and others are concerned with how well prepared I feel I am to go out and live as the person I want to be. But to me, asking that question seems to miss the point. I guess, the point is I don't have to wait to be the kind of person I want to be, Jeremy; I am that person now.

"I think mostly, in our Oaktree Group, I haven't been preparing for life; I've been living it. I've been living it, looking at it and at the same time coming to terms with it, as best I can. You know, working, making my decisions and then looking, with you, about how things are turning out; facing my feelings—all that. I've been doing that since I started in the Urban Little Schools. It seems just natural to go on doing that.

"Of course that's not as easy as falling off a log. Sometimes it doesn't feel comfortable to do what might feel like paddling upstream—feeling alone, like I said. Sometimes it feels, well, like I am tired and want to be taken care of. You know. I see being in high school that way—do what you're told and then they'll take care of you.

"Well," Chris reflected, "I've been pretty well taken care of, most of the time. But in the Urban Little Schools, it seems to me I've learned to take care of myself—to do what makes sense inside. And I feel I'm prepared to go to college.

"I probably can go to any college I can afford. At least when I interviewed this fall, the five I looked at seemed to want me. I felt I'd get accepted. All but one offered scholarships. Well, not in so many words, but I felt that if I applied for financial aid I'd get it. Funny how admissions people were so interested in the Urban Little Schools; asked me a lot of questions and really read my portfolio as I was sitting there showing it to them. You remember I went on that bus trip visiting colleges for a week last fall. It was a part of that "Take Control of Your College Education," Special Events series. That was one of the best S.E. series we've had. I think all the kids got a lot out of it. Neat fun, too, to take that week's bus trip visiting colleges day after day—just the six of us and Miguel.

"I left that S.E. series with a kind of rough tentative plan about college. First I plan to concentrate on making the most of the college 'general education' phase—the first two years of college. I can do that here in Twin Rivers at the Community College. It'll cost me about nine-hundred dollars a year for tuition if I do it half-time while I work. Then after that 'general education' part I'll be in a position to choose the best college for whatever my major study will be. During those four years of 'general education'—that's two years of college at half-time—I ought to be able to decide on my major.

"I was really moved the other day. When I was taking my grandmother to the store she told me that she had been putting aside twenty-five dollars a month for my college education. She's been doing it for several years, out of her Social Security. But I'd like to do it all myself—work for a year or two full-time, before starting at community college, maybe doing clock and watch repairing and perhaps jewelry work. Then I'll have enough money to do it, so long as I work part-time when I'm going to college. I guess I don't want to take my grandma's money. Maybe she can use it for someone else in the family."

Chris looked out the window again. Both men were quiet for about a minute.

Chris began again. "I feel good about the way that we learned the basic high school courses. Well, it was a slog sometimes to face one more session of that physics lecture series on videotape, with its accompanying exercises on the computer. I'm glad I could do that course at the Self-directed Learning Center and not here or at home. Over there, I can go into a study carrel and sort of completely apply myself—just the video player, the computer and me.

"As you know, I didn't use the tutors all that much. I guess it was because I sort of took to most of the self-study materials easily. I'd been using them since I was five or six. Well, our math tutor helped me see the theory—I mean the logic of it all rather than just all the number manipulation. That helped me with the math courses on TV tape and on the computer.

"I feel good about how you had us take those sample Scholastic Aptitude Tests and ACT tests about a year and a half ago. I needed more geology to have the background the college people seem to want—like that man from the preparation service told me. When I learned more of that at the Self directed Learning Center and tried the sample tests again I feel it helped me a lot to get the high scores that I did when I took the real tests.

"I hope you'll do that again—have that fellow take our kids through the tests college people judge applicants with. That was good practice, too. I needed to get the hang of taking timed tests—all that pressure."

"Thanks Chris," said Jeremy. "Could we get back to that question about the kind of a job you might like? That's a question most parents seem to ask over and over, in all sorts of ways. As I see it, that question misses the point about deciding on one's work or career. But they ask it anyway. I feel that the right job will come after one's house in order, so to speak; after one has done the kind of exploring and learned the basic skills of independence, as you have been talking about. I guess so many parents who are considering an Urban Little Schools education for their sons or daughters, ask that question because they're afraid ULS graduates won't be able to fit in.

"OK," responded Chris. "But first I'd like to just relax and sit here a bit."

They both did that.

"You know Jeremy, it feels so good to be quiet like we just were. Huh. Maybe that is one of the best things I am getting out of our Oaktree Group. We're quiet a lot when we meet together.

"But I still don't know if I'm answering your question about 'what I want to be.'

"I guess that's just it. Somehow what I want is the.... Well, I don't want to head toward some kind of an image. I want to do sort of what we are doing here right now—what we do so much in the Oaktree Group—like you said, exploring ourselves and what work is all about. I want to go through things and have space to talk about them, share them, feel them myself and share my thoughts and feelings with someone like Carol, or you.

"Yeah, that's it Jeremy, if I head for some sort of an image or role or whatever, I might find myself putting it on, like a cloak. I'd wear it and try to kid myself and everyone else that it was me. You know the other night when Paul really opened up, cried—in the middle of all of us? Well, he was letting it out. It seems to me that he was being with the part of him that he needed to be, ...well, that he needed to feel.

"Yeah. Guess the other thing that I need in the future is *space to be.* Like I said, being in the Oaktree Group has given me a lot of space. For example, like I said, when I go to college, I want to go part-time—take just a few courses each term and work the rest of the time. That way I'll leave enough space for me to sort of follow what comes up, to explore—maybe take some ideas to the library and read a lot more around them. I can take a semester off college work and learn on my own, if I want to. That way I probably will get excited about some subject, something that I might major in, during the last two years of college.

"Carol feels she'd like to go to college part-time too. We both plan to. It should be kind of special for us, both working for a year or so while we save for college and then going to community college half-time for four years while we do the 'general education' part of college.

"Carol's mother is behind her a hundred percent in this. Carol's kind of explaining it all to her mom as we think it through. Her mom never went to college and really doesn't know much about it. Up to a few months ago, she saw college as kind of like an expensive extension of high school—something they can't afford to give to Carol. But now her mother sees how Carol can get a college education, use it to get jobs and all that, *and* pay for it herself as she goes along. Neither Carol nor I want to take out those loans some kids use to pay for their college educations. After college we want to be free to live on a small income, if that goes with living the kind of life we want. Don't want to have to take high paying jobs—if we can find them—partly just to pay for college debts.

"It would help Carol's mom to do what some of us did last year when we spent two weeks going to college—trying it out. I remember how it hit me—the feel of what it was like to be caught up in that college world. I remember how it can submerge you, how you can get swept along, like a wave's got you. Maybe college teaches kids to lead frantic lives, to never have enough time. It looks to me like you learn to get things done as quickly as you can. You know, it comes down to doing it quickly and so it pleases the professor. I won't have to do that when I go to college the way we've planned it. I won't have to fit into the usual way of learning—hurry up to pass the tests and all. It's kind of exciting to think of what I might learn by *using* college to learn in a kind of step by step way, rather than having it just submerge me. Yeah, step by step—a lot like we learn in the Urban Little Schools except the Urban Little Schools are set up to help people do that. At college you have to do it for yourself. But I think I can do it."

Chris paused, "You know, Jeremy, at first it was fun to talk abut these things. Now, all of a sudden, it feels sort of heavy."

"Heavy?" repeated Jeremy.

"Yeah," Chris went on, with a more sober sound to his voice, "when you stop and think of the future....Well, maybe there won't be one.

"I know that sounds pessimistic. But that's the way it seems to me sometimes—what with global warming and its climate changes already beginning to change all sorts of the things people depend on; what with the population expanding still more; all the violence on the streets; and how now that the secret is out, almost anyone with plenty of money can get their hands on nuclear or other mass destruction weapons. Seems to me people sense all this and are running more and more scared. The thing that worries me is that most don't seem to know how to handle that kind of fear. Like they want to blame it all on someone else or some group, and then get 'em."

Chris paused and then continued.

"It's good that in the Oaktree Group we share what each of us thinks about things. Helps me not to lose hope entirely. I mean it's important for me to share my feelings about how scary the future looks unless people wake up and see things that are happening, more clearly—see things like those scary realities I just mentioned. After I share my lousy feelings with people who listen and accept what I say—like I did just a minute ago here—I so often can feel my sense of hope. I mean when I share with people who sort of believe in me, feel I'm OK—you know, with you and our Group, for instance. Then being alive feels good. I guess it's then that my hope can move to be focused on things right with me now—like my relationship with Carol, what I'm learning, how I might start my own business.

"Yeah, and maybe I can help other people see things more clearly—starting with seeing themselves. Maybe I can help them see themselves and see what's going on in the world around them, a bit more clearly. I guess that means helping people see a bit of what we're up against—you know, like how hard it is so often, to be true to yourself inside—all that. The only way I think of helping people that way is to be me, to show people by what I do, what I see when I don't kid myself. I want to do the kind of job that will allow me to—you know—be open with people as much as I can; like how we share so often in the Oaktree Group or when I work with Glenn.

"Like I said, I just feel OK here about letting it out, being open. I really feel others listen to me. We do it a lot in the Thursday evening group and then in these person to person times with you; we do it in our journals; just all the time.

"Yeah, I want to go on listening and sharing the way we do. When I leave, it will be with people like Carol and some other good friends. Whew, it's good to know that Carol and I can be with each other and.... Well, it's hard to explain. The two of us just laugh and joke around and then sometimes, the very next minute, really feel something. Like we feel scared; or really feel how special it is to be together. Wow. That's terrific—even when sometimes we have to work through the bad feelings toward each other after an argument."

• • •

Chris, in this conference with Jeremy, gives us one example of how life might look for a young person who grew up through the Urban Little Schools. Each ULS graduate's experience would be as unique and varied as Chris's.

9

The Backup Organization's Work—Including Selecting and Training Teachers

If the Urban Little Schools backup organization does its job capably, then its teachers out in the neighborhoods will be freed to concentrate on their work. In this chapter I shall talk about how an effective backup organization might do this within one city school district. Then it could branch out to other cities in the region or in the whole nation.

I lead off, in this chapter, with a list of the backup organization's various jobs. Next I discuss how such a backup organization might come into being and could take the leadership in bringing strong pilot Urban Little Schools to a community. Following this, in detail, I shall discuss the following roles of a backup organization: developing independent learning materials; writing a contract for autonomous Urban Little Schools; facilitating continual evaluation of ULS units; teacher selection and training.

In a nutshell, here are the key specifics of how an Urban Little Schools backup organization, could work:

- The non-profit backup organization would have final responsibility and authority for each ULS unit. This authority would include teacher hiring, training and, possibly, terminating teachers' employment. The backup organization would issue limited-term contracts to teachers who had proven themselves, beyond the provisional stage. For example, the backup organization might use a "2-3-4 limited tenure plan" after approval of state teacher credentialling authorities—two years training, three years probation period to double-check teachers' fitness and then four year contracts from then on out.

- The backup group would raise funds for its non-reimbursed operations, such as hiring and training teachers plus startup of pilot schools, through grants and donations.

- Initially the backup organization could work to enlarge and deepen community discussion of a possible Urban Little Schools tryout in its city. Then the backup organization would facilitate the work of a constituency of people committed to trying the ULS Idea.

- As the discussions proceeded, the backup organization could bring people together to draft a proposal for trying out the Urban Little Schools in the community's public school system. The proposal draft would be discussed concurrently, with the state department of education and with the local board of education. (Local school districts have decision power within the state's statutory authority.) If the pilot schools were set up as Charter Schools within the school district, the tryout plan would need to fit the state's Charter School proposal guidelines.

- The backup group could help the people and groups involved, translate the proposal to a binding contract for developing pilot and subsequent Urban Little Schools within the local school district, after the district had agreed in principle to support the work and autonomy of the Urban Little Schools within its system.

- It would direct the selection and on-the-job training of pilot school teachers; would provide for their supervision; would provide stipends for pilot school teacher trainees and if funds were available, for subsequent trainees as well. This startup teacher development would include working out provisions for teacher credentialling with the state department of education which might be done in two stages: first a tentative arrangement and second, after pilot Urban Little Schools had proven themselves, more permanent arrangements could be made.

- The backup organization would help newly selected ULS school teachers develop their small schools in buildings which the backup organization would have leased according to its contract with the district.

- The backup organization could help interpret the new elementary Urban Little Schools to neighborhood parents who might want to consider enrolling their five-year-olds. Perhaps this program would not be necessary if the teachers ended up doing it casually with their neighbors on the nearby streets during the time they were setting up their schools.

- The backup organization would make sure the pilot Urban Little Schools were tested adequately before offering them as models for subsequent Urban Little Schools in the district and beyond. This individual school evaluation would be a part of continuing evaluation for all subsequent Urban Little Schools on an annual or biennial basis, as specified in the contract with the host school district. Thus the backup organization would demonstrate, continually, how each Urban Little School was delivering on the specific goals stipulated in the contract with the host school district.

- It would identify, acquire and develop reading, writing and math independent learning materials for elementary Urban Little Schools. Examples of such materials in the math area might be games and individualized arithmetic learning options for children. These would be practical skill-oriented print materials and computer programs which could help children ably learn to handle such tasks as the arithmetical thinking and calculation needed on the secondary jobs they would take later.

- At the same time, the backup organization would begin planning for the secondary Self-directed Learning Center facilities. The backup organization's independent learning materials task group would select from available computer software and other learning materials, plus consider designing whatever additional individualized learning materials were needed. The high school basic academic subjects would be set up in course modules. One to one with their secondary teacher, students would consider their test scores and other course evaluation to determine successful completion of each module. These Self-directed Learning Centers would have to be ready in about seven years after the pilot elementary schools opened—ready when the first elementary Urban Little Schoolers entered the newly formed pilot secondary ULS groups.

- The backup organization would help interpret the new pilot schools to visitors. This work could be coordinated by the backup organization's host or hostess who worked in each pilot elementary school.

The Beginning: A Backup Organization Grows out of Initial Grassroots Interest in the Urban Little Schools Idea

Serious talks about bringing Urban Little Schools to a community might be initiated by child advocate groups, local urban planners or by an urban university which might consider sponsoring an Urban Little Schools tryout in its adjacent declining neighborhoods.[1] Then too, preschool parents, representatives from the local library system, plus school district board members and the superintendent, might want to discuss the ULS approach. Public school board members and top administrators might find themselves open to exploring reform through fundamental redesign, such as this approach offers, because previous "quick-fix" attempts to remedy failing urban schools weren't solving the problems adequately. Also the thrust for dialogue and exploration of the ULS approach might come from people who had specific concerns, such as parents from a particular minority group who might acutely feel the lack of city schools good enough to help all their young children make something of themselves in the mainstream of society. Topics for the dialogue might be suggested by concerned individuals who had read this book. Individuals who were able to provide talent and money should be invited.[2] I foresee hope running high in these discussions. As I explained at the end of Chapter One, several factors are coming together to make citizens open to redesign of failing urban schooling.

How might the kind of community enthusiasm for the Urban Little Schools tryout I am discussing, be turned into reality? I suggest the first practical move would be to form the backup organization whose work is summarized above. Such a backup organization could coalesce interest and enthusiasm into practical steps toward starting the first pilot elementary Urban Little Schools. I assume that by the time a backup organization was considered seriously, enough seed money would have been promised to begin the new backup organization and in addition, more substantial grants were on the horizon.

Once the decision was made to create a backup organization but before the die was cast, the group behind the proposed backup organization should give serious consideration to selecting the best possible leaders. They should consider selecting leaders in the following two categories: a Director who was committed to the ULS vision and who could effectively lead the initial community discussion and planning phase while at the same time building an effective organization; two Startup Leaders for the pilot school phase and to subsequently oversee the teacher trainers who would help additional teachers start new Urban Little Schools based on the first pilot school models.

Now let's think about these key people—the backup organization's Director and its two Startup Leaders: Their job descriptions illustrate how key backup organization leaders need to have differing skills related to their roles. The Director should be a person who is comfortable taking final authority. This person should be someone who could handle ably and sensitively, the organizational and administrative aspects of such tasks as these: designing a strong backup organization to help Urban Little Schools thrive in a cooperative but autonomous relationship with the school district; raising funds; working out a teacher certification program with state education officials; working with the teachers' union to facilitate smooth intra-organizational transfers for district teachers to become ULS teachers; spreading the word about the Urban Little Schools, locally, nationally and internationally; hiring and facilitating the backup organization staff; and maneuvering politically in the local and state power hierarchies, when that was called for.

The two Startup Leaders should be people who would be able to select and train the pilot ULS teachers. The Startup Leaders should be people who know and understood children and who enjoy working individually with children and with responsive teachers. In addition, the Startup Leaders would need to be able to help others solve problems and be open responsible people on whom all those involved could depend.

These Startup Leaders should have had experience teaching in ways sensitive to each child under their care. Thus, for example, they would find it natural to help every single child learn to write and to read in ways that best fitted the child. If one or both of the new Startup Leaders hadn't had experience individualizing children's learning to write and read, they should spend a few months learning how to do it, before beginning their jobs as teacher trainers. This book can show a Startup Leader how to go about getting that experience. Chapter Four, Chapter Five and Supplemental Article #3 could comprise the handbook prospective Startup Leaders could follow in teaching themselves how to individualize children's learning in writing and reading. They could try out how to individualize by teaching four-year-olds who had the required readiness. These children could be selected from the district's preschool program.

Where might good candidates for the two Startup Leader positions be found? A good candidate might be working as the head of a nursery school which was known to be especially responsive to each of its children. Startup Leaders, of course, wouldn't have to be administrators. They might be preschool teachers who showed they not only could work with children responsively but enjoyed working that way with adults who might want to learn to teach the ULS way. [3]

Defining and Developing Task Groups

The backup organization should bring together interested and knowledgeable people for serious ULS planning and organization sessions all focused on how best to begin the pilot Urban Little Schools and then to extend their influence. Out of these initial discussions could come names of people who the backup organization possibly could then hire as consultants. These consultants would be called on to work out the development of task groups to consider and plan needed organization, facilities, and learning materials. Task groups should be set up to focus on specific needs such as the following:

Drafting the Contract between ULS and School District

A task group should work out procedures to plan the specifics of how local Urban Little Schools would relate to the host public school system, assuming, as we are, that the Urban Little Schools were to be part of the school district. These detailed plans probably would include drafting sample contracts to help interested community members, school board members, and the school district superintendent discuss how best to agree on a contract with the school district so the basic needs of all parties could be met.

Any contract which was finally signed should allow the Urban Little Schools to be essentially autonomous while specifying the backup organization's role and consequent authority in the pilot school tryout operation and beyond. Important details which later might cause tension unless agreed upon in advance, should be negotiated into the contract.

For example the contract should stipulate the district's willingness to have the backup organization explain the proposed ULS tryout to the district's preschool staff. This introduction should explain how the Startup Leaders might observe in the preschools with the view of possibly offering some preschool teachers and assistants, positions as elementary ULS teachers. To avoid awkward situations later, the district should agree, in the contract, how the observation of preschool teachers might take place. The contract also should specify that the district's tenure rights of transferring teachers would remain, in case the teacher transferred back to teach in the district's conventional schools.

A well thought-through contract should lay out the basic plan for financing and for evaluation of the Urban Little Schools. It should be made clear how much money the district agrees to pay per ULS pupil. It should be clear, too, that the backup organization will fund startup expenses of pilot schools and will lease equipment and facilities to the district. The backup organization should lease to the school district such things as buildings, computers and the computer software it would select and develop for Urban Little Schools and their secondary Self-directed Learning Centers. This leasing would help to keep the Urban Little Schools basically independent of school district bureaucracy. Also the backup organization's initial funding for facilities and materials should help city school boards feel easy about trying out pilot Urban Little Schools because the district would not have to pay for such expensive things.

The contract should stipulate further that the backup organization would evaluate the pilot Urban Little Schools adequately before it developed more of them. How this was to be done should be laid out specifically. This evaluation probably would mean that the backup organization wouldn't seriously move to start more Urban Little Schools in the district until the first entering group of five-year-old pilot school children were at least eight- or nine-years-old. By this time sound predictions probably could be made as to whether the pilot school examples were ready to be used as models. Likewise, pilot secondary Urban Little Schools shouldn't be replicated until they had become tested adequately with children who had already gone through elementary Urban Little Schools. [4]

The contract might specify the scale of the startup. I suggest beginning with two pilot elementary Urban Little Schools. More, of course, might be set up if there were adequate funds and people available to mount a quality tryout of greater extent. But if the backup organization were to focus on just two pilot schools for the first three or four years, such a scale should help the backup organization to finance the pilot operation and to secure funding for expanding in a few years, to more Urban Little Schools in the district. This would be the case, because at first the backup organization only would have to lease and develop two pilot elementary school sites. Also once the pilot schools were up and running, benefactors and charitable foundations could see model schools which lived up to the Urban Little Schools' promise. (Startup of Urban Little Schools modeled after the pilot schools is explained in detail in Chapter Twelve.)

Considering Potential Problems

Another task group might be brought together to discuss possible specific future problems—to anticipate difficulties which might arise within the Urban Little Schools and in their neighborhoods. Then, using these possible problems as hypothetical discussion vehicles, the task group could see if the plans which were being set in place, could meet such contingencies. Examples for discussion might be a crisis within a particular elementary Urban Little

School caused by a charismatic and extremely able lead teacher's leaving; or it might be a difficult situation for teachers arising from a neighborhood fight which divided school parents, even though the teachers tried to stay out of it.

Governance Issues

One more task group should give serious thought to governance of the Urban Little Schools enterprise within its host district. I assume that final authority for the Urban Little Schools would be in the hands of the backup organizations' Director. But what about the role of the backup organization's board of trustees which might oversee the Director? Also it would be important to consider how individual ULS teachers could be empowered to have a significant voice in governance.

The governance task group should plan a working interrelationship of the various ULS units in the district which gave the grassroots school units a voice in overall ULS policy matters. This might be done by bringing elementary lead teachers together periodically in a council along with the Floating Teachers who backed up the secondary ULS teachers.

As soon as possible, this governance task group should contact a lawyer and begin applications which eventually would allow donors to contribute funds to the backup organization and then deduct these charitable contributions from donors' individual income tax liability. In my home state of New York this would mean the following: First the backup organization's lawyer would draw up articles of incorporation and by-laws for the backup organization to become a non-profit corporation. These documents would stipulate such things as the purposes of the organization, the roles of the board of trustees and officers of the corporation, along with other specifics. Once incorporation was approved by the state authorities, application for The Internal Revenue Service's Section 501(c)3 status, should be submitted to the IRS. After the backup organization had secured this status, donors could deduct their contributions.

Other Administrative and Facilitative Jobs

Another task group might be formed to define and handle various administrative and facilitative jobs such as the following: selecting and rehabilitating buildings and other space to be leased as Urban Little Schools; working with city officials to make sure ULS elementary units would be allowed within the city's housing code rules; working with city and state fire and school safety officials; planning budgets for each school and for the backup organization which channeled incoming money to highest priority uses;[5] and helping visitors to get the most from their observations in the pilot schools.

Acquiring and Developing Independent Learning Materials and Facilities

A task group of major importance should sift through all of the relevant self-directed independent study materials extant. In so doing it would plan which educational software and other independent learning materials, not now available, might be developed by the backup organization. Because there would be so many materials from which to choose, probably the task group would not have to spend much money developing its own software, videos, and other such learner-operated lessons or courses.

To help teachers implement the elementary individualized reading and writing program described in Chapter Four and Supplemental Article #3, the backup group would need to supply the following: plenty of computers with which children would write; learning games such as Consonant Bingo and Fish; high interest but low vocabulary-level books which children found easy to read, such as *The Boxcar Children*, which is analyzed in Supplemental Article #3; software to teach specific reading and writing skills such as consonant-vowel-consonant phonics practice, spelling, dictionary use, and grammar; consumable workbooks and other practice material to teach the fundamentals outlined in Stage Two of Supplemental Article #3.

The new individualized math program, developed by the learning material specialists at the backup organization, should be geared to help children develop the practical skill and understanding of math needed for them later to succeed on their secondary ULS jobs and at the Self-directed Learning Centers. The individualized math program might start initially with the district's present math curriculum sequence and its textbooks as a base. Supplementing this, the new program could feature individual study options for children. It could utilize computer learning games, especially in helping the children memorize arithmetic facts and in understanding the number system. Also the new program should introduce the fundamentals of geometry and algebra. The math program probably would evolve and change over its first few tryout years as teachers gave feedback to the specialists working on the program.

New materials and methods for both the reading-writing and the math programs could be tested with the help of some children who could try out what was designed and share their reactions with the developers.

The independent learning task group would design the secondary Self-directed Learning Centers. In these Centers most of the learning of traditional high school basic subject matter would take place. The task group should address how best to provide independent learning materials, program options, and how to provide tutors for the Centers. Also, the designers should set up each course so students as well as their secondary ULS teachers could follow the individual student's progress. With this constant feedback the teacher and student, in their one to one meetings, could determine whether additional help might be needed for the student to succeed. Then, at the completion of each basic course, a successful completion certificate should be issued, to file in the student's portfolio.

Developing quality secondary Self-directed Learning Centers would not need to be a hurried crash program. Developers would have at least six years to bring together and test the very best secondary school self-directed academic programs. Children who started at five-years-old wouldn't begin to use the Centers until they become secondary students at about twelve years of age.

I demonstrate, in Supplemental Article #4, how such a search for independent learning software, video lessons, and other self-directed learning materials might begin. The article explains the AskERIC free information service which can be accessed by sending an e-mail request, to <askeric@askeric.org>.[6] In the article I show a recent AskERIC e-mail request of mine, where I used the AskERIC service for help in searching for secondary level independent learning materials, along with books and articles which might explain how others were using independent learning at the high school level. As the reader can see in Article #4, I received back (within forty-eight hours after the acknowledging e-mail) lists of catalogues and other sources containing thousands of independent learning items.

As part of the independent learning task group's search they should consider how to use complete ready-made kindergarten through twelfth grade individualized computer learning curriculum materials which are available. An example is the curriculum software produced by IBM's K-12 Division. IBM has a line of software featuring basic learning typically taught in a complete K-12 curriculum, with built-in feedback and evaluation. IBM also has a team of consultants to help schools set up programs using their software and hardware products. [7]

In addition to searching for available self-study materials, the independent learning task group should explore questions about how to individualize in specific secondary school academic fields. From this exploration, the backup organization people could put together the study program options they needed to provide in the Self-directed Learning Centers. For example, a task group committee should explore, with scholars and high school teachers, the question of science laboratory experiences—to what extent, how and where should secondary ULS young people do laboratory work in the basic sciences?

Another question the independent learning task group might address would be how to find and support some outstanding high school teachers who could prepare television versions of their best courses, to be used at ULS Self-directed Learning Centers. The goal should be to make the televised courses at least as clear, informative and interesting as the best high school lecture courses might be. These might supplement available courses already in television format, such as are produced by The Teaching Company.[8] These video-taped courses would need to be complete with accompanying textbook assignments, library assignments, study options, ideas for term papers and other work. The courses would have to satisfy the state's high school graduation requirements and would have to prepare the students to handle well the material covered in college entry qualification tests. Some of the high school teachers who had submitted TV tapes of their teaching might be good candidates for tutoring in Self-directed Learning Centers during the late afternoon or evening periods when most of the ULS students would be using the Centers.

Evaluating Urban Little Schools
Carefully and Continuously

The backup organization would plan and direct effective evaluation of Urban Little Schools in its own school district. It also could handle the school evaluation in affiliate districts, if requested.

Evaluation results would be addressed to the Board of Education, through the school superintendent. The Director and superintendent together, should select outside consultants who would annually or biennially evaluate, in detail, the district's Urban Little Schools. The consultants should be people who both the backup organization and the local school board could trust and respect. Evaluation consultants should be independent of the district's administrators, managers, their support staffs and, from ULS people. The evaluation could be based on criteria laid out in the contract drawn up between the school board and the ULS backup organization when the Urban Little Schools were being set up in the district. As mentioned, these criteria and basic exit requirements from elementary and secondary Urban Little Schools might be selected from the lists in Chapter Ten and Supplemental Article #2.

Evaluation should also include follow-up studies on two groups who were no longer enrolled in Urban Little Schools: (1) students who had left the Urban Little Schools because their families moved; (2) graduates of the Urban Little Schools. The idea here would be to find out how well prepared the departed students had been for their next steps after leaving their Urban Little Schools and, particularly in the case of graduates, how their lives reflected the ULS goals.

Graduates of Urban Little Schools might be polled regularly in statistically sound ways to provide follow-up data to see how their ULS education was working in their lives. Along with questionnaires, selected graduates could be interviewed. If there were enough funds for this research, a control group of matched students who had not gone through the Urban Little Schools might be used.

This continuing one to one contact with graduates also could result in videotapes and written stories showing and telling the lives of ULS graduates. This record not only would illustrate the statistical evaluation, the videos and written accounts could help prospective parents get an idea of how a ULS education might influence their sons' or daughters' lives.

This followup study might turn up ways which could aid the backup organization to support some graduates as they related to others with trust and integrity yet still got ahead in the market economy, which often seems to denigrate these values. To this end, ULS backup organization people, when they talked with graduates, could seek answers to questions such as the following: What do you think about establishing some kind of a follow-up support for graduates? If you would welcome this kind of support, should it be one to one? Should this be something available for just a short time—a transition benefit—or should it be longer term? How might graduates help each other?

Selecting and Educating ULS Teacher Trainees

Trainees should be selected who demonstrate a predisposition to teach children in the ULS way. Then trainees should be helped to use that way of learning, for themselves, in their own training. Two key principles should guide the training of ULS trainees: (1) trainees should learn to teach with the same process that they later will use in helping their students to learn; (2) trainees should learn on the job guided by experienced ULS teachers. These two principles mean the Urban Little Schools would not be able to use the conventional teacher education programs, done at typical university schools of education. Let me explain:

First, let's consider how the first principle rules out conventional teacher training typically done in university schools of education. In general, the process of teaching and learning used in the typical teacher training program at colleges of education basically is not similar to the ULS teaching-learning process but is consistent with how children are trained in conventional schools.

I am speaking of the typical teacher's college process where for example, the name of the game is to find out what the professor wants specifically and then, when tested, to give it back. Then too, school of education teacher trainee students are fitted to the school of education curriculum rather than the reverse. The college of education's curriculum typically is fixed. Any serious individualized work therefore would have to be done in addition to the roster of courses and other requirements all have to do successfully.

Second, in this conventional teacher education process the professors seldom listen seriously and regularly to their individual students in ways which could help students take responsibility for their own learning. One to one openness and individualized planning based on it, is difficult even if professors wanted to do this. The typical education college system presses teacher training professors to maintain social distance from their students because professors have to give crucially important grades or other evaluations that designate which students are better than which other students. This omnipresent judgment-by-professors atmosphere doesn't lead students to feel the easy emotional safety with their professors which is essential for most students' critical self-judgment. With their professors, students need to feel free to discuss how they are meeting their goals, including ways they feel they aren't measuring up to their goals, maybe occasionally touching on self-doubts that might arise. If such an open atmosphere did exist, students and professors could work together in defining problems and in working out ways to overcome difficulties and roadblocks.

Third, the method used to teach trainees in the typical university school of education emphasizes study in a series of lecture-and-test-format education courses taught away from children and their schools. This focuses students' energy on pleasing the teacher rather than step by step learning to help every student succeed. In these typical programs, much less emphasis is placed on trainees taking responsibility for teaching children under the watchful eye of an experienced master teacher who teaches in the ULS way. "Master teachers" selected for the trainees' student teaching semester, are usually those regular teachers who wish to have student teachers, rather than teachers who might be particularly responsive to individual children.

Because typical college of education training would not be suitable, the backup organization teacher training task group would need to work out its own teacher training program consistent with the Urban Little Schools way. This means keeping in close contact with the state department of education teacher certification office, as the planning for teacher training takes shape. If pilot Urban Little Schools were started as Charter Schools, the backup organization's plan for teacher training could be submitted as part of the Charter School proposal package to the state.

In most of the states (forty-one by early 1999) there are alternative teacher certification plans in place which might be used to secure certification of trainees. Typically these plans emphasize what is described in the next section as basic to the Urban Little Schools plan for teacher training: extensive involvement of the trainee with hands-on teaching all through training, plus trainees working with experienced teachers, who are good examples of the kind of teaching desired.

Selecting and Training Teachers Once Pilot ULS Models are Up and Running

Once the first pilot elementary Urban Little Schools were up and showing the way, many or most teacher trainees needed for expansion to additional elementary Urban Little Schools could be selected from volunteers and assistant teachers in existing elementary Urban Little Schools.[9] The backup organization should set up a task group to put substantial effort into attracting volunteers to try out teaching in an Urban Little School. Along with seeking television and newspaper news and feature story coverage, invitations to volunteer might be placed in libraries and other places where people might see them—people who thought they might be able to teach in the ULS way. These notices should sketch the ULS idea, emphasizing how listening teachers conference regularly with students and exchange a substantial journal at least every other week with each of their twelve children. [10]

Having a number of volunteers and assistant teachers from which to choose would allow ULS people to select new teacher trainees after the likely candidates had shown they could relate to children in the ULS way. That is so important: only accepting teacher candidates who had proven they could do the basic job because they had been seen doing it. Also, of course possible candidates could try themselves out as they volunteered, to see if the job was for them.

This tryout could start for some people, by their first observing in an elementary Urban Little School. These observers might be helped by a ULS host or hostess if one worked in the Urban Little School being visited.[11] If observers became more interested they could read about what they were observing, in this book. After such an introduction, people who felt they might fit in well as ULS teachers should be able to weigh the merits of volunteering in one or more Urban Little Schools.

Perhaps, also, parents of ULS children would be drawn to consider teaching in schools like their children attended. By volunteering, parents who thought they might be good as ULS teachers could determine whether they fitted and whether they wanted to do the work. The ones who demonstrated they could relate to children in the ULS way should be encouraged to take the next steps toward ULS training.

Some people might not be able to take time off from working to volunteer at an Urban Little School. These people might need to keep working in order to pay the bills. Some of these likely candidates—strong people who related to young children sensitively and who knew firsthand what poorer families face—might be hired as assistant teachers for, say a year, if there were enough money in a ULS budget. These would be people who seemed to be close to the ins and outs of living—people who knew children, themselves and life. During their assistantship year they could help individual children learn while they tried out the job of Urban Little Schools teacher. It is hoped that the backup organization could secure enough money to pay a modest stipend to trainees who needed financial help. If needed, that training might include part-time work toward a college degree.

Some ideal candidates who had not been to college would need to take college courses while they were being trained and during their first years as a ULS teacher. As they succeeded in college they would be able to understand more fully what ULS children have to look forward to. These new ULS teachers who might need time for further college work could teach in partnership, each teacher taking a half share in one full-time position. This is explained further at the end of Chapter Twelve. The state department of education should be asked to consider authorizing a temporary teaching credential until the new teacher graduated with a college degree.[12]

Several different self-directed college education alternatives are available, which might fit trainees in various life situations. I am referring to independent learning programs such as are offered by New York State

University's Empire State College, its Regent's College or Goddard and Skidmore Colleges' Adult Degree Programs. In these kinds of programs, students plan a particular study with an individual college faculty member, decide on how to evaluate their work and then carry it out with frequent contact with their faculty mentors along the way. Sometimes students use distance learning via the Internet or other audio visual means, to secure their training. In some programs students receive college credit for relevant non-college job experience. [13]

Teachers-in-training for Urban Little Schools would be taught one to one by experienced ULS teachers. These teacher trainers would be released from their normal teaching of children, usually for a three year period. The teacher trainers would work step by step with each of their teachers-to-be. Trainees, in this close trusting kind of relationship would be trying out the same teaching-learning process they would later use with children under their care.

The trainees should spend considerable time with experienced teachers in Urban Little Schools that were up and running well, perhaps working alongside regular teachers in an apprentice role. Then the trainees would feel involved in the teaching and learning going on in these schools, not just feel they were an observer. Trainees could see what they needed to learn so they could make the ULS Idea work for children when they began teaching on their own.

Out of this immersion in ULS teaching, each of the trainees and their training teacher should be able to figure out what the trainee needed to learn and then, how to learn it. For example, trainees might interview children, photograph and videotape secondary young people on their jobs, and exchange journals with children. Trainees could spend time with parents, learning how to create trusting open sharing relationships with them. All the trainees, of course, should learn well how to help every single ULS elementary child master the basic academic skills.

Trainees might take advantage of the backup organization's optional weekend training workshops which would be designed to help teachers-to-be come to know others and themselves with sensitive awareness. They might, for instance, spend a weekend doing expressive dance, another weekend learning how to peer counsel one to one, another workshop doing autobiographical writing, and so on. Some trainees who were working as apprentices might participate with regular elementary ULS teachers in the day-long child study meetings each month where experienced teachers fine-tuned their sensitivity toward each child in the school.

As trainees and their teachers worked together, they would keep a training portfolio specifying the learning each trainee did. This would be the same kind of cumulative record-keeping process the trainees later would use with each child under their care. This portfolio would be the key document used to establish the new teacher's readiness to begin as a probationary teacher in the Urban Little Schools. It could be used with state teacher certification officials as the primary data on which a temporary or a provisional teaching certificate could be issued.

The teacher certification plan which eventually would be adopted would have to be worked out in close cooperation with the state's department of education, which would eventually have to approve any plan.

Teacher tenure? Urban Little Schools should operate on something like a "2–3–4 limited tenure plan." In most cases this would mean two years of full-time training, or its equivalent, usually with the second training year having the trainee work in responsible teaching roles and perhaps being paid a small salary. This would be followed by a three years' probationary period at almost full salary to insure that the trainee could make the ULS way work for children. After the probationary years there would be four-year contracts at full pay. The contracts could either be with the host school district or with the backup organization. As noted, if a leaving teacher had transferred to ULS teaching from another teaching job in the district the teacher should be guaranteed reinstatement of former job tenure upon return to the teacher's former job.

This ULS "2–3–4 limited tenure plan" is a check on teacher adequacy. Without such a safeguard, schools and their children can become burdened with well-paid inadequate or marginal teachers who typically are granted lifetime tenure after five to seven years work.

Notes

1 See Supplemental Article #1 for a discussion of how an urban university might sponsor Urban Little Schools to bring a vital new life to adjacent blighted neighborhoods and to provide diversity and an outstanding education for neighborhood and university families and students. University teacher trainees would benefit from seeing the contrast between Urban Little Schools and conventional schools.

2 Federal Reserve Bank figures show that almost forty percent of American wealth is owned by one percent of its citizens. Thus there are some 2,500,000 people out there whose families could back a complete Urban Little Schools tryout without significant financial strain. (Figures cited in *New York Times*, April 17, 1995 and reported in *Trends 2000* by Gerald Celente—New York: Warner Books, 1997.)

3 For more about the Startup Leaders' work see Chapter Twelve, "Startup..."

4 For specific evaluation criteria see Chapter 10, "Beyond Rhetoric: Specific academic, job-related and character goal criteria...," and Supplemental Article #2, "The Academic and Job-related Exit Requirements List."

5 See sample elementary and secondary ULS budgets and budgetary criteria in Chapter Eleven, "Budget Priorities and Realities of the Urban Little Schools."

6 ERIC stands for Education Resources and Information Center.

7 For more, visit IBM's Web Site: HTTP://www.solutions.ibm.com/k12. Viewers can request IBM's "K-12 Educational Solutions" booklet, by writing to IBM K-12 Education, Hill Northside Parkway, Atlanta, GA 30327.

8 The Teaching Company: 7405 Albion Station Court, Suite A-107, Springfield, VA 22150.

9 This does not exclude teachers from the host district who might want to apply for ULS teaching.

10 Possible applicants should know that ULS teachers need to be adept at writing in order to write six or more journals each week which are models that will lead and inspire students to write freely with correct use of conventions.

11 See Chapter Four for a description of how hosts and hostesses might work.

12 It might be easier to handle certification and other legalities if Charter School status were granted, in those states where effective Charter School legislation is in place. For a discussion of the Charter School possibility as a way to begin Urban Little Schools, see the Charter School discussion at the end of Chapter One.

13 For directories listing distance learning opportunities for undergraduate degrees: Phillips, Vicky. (2000). *Never too Late to Learn*. NY: Random House. For graduate opportunities: Phillips, Vicky and Yager, Cindy. (1999). *The Best Distance Learning Graduate Schools: Earning your degree without leaving home*. NY: Random House.

10

Beyond Rhetoric

Specific Academic, Job-related, and
Character Goal Criteria Against Which
Each Urban Little School Can be Judged [1]

To What Extent is the School
in Harmony with Each Child?

If evaluators were to ask only one question when determining the extent to which an Urban Little School unit was meeting its goals, they might ask themselves this: To what extent is the school in harmony with each child? This question translates to further questions such as these: To what extent is this a school in which there are no academic losers? Do the teachers know each child in the school with heightened awareness? Do teachers listen carefully and sensitively to each child? Do children listen to other children when in serious discussion? Do the next steps each child takes in learning fit with what has already been learned and with the child's learning style? Are children becoming self-directed, becoming able to take responsibility for their own learning? Are they coming to be able to compete successfully and with integrity in the world?

The Academic and Job-related Criteria

1. We can expect ULS students to show in many ways that they hold books, reading, and writing to be a valued personal experience. This should be apparent in what young children are helped to write from their first written pieces onward. Then too, we can expect that choosing library books for personal reading often will be weekly highlights for those children who are independent readers. We can expect that sharing in writing with their teachers will be something these students look forward to almost all of the time. This will be shown by the quality, genuineness and involvement of what they write. (If outsiders look at what children write, it is assumed that children's permission has been given.)

2. Students will come to know skills of independent learning and self-reliant living in ways such as knowing the library as if it were one's own home turf and learning to use other tools of self-sufficiency in skillful ways. Another way young people will demonstrate their self-reliance is how fast and adequately they can learn the skills needed for a new ULS community job.

   We should expect that the young people increasingly will learn practical self-sufficient skills by working side by side with carpenters, dressmakers, electricians, or chefs, for example. Also at graduation we can expect young people to know how to be self-sufficient in the following ways: They will know how to conserve money in ways which will help them to be less dependent on a lush money income. They will know how to make thrifty and wise purchases at garage sales or other sources of recycled goods. They will be able to keep a budget which cuts their expenditure but also educates them as to where the money is going. They will know how to fix many items that increasingly people throw away such as broken furniture and clothes needing minor mending. They will know many of the basics of house wiring, tailoring and dressmaking, plumbing, carpentry and fixing one's automatic washing machine, bike and car.

3. Students will learn how to use advanced communications technology appropriate to their skill level. They will know how to use a computer's word processing facility in their writing and on jobs. They will know how to use the computer to make graphics and to do other things to enhance their ability to communicate. They will learn to reach others in

computer networks as they share information and ideas. Students will learn much traditional academic subject matter in multi-media interactive instructional learning situations which they manage through a computer. Thus a young child might learn the arithmetic times tables through games on the computer; another student might learn to speak German by conversation exercises in a computer's learning program. In addition, students will be able to learn successfully in traditional lecture-textbook courses given on videotape. Finally, students who are working independently with computers, videotapes etc., will be able to define their learning problems clearly so they can ask specific questions of tutors at the ULS Self-directed Learning Centers.

4. We can expect students will not see themselves as losers or in some other way feel they are categorized as not measuring up academically, as they go through the Urban Little Schools. In the elementary schools, to illustrate, this means that if children stay on in their elementary school for a year or two after they reach the age of twelve, we should not expect them to see themselves or to be viewed by others in a disparaging way.

5. When the host school district tests the graduating elementary children, none will be expected to score on the district's achievement tests below the sixth grade level in reading, writing, grammar, spelling and arithmetic.[2] Also, all will be able to use reading and writing to prepare and write a communicative essay on an unfamiliar subject. In writing the essay they will be able to use fundamental research tools such as a standard elementary school dictionary and encyclopedia. [3]

6. Each secondary ULS graduating student will score in the top half of academic achievement tests used in the district and on college aptitude and basic academic knowledge tests used.

7. Each student with a ULS education can transfer to conventional schools and do well there academically, unless of course, some disablement or other such limiting circumstance prevents this.

8. Students can expect to grow in ability and desire accurately to judge themselves both academically and in other important ways. This is as opposed to turning to others to secure crucial measures of their worth. For example, when students periodically study sequenced samples of their own writing (kept in their record portfolios) they can and will

want to come to their own conclusions about the extent to which their writing is becoming more communicative and fine tuned.

9. ULS students will show they are learning how to learn and that they are finding the process satisfying. Increasingly over the years, as they go through their education, we should expect they will be able to plan it themselves with facility. This might include asking others to help them in ways which sharpen their own abilities to analyze—such as asking their key teachers or employers to help them to assess skills in a specific area.

The Character Criteria

10. As they progress through their Urban Little School, students will come to see what *is*, both within themselves and in their worlds, rather than limit their awareness to what they or others might want them to see. Students will tend to do this even if what they have to face evokes fear in them. Examples at the secondary level might be: (1) how young people often will see early warning signs of an emotionally heavy problem before the problem becomes so large it might be too late to handle it in a relatively easy way; (2) how they will tend to look to facts and evidence at hand to define a problem that besets them. They won't, on the other hand, tend to scapegoat—won't be quick to blame others for their problems or discomforts. Thus we shouldn't expect ULS students to be swayed by those who seek to curry their favor by oversimplified or false promises of happiness, power or security.

11. Students can expect to see themselves as strong when they reach out for help to a trusted person in appropriate circumstances, such as in a one to one conference with a their teacher. Students might share, with this trusted person, their feelings of pain, fear, self-recrimination, loneliness or other unpleasant feelings. This might be despite how, at the same time, a student might feel the conventional prohibitions against "showing weakness," when one is honest and open about self-doubts or other self-diminishing feelings.

12. As students go through this schooling, increasingly they will be genuine. Students' need for an emotional mask or other protective facade

will be minimal at an Urban Little School. Thus we should expect an air of openness in an Urban Little School, where people speak the truth both by the way they lead their lives and by their words. At the same time we should expect students to be sensitive to others' vulnerability in, for example, how frank criticism might be received. We should expect that young people are learning to be true to themselves as they conference and exchange journals with their teachers and in other ways are learning to have a clear sense of themselves.

13. We can expect ULS students are becoming good listeners and good questioners. This means things such as how they pay close attention to what another says including sensitivity to facial and other non verbal expression. ULS students will help those to whom they listen to reflect on what is being said. They might do this by not interrupting and by encouraging silence for reflection. In serious conversation, these students to an increasing degree, should be expected to ask penetrating questions which can help the other person probe and gain perspective. Their questions will tend to emerge from their genuine interest and concerns as opposed to their trying to act "the good counselor."

14. We can expect ULS students increasingly to feel undiluted compassion. They will feel it's OK to be this way openly. They will not tend to show signs of indifference toward a person who is hurting or to another who seems to be going through a difficult time. This is just the opposite from those people who seem to get satisfaction from exploiting so called weaknesses or perceived vulnerability in another or who pick on or bully those they see as vulnerable and less able to defend themselves.

15. We can expect young people to become increasingly clear and effective in talking about what means most to them. They have been doing it often, in writing or face to face, with a teacher who can evoke their trust. This should be apparent in the serious essay about themselves which young people are expected to write near the time they leave their secondary Urban Little School.

16. We can also expect students increasingly to accept themselves as they are, based on their self-understanding and self-awareness. This includes accepting what sometimes is called one's "dark side." Such acceptance

should help them in changing aspects of themselves they don't like. If that isn't possible they will be able to come to live with their "dark sides" in ways which permit them and others to cope with what otherwise might be a destructive force toward themselves and others.

As they become more tolerant of themselves, we can expect them to become more tolerant of others who might show self-diminishing, anxious or heavy feelings. We should expect, therefore, that in an Urban Little School there will be an air of acceptance of others; there will be minimal destructive gossip, critical judging or put downs of others.

17. As children progress through the Urban Little Schools, we should expect they increasingly will do what inner necessity says has to be done despite having to face fearful feelings which might trigger anxious emotions such as "I can't do it," or "It just feels too big." At least two key character traits and skills are involved here: first, ULS students increasingly will be able to respond to the signals that tell them something they might be pulled to do is contrary to their inner sense of direction, and second, they will be able to do what is needed in order to figure out how to see the situation clearly and handle it. Here is a case in point:

A twelve-years-old boy is faced with a problem involving drugs and some pals on his street. The boy wants to do what he senses is right, yet he finds it difficult and scary to get himself to do it.

He shares his feelings with his ULS teacher in one of their conferences. As they talk, the boy finds himself crying and shaking, releasing a dam of debilitating nervous tension which had been building up within. The boy begins to feel more clear about doing what he senses is right for him to do. At the same time he finds it easier to accept some of the fearful powerless and lonely feelings that seem to have been triggered by the situation.

The boy leaves his conference with his teacher able to go ahead, able to follow inner necessity. He seems to be in touch with a strength to do what he senses is right, even if it is scary to do so, even if at times, aspects of the challenge seem too much to bear, or even if he might feel "little" and alone. The situation no longer seems impossible.[4]

How do Employers of Secondary Urban Little Schools Young People Judge the School?

18. We can expect employers to feel positively about having Urban Little Schools young people working with them. This means such things as: (1) ULS young people can figure out what needs to be done, ask pertinent questions and get on with learning the job; (2) young people's work contributes to the employer's goals; (3) having ULS young people helps set a workplace tone where people can listen seriously to each other, can count on each other and thus can help make work as productive and satisfying as possible.

19. Also we can expect that employers feel the ULS secondary teacher and backup organization are of help in making job placements successful. This could mean things like these: (1) Employers feel a request from them is handled with priority. (2) They feel the teachers make it their business to understand the jobs employers want students to do. (3) Employers feel that the teacher and backup organization have helped in all the ways they could to enable a student to learn the job and to make a success of it.

How do Parents and Neighbors Judge their Urban Little School?

20. We should expect parents who take their children's schooling seriously, to know how their child is developing academically and job-wise. Specifically, elementary parents might be asked to explain to an interested person they liked, how their child was learning to be independent in reading, writing, in library use and in doing arithmetic—perhaps they would even be able to explain what the child had accomplished so far and what the next steps seemed to be.

    Secondary parents also might be asked to explain to an interested person with whom they were comfortable, why or why not it seemed at this point their child should be accepted at most colleges or to other more suitable training schools, and if accepted, why the young person should be able to succeed there. In addition, the parents should be able to explain (1) how it appears to them that their child is on the road to be successful on an adult job which fits the young person; (2) how their child is coming to know how to secure such a job; and (3) how the young person seems to be learning how to re-train for a possible next job.

21. These parents should be able to cite evidence or example to summarize how well they see their child becoming the following: (1) a person with whom it would be pleasant and rewarding to work; (2) a person who they feel could raise children well; (3) and a person who would be a good example to others.

22. This question could be asked of parents or family members: "If you had it to do over again, to what extent would you, yourself, like to go through the Urban Little Schools?" "Why do you answer as you do?"

23. We can expect that these parents who take their children's schooling seriously, feel their Urban Little School is receptive to them. Specifically, this might mean: (1) The parents feel easy about coming into the building at any time. (2) They feel that teachers seem to want to listen to them. (3) They feel no significant intimidation caused by the school when they consider talking with teachers about a problem which might seem to be the fault of the child, the school, or of the parents themselves.

24. It is expected that parents and neighbors will feel their nearby Urban Little School is a positive force for neighborhood betterment. Here are some possible questions to get at the issue of whether their school helps the neighborhood: (1) "Do parents or others in ULS families know their neighbors more than before their children began in their school?" (2) "Do neighbors close to the Urban Little School trust each other more than those in comparable neighborhoods without an Urban Little School?" (3) "Do neighbors find it easier to work together here as compared with neighborhoods without an Urban Little School?" (4) "Do neighbors close to their Urban Little School tend to feel they can count on the people who live nearby—more than one might expect?"

Other questions which might elicit close-by neighbors' feelings could be the following: (1) "Does it help your neighborhood to have this Urban Little School here?" (2) "Is there any way having your Urban Little School nearby has hurt the neighborhood?" (3) "Are ULS children you see, well behaved as compared with other school children?" (4) "How do your neighbors see your nearby Urban Little School?" (5) "Is the Urban Little School a credit to the physical appearance of your street? That is, are the grounds kept neat and orderly, the building well maintained—things like that?"

Notes

1. See Chapter Nine for a discussion of how some the goals listed in this chapter might be written into a contract with a local school district. The contract would ensure autonomous status for its Urban Little Schools component so long as the ULS units measured up to the goals

2. We are not speaking of seriously disabled children with limited abilities here.

3. See Supplemental Article #2, "The Academic and Job-related Exit Requirements List," which details the minimum standards elementary and secondary ULS students need to meet.

4. As is the practice in the Urban Little Schools, the boy in a situation like this will be asked to talk with his parents too about this difficult situation he is facing and how he intends to deal with it. In the Urban Little Schools, parents won't be kept in the dark about serious matters shared between young people and their teachers.

11

Budget Priorities and Realities of the Urban Little Schools

How can the Urban Little Schools accomplish what they do and still cost most school districts no more than they already pay per child? How practical and realistic is the funding plan implicit in the Urban Little Schools design? In answering these questions, this chapter emphasizes the trade-offs—why, in the Urban Little Schools, there are more of some things and less of others. Explanation is done at the bottom line, of dollars and cents practicality. A sample elementary ULS budget is presented, line by line, as is a budget for a secondary Urban Little School. Following each will be an explanation of the items in that budget.

Budget Priorities

Three budgetary priorities underlie both of the budgets presented in the chapter. The priorities determine the trade-offs—where the Urban Little Schools' money goes and as a consequence of that, what has to be given less money. These priorities are ranked below in order of their importance:

1. Urban Little Schools need to provide for a teacher–student ratio of at most one to twelve to facilitate the close listening and working relationship between each child and at least one teacher on the staff. (In legal terms, I am speaking of one teacher for every twelve children in average daily attendance.)
2. Plenty of flexible teaching space is needed in the elementary schools. Secondary Urban Little Schools need less space because the older students are working in the community or at the Self-directed Learning Center much of the time. The school space for older children needs to facilitate each young person's independent learning or job-related activities.
3. And finally, enough money is needed to provide the learning materials and opportunities that can make the teachers' work with individual children count. Money needs to be at the ready to help teachers respond to unforeseen projects, too. It is to be expected that ideas for projects will pop up quite often, as children and teachers conference one to one and share journals in their planning of next learning steps.

As you see from these priorities, Urban Little Schools money is spent to make the one to one teacher–child process vital and effective both academically, on jobs, and in the lives of children and their teachers. Spending money according to these priorities means that Urban Little Schools do not have funds to pay salaries for such people as psychologists and social workers and their staffs. There is little money to pay wages for special subject teachers. Urban Little Schools do not spend money for libraries and librarians in each school, school busses and drivers, cafeteria workers, hall guards or similar expenses.

Also, in the ULS budgeting, there is much less need to fund administrative people both at individual school units and for central office staffs. There is less administrative work as compared with conventional schools, partly because through the backup organization they report directly to the superintendent, bypassing layers of central office people. In addition, the teachers absorb administrative work the lead teachers cannot do while focusing on their priority job. The lead teacher's priority job is to lead the child study process—to help all staff people to be sensitive to each child in the school and, from such an awareness, create a school in tune with every single child.

However, the Urban Little Schools need to pay for two necessary school district services they cannot perform for themselves. First they have to reimburse the district for money it spends to pay for the review team of outside people who annually or biennially review and evaluate its ULS component. These outside educational auditors must be people of impeccable integrity who have shown by their record that they are capable of taking the ULS list of expectations which are written into the contract, and finding out the extent to which these goals are being realized.

Second the Urban Little Schools needs to pay the district for the cost of educating severely disabled children. However, even in this area, much of this can be absorbed into the regular ULS teachers' work except for those disabled children needing a full-time teacher's care. Most disabled children can be taught in regular ULS groups because ULS education adapts to children's special needs as a matter of course. The education program is not oriented to provide the same learning journey for all the children in a group.

All this is not to say that some of the people and facilities funded in the conventional schools are not of value. Expensive purpose-built buildings, art teachers who can inspire creative work, music teachers who can help children relate to music with spirit, are valuable. But these and other personnel and facilities are lower in priority than is close one to one work between each child and a teacher who can make this result in children's succeeding.

Following these priorities doesn't mean that ULS children have poor training in areas such as art and music. But keeping to the priorities means that ULS teachers often turn to outstanding community people for help in specialized areas. Such community people work with ULS children both in the schools and their homes or studios. It is often more effective and less costly to pay people hourly to work at their convenience and perhaps in their own space, than it is to hire a special subject teacher as a school district employee. In this way truly outstanding specialists and craftspeople can be brought in to work with children—people who have proved they are responsive to children. Also a self-employed craftsperson can work with a young person over long periods of time in an intensive master and apprentice relationship, because of the ULS flexibility.

Budget Realities

However, no matter how the priorities are changed some school districts in some states won't have enough per pupil money to pay for Urban Little Schools. My estimate is that at least 60% of US children go to school in states where Urban Little Schools could be funded without additional money in all but their most underfunded districts. That is, roughly speaking, thirty million elementary and secondary school children could be funded to attend Urban Little Schools without increasing the amount already being paid per pupil by their districts.

The two crucial figures to consider when deciding whether Urban Little Schools can be funded without additional money are the amount being spent per pupil in average daily attendance and the average teacher's salary. Generally speaking, in districts where the amount spent per pupil is less than the national average, the average teacher's salary also is at least somewhat less. Also rent and costs for other essentials are less, typically, in these underfunded districts. Thus even in some districts where the per pupil expenditure is less than average, Urban Little Schools might be funded without extra expenditure.

But even though teacher salaries and other expenses are less, in some states the amount spent per pupil is so low that Urban Little Schools will need additional funding in many of the state's districts. Some of the districts, of course, might have rich tax bases far in excess of the state's average and those districts could afford Urban Little Schools. On the other hand, many school districts in the states at the upper end of the scale from the underfunded states, not only could afford Urban Little Schools easily, they could lower the teacher child ratio from one to twelve to something like one to nine. In New York State, for example, Urban Little Schools teacher-pupil ratio could be lower than one to twelve, in almost all districts. The Washington, DC district, with its per pupil expenditure well over $10,000, is another example.

In those districts where the per pupil expenditure is above the national average, some of this additional available per pupil income might be used to help fund the ULS backup organization. This would decrease the backup organization's need to turn to outside sources to fund its non-reimbursable expenses such as the cost of its administration, startup costs for pilot schools and the development and support for the Self-directed Learning Centers. As you will see from the sample ULS budgets, the backup organization is reimbursed for its leasing and modifying school space, for its replacement and maintenance of learning equipment and similar expenses. This reimbursement is done in a series of payments over several years.

The sample budgets, can be used as a guide when one wants to know if Urban Little Schools could be funded at no additional per pupil cost in a particular school district. These two budgets, one for an elementary and one for a secondary Urban Little School, are based on the average per pupil expenditure in the US for a recent year, and the average teacher salary for the same year. When one wants to determine if a particular district's per pupil expense might support Urban Little Schools, first substitute the district's average teacher's salary-benefits and amount paid per pupil in these sample budgets. Next adjust the budget according to what it might cost to lease space and to pay for other costs in the community. Then see if Urban Little Schools would be feasible within the district's current budget boundaries.

Budget for an Elementary Urban Little School

You will find below an annual budget example that reflects the priorities and principles I have been discussing. Let's imagine we are funding an elementary Urban Little School which enrolls 44 children, like the Fircroft School in Chapter Four's illustration. It is realistic, to say our Urban Little School can have a minimum annual budget of $307,693 with which to work because of the 44 children's entitlement from the school district's budget. This figure is based on the average US school district's estimated per child expenditure in 1996, which was $6993 (44 x $6993 = $307,693).[1] From that minimum annual budget of $307,693, $24,000 is allocated for education of severely disabled children in the district's special education classes and for the annual or biennial evaluation of its Urban Little Schools. This figure is calculated on the basis of $600 per child attending the Urban

Little School. Then the Urban Little School is free to spend the rest of the money, derived from its per child entitlement, according to its priorities. Here is the first year's budget breakdown for an elementary Urban Little School such as the fictional Fircroft School in Chapter Four:

$ 24,000	for educating severely disabled children and for evaluation
25,000	to ULS backup organization for rent and an amortized payment for modification of teaching space
193,736	salary-benefits for four teachers
18,000	to ULS backup organization for leasing and updating of equipment and furniture
24,000	for consumable educational material and other educational expense plus custodial, office, and utilities expense
4,400	for a grant to the nearby branch library ($100 x 44 pupils)
18,557	reserve for contingencies

$ 307,693 ($ 6993 per pupil x 44 pupils)

Notice, in the above breakdown, $25,000 of the per pupil entitlement is spent to repay the backup organization for some of its annual cost to lease space for the school. Enough money is also included in this budget item for the current year's payment to the backup organization for some of its initial outlay for necessary building changeover. (When these initial costs are repaid in full, the money budgeted here for initial changeover can be spent for other needs.) Changeover modifications on the large old house, leased for the school used in this hypothetical example, were necessary to suit the fire code. In addition, several other building changes were needed. A ramp for children in wheelchairs was built and a large, open multi-purpose room is now situated at the rear of the building. This was done by enclosing what was a screened-in porch. The building is now protected by an electronic security system and wrought iron grills cover all ground level windows. Payback of these kinds of costs, which the backup organization paid at the startup of this Urban Little School, is spread over the first five years of occupancy.

Notice also that this elementary Urban Little School contributes $4,400 to the nearby branch library ($100 x 44 children = $4,400). This grant can be used as a discretionary fund by the local librarian. More importantly, it serves as a tangible symbol of the bond between the ULS and the public libraries.

$18,000 is paid to the ULS backup organization for the leasing and updating of equipment and furniture. The backup organization bought these things initially and now provides for their maintenance. For example, the backup organization updates the computers (almost all were secondhand when first purchased by the backup organization) and handles the servicing contracts on those items. In addition, the backup organization provides a petty cash fund for teachers, who wish to buy needed materials, such as paying for garage sale purchases. Title to all the major movable assets in each ULS elementary and secondary building space is vested in the backup organization.

The backup organization's ownership of the ULS assets is a safety net feature in case all efforts fail to maintain the Urban Little Schools as part of the school district and the Urban Little Schools have to become private schools. If this happens, each of the Urban Little Schools can go on, financially speaking, by leasing its facilities, furniture and equipment directly from the backup organization, as the school district did before the split.

$24,000 is allocated to pay for other costs. After paying for the basic expenses such as utilities, enough should remain in this account to pay for help from exceptional and specialized community people such as local craftspeople. Also, there is money to finance special projects. Elementary teachers can use money in this account to pay a local bicycle repair person to teach two of its children in her shop for three hours a week as a prelude to one or more of the children working in the shop. Money is available for the lifeguard who works with children at their weekly swimming times. If teachers and young people want to publish a magazine of the children's writing, there is money to do that.

$193,736 is allocated for teacher's salaries (including their fringe benefits).[2] ULS teachers are paid according to the district's pay scale; typically, each teacher's salary varies according to years of experience and training, as is stipulated in the district teachers' contract. The $193,736 pays for four teachers including one lead teacher. This teacher's leadership role, as mentioned, is to help all of the school's workers heighten their sensitivity toward each child and in this child study process make sure the school is in harmony with every single child. The lead teacher handles some of the inevitable general administration, in cooperation with teachers. In addition the lead leader is the key teacher for eight of the children, one to one. The three remaining key teachers each have responsibility for about twelve children. Prime time teacher assistants are hired with whatever unspent money is left in the budget. An assistant is hired at a modest wage on a year to year basis, by the teachers who will work with the assistant. An assistant might work from 9:00 to 1:00 daily or at another time period which is good both for the school and for the person assisting.

Notice that no money is allocated for substitute teachers. This is because when a teacher is out due to illness, normally the other teachers step in. This is partly due to the flexibility in the elementary Urban Little Schools. Also, because of the child study program, all teachers know all of the children well. Then too, another reason substitutes are not needed typically, is because of the assistant teachers, volunteers and teachers in training who almost always are a part of the scene. Add to this, how elementary ULS children are learning how to be self-reliant. When their key teacher isn't close at hand, at least the older children in a particular teacher's group of twelve usually can take significant responsibility for themselves.

One final note: Because the Urban Little Schools are independent from the school district financially, they have to make sure that there will be enough money to finance commitments such as their teachers' salaries or unforeseen expenses. They need a financial cushion in the budget for that. With this in mind, the lead teacher sometimes will admit two or three children more than the forty-four children projected for each elementary Urban Little School—a financial safety measure in addition to the budgeted reserve for contingencies. The added per child income from having two or three children over forty-four, pays for times when the enrollment might dip two or three below forty-four pupils due to parents' moving. This additional money is carried forward to the next year if not spent this year.

Children begin in Urban Little Schools at odd times during the school year, whenever they turn five-years-old. This minimizes the need to keep large reserves in the discretionary account to cover money lost due to children leaving during the school year. Because they enter at odd times during the year, entering children can slip right into the established routines and learn from the other children who are familiar with how things work.

Budget for a Secondary Urban Little School

Here is the first year's budget breakdown:

$	5,000	for educating severely disabled children and for evaluation
	7,000	to the ULS backup organization for rent and toward cost of initial modification of school space
	50,554	salary-benefits for one secondary ULS teacher[3]
	4,445	to pay 1/10 salary-benefits of Floating Teacher
	5,500	to the backup organization for leasing, updating and servicing of self-study equipment at this secondary Urban Little School and at the centrally located Self-directed Learning Center where its twelve students study
	3,100	for tutoring which takes place outside the Self-directed Learning Center and for self-study material needed for this individualized help
	5,000	for non self-study educational materials, plus office, utilities and other miscellaneous expense; this includes money for custodial expenses
	2,917	contingency reserve

$ 83,916	($6993 per pupil x 12 pupils)

Much of the discussion about the budget and priorities that fits an elementary Urban Little School applies here. But the secondary ULS budget differs in some respects because there is a change in emphasis and structure in the schooling for older young people, explained below:

1. Each secondary Urban Little School unit is a one teacher operation. This can be a partnership between two teachers, each taking pay in proportion to the amount worked.

2. For every ten secondary Urban Little Schools, there is one Floating Teacher. Because the Floating Teacher comes to know the young people and the teachers, the Floating Teacher can help make sure that each young person and teacher have a good working-together fit with each other. In addition, the Floating Teacher handles some of the administrative burden and in other ways takes a facilitative role. $4,845 is allocated from the budget of each secondary Urban Little School to pay one-tenth of the Floating Teacher's salary and fringe benefits calculated on the basis of the conventional school year of 175 workdays.

3. All of the secondary ULS students work in the community, usually about a third of their time. When they (and their teachers, too) take their vacations will depend on their needs and the needs of the people with whom they work. Thus some of the young people might choose to take less than the usual summer off or its equivalent, because of their involvement with jobs that are year round in rhythm. Other young people might take a few weeks off during the winter if this better fits with their jobs and their other commitments.

4. No funds are granted to the nearby branch library, as is done by ULS elementary schools. This is due to two factors: First, the secondary young people often work in the library as non paid employees for an extended time on jobs which allow regular library personnel to do other needed tasks. Second, much of the basic academic studying done by secondary young people is carried out at the backup organization's Self-directed Learning Center, not at the library.

5. Some of the cost for supporting young people on their jobs is paid out of their earnings. This is not reflected in the budget above. Here is how it works: Employers pay all moneys earned by young people directly into the central fund of the ULS secondary schools in the district. Expenses for such items as transportation to and from work, special clothing, lunch money, tools and the like are paid from this fund. This money also pays for the secondary teacher's expenses in guiding the community work program. The teacher is paid per mile for the use of a

private car and for such necessary items as an occasional lunch with an employer who works with a young person in the teacher's group or who might be interested in doing so. The money also covers part of the expenses related to the work program such as an extra telephone line to the secondary ULS learning headquarters, telephone instruments in each young person's office area, and perhaps a third computer or an additional printer with specialized software for all to use. Any surplus in one year is divided equally and paid monthly to all the ULS secondary young people in the district, during the following year. Payments are made electronically to each young person's savings account.

6. Because much of the teaching of basic high school subjects is done through self-study materials, money is allocated in the budget for tutors in addition to the tutors available to help young people who use the centrally located Self-directed Learning Center. Sometimes young people work with these additional tutors one to one or in small groups, at the Self-directed Learning Center or at the tutors' homes. Often this kind of tutoring is done to teach young people how to learn independently from textbooks; then, too, usually foreign language learning is done with the help of a tutor who speaks the language fluently.

7. Because secondary young people use the Self-directed Learning Center to learn most of the traditional high school academic subjects, $5,500 is paid to the backup organization to help keep the local Center functioning and up to date. Any additional expense to keep the Center working well is covered by the backup organization. As is the case with all major ULS assets, the Center's equipment and furniture is owned by the backup organization. The space also is leased by the backup organization.

Some readers might wonder how the backup organization can keep the Self-directed Learning Centers up to date, staff them, rent space for them, all on the limited income the backup organization receives from the secondary ULS budgets. One answer is that the backup organization's Self-directed Learning task group might receive considerable additional income from its licensing of the sale of software and other self-directed material and processes it develops for its learning centers. The backup organization not only can sell these learning materials, but it can earn money by providing a service for conventional schools which wish to use these and other independent learning materials. Each summer, for example, the backup organization might conduct workshops for people from schools and industry showing how they might bring about efficient and motivating self-directed training. Backup organization consultants could help schools and businesses set up independent learning facilities on their own sites, too. Much of the income from these services and from sale of software, then would go to keep the Self-directed Learning Centers functioning well.

Incidentally, some secondary ULS young people could work with the Self-directed Learning Task Group as one of their job experiences. There they could learn how to create the kind of materials from which they learn. Some young people also could go out on-site with consultants who work to help others use the materials and processes in industry and conventional schools.

My prediction is that the Centers can be self-supporting. I foresee that the backup organization will receive enough funding to cover the costs of maintaining and further developing the Centers after startup. This will be because of funds received through sale of materials and services plus money from the school district through per pupil funding allocated to each of the district's secondary Urban Little Schools. In our example above, $5,500 is paid from this secondary ULS budget to help fund the Self-directed Learning Center at which its students study. The only way to tell if my prediction is true, of course, is to wait and try out the first Center when it will be serving a full complement of secondary young people. This is something which won't happen until ten years or later after the first five-year-olds enter the first pilot elementary Urban Little Schools.

The Necessity and the Reality of Outside Funding

How realistic is it to expect outside funding for the backup organization's services not covered by the district's per pupil payments? Another prediction: in this case it is my speculation about how easy it should be to fund the backup organization over the long haul.

As has been discussed, four aspects of the backup organization's work will have to covered by outside funding: school startup, teacher training, helping other school districts to begin their ULS programs, and general administration and development of the district's Urban Little Schools. The local school district then will be able to have well evaluated and successful Urban Little Schools without any additional funding beyond what the district now pays per pupil.

I assume the outside funding needed for these four parts of the backup organization's work won't be difficult to secure once the Urban Little Schools are evaluated as delivering on their academic, job-related and character goals. Outside funders should be pleased to be a part of this effort which is making such a needed change and doing it so well.

• • •

Before we leave this chapter, I need to say something about the meaning for each child implicit in all this concern for money which has been occupying us. As one gets involved in finances it's easy to lose sight of the beautiful educational concept the money is paying for. When that happens to me, I need to remind myself how something very special happens for children as a result of the careful concern for finances and the other practical matters we have been discussing. The financial nuts and bolts support Urban Little Schools where children learn to make personal independence and honest self-direction work as they plan and take responsibility for their own learning while working one to one with a teacher who listens.

Notes

1   US Department of Education, National Center for Education Statistics. (1996). *Digest of Education Statistics*, Washington, DC, p. 166. This figure is compiled from estimates submitted by the state departments of education.

2   This is a calculation based on the average US teacher's salary in 1996 of $38,434, increased by a fringe benefit package of $10,000, bringing the total teacher's salary-benefits to $48,439, and the salary-benefits for the four teachers in this school to $193,736. The $38,434 average teacher's salary figure is reported in US Department of Education, National Center for Education Statistics. (1997). *The Condition of Learning*. Washington, DC. p. 179.

3   $50,554 is the annual salary-benefits figure for a secondary ULS teacher. It is the salary and benefits for working 185 days—10 days longer than the usual 175 day school year worked by the ULS elementary teachers. (The $50,554 figure is calculated as follows: $38,434, which is the average US teacher's salary in 1996 + $10,000 benefits package + $2120 for 10 additional working days = $50,554.) NOTE: Secondary ULS teachers may schedule their 185 working days in any way they find best enables them to work with employers as well as students. Thus a teacher might decide to work four-day weeks for most of the twelve-month year with a three-week vacation and the usual holidays. This rhythm would enable the teacher to work closely with employers who work a twelve-month-year.

12

Startup

Selecting and guiding teachers to create pilot schools.
Helping more teachers use pilot models in building
their new Urban Little Schools.

The teacher education guidelines explained in Chapter Nine will be used in selecting and training startup teachers to begin the first pilot Urban Little Schools. In summary, those basic guidelines are as follows:

- All candidates for jobs as ULS teachers will be observed working with children to see how they relate to individuals and to groups. Only the ones who demonstrate they are strong responsive listening teachers, who relate to children in ways which fit the Urban Little Schools model, will be offered positions as ULS teachers-in-training.
- In their training process, new teachers will be guided one to one by teacher trainers who themselves have demonstrated they can teach children in the ULS way. Trainee teachers will learn in practical hands-on ways. As a part of their training, new teachers will learn how to determine what is the best next step in learning for each child; then how to help the child master the new learning. This is the same process teacher trainees will be using in their own learning to be ULS teachers.

Finding the Right Teachers
for the Pilot Elementary Urban Little Schools

The teachers selected for the pilot elementary Urban Little Schools would be seen as models for all the teachers trained and hired subsequently. They should be people whose lives show they respect the uniqueness and value of each human being. In their teaching, they would need to exhibit the kind of characteristics expected of the best Urban Little Schools teacher, as discussed in Chapter Nine.

Some of the best preschool teachers and assistants I have seen fit this description. In addition to living a life of integrity, the teachers about whom I am speaking are able to get into the shoes, so-to-speak, of each four- or five-year-old child in easy-feeling ways. These teachers seem to sense where their children are coming from, psychologically speaking. They can relate spot-on to a young child in ways that sometimes don't need words to communicate. They are capable people who have mastered the skills they will be teaching their ULS students. For example they are able to write with the ease and proficiency needed to write substantial journals to their children—writing which is a good model for the students to follow.

Therefore, to find the first teachers for pilot elementary Urban Little Schools, the backup organization's two Startup Leaders might observe in the host school district's preschool program. They would be looking for experienced teachers or teaching assistants who seemed particularly responsive to individual children and who demonstrated this by the ways they worked with children in their classrooms and by how they talked about individual children. Of course this doesn't rule out selecting capable people in other settings such as Head Start classes, who have shown they related to young children in ways which fit the ULS model. They too should be observed sufficiently to make sure that they are naturals for Urban Little Schools teaching. Then there are people of all ages and from all walks of life who might be good ULS teachers. I think of Betty Lise, described in the memoir, who I observed with children on my home street, when I was directing the SIEE School. Betty became one of our best teachers when she worked afternoons from her high school.

Wherever Startup Leaders find teachers who seem ideal, I can't emphasize enough that *all people selected to be pilot elementary Urban Little Schools teachers should be observed working with children*. I don't mean just for a few minutes. I mean every candidate should be seen with children in different situations which show how the prospective ULS teacher relates to individual children as well as to groups of children.

For example, after watching in preschool classrooms, the observer should accompany preschool teachers out to the playground if they go out with their classes—the observer should be close enough to feel the kind of respect there is in the air between the teacher and individual children in this and other situations where teachers can be seen relating to young children one to one. Also the observer should pay attention to the ways candidates have organized their teaching. Is it responsive to individual children? Are there numerous times when the candidate might listen to children one to one and does this? Of course when assistant teachers are being observed this is harder because the style of teaching is usually set by the head teacher in the classroom.

Candidates in other ways should show a sense of heightened sensitivity toward each of the children under their care. For example this might come out as a candidate was encouraged to talk about individual children. Is there a special person in the child's life from whom the child feels unreserved love? Does the child have a special place at home where the child has a sense of privacy? What does the child typically do on weekends and in vacation periods and with whom? Why might someone enjoy being with this child?

Contrast these kinds of observations and discussions with the usual ways new teachers are selected and hired. The conventional way is to narrow the field by reading paperwork submitted by the college of education placement offices which mail out placement packets for both beginning and experienced teachers they have trained. The assumption is that the college has screened the teachers they have trained—only recommended those who would be good teachers, for a credential.[1] These papers offer employers' letters of recommendation (usually only those letters requested by the candidate), college grades, lists of coursework taken, degrees earned and the candidate's one-page statement. The next stage is an interview, typically by a panel of principals from the district. Finally the candidate is notified by mail as to the district's hiring intentions.

Possible Startup Sequence

A Good ULS startup Plan Must Enable these Things to Happen

- Pilot school Startup Leaders, if they are not already, will must become adept in individualizing how children can learn to read and write so learning fits each child.
- These Startup Leaders will have to recruit teachers who have demonstrated they are natural listeners as they work effectively with five-year-olds.
- The teachers have to be given preparation time to set up their pilot schools and to train themselves under the guidance of a Startup Leader who is good at working well one to one with each of them. Thus new teachers will try for themselves the ULS way of learning which they will use with their children. For some this self-directed learning will mean mastering computer use, becoming old-hat familiar with the children's room at the library, etc.
- New teachers will have to learn how to individualize the teaching of reading and writing, from a Startup Leader who is good at this work. Teachers will need to practice enough so they can be fast and sure with diagnoses and then can decide what the next learning steps for a child should be.
- Training for the second wave of Urban Little Schools has to take place as soon as the pilot schools prove themselves. Teacher trainers should be former pilot school teachers who know the ropes. The trainers can select teachers for this second ULS group of schools as soon as the pilot schools prove themselves. There should be enough former pilot school teachers available to select and to start training a significant-sized group of teachers for the second wave schools. Teachers selected for these second wave schools will have to be given enough time, before the first child arrives, for their self-directed preparation to do what they see the pilot teachers doing.
- Likewise, while the pilot elementary schools are up and running, the teachers for ULS secondary schools will have to be preparing themselves to take the first graduates from the pilot schools, in seven years after the first children start in ULS pilot elementary schools. These new secondary teachers should have taught in the pilot schools so they will know how to help children take their skills and abilities and apply them to independent learning and jobs at the secondary ULS level.

- All this while the instructional media specialists at the backup group will be collecting and developing self-directed learning materials for the elementary reading, writing and math program and for the upcoming secondary Self-directed Learning Center.

The plan outlined below satisfies these conditions. It begins with two pilot elementary Urban Little Schools within the host school district. This start grows to be seven elementary Urban Little Schools and two secondary pilot Urban Little Schools in eight years. These schools then could be used to train more teachers who could start more Urban Little Schools.

If more Urban Little Schools were wanted initially, the scale could be increased. Several clusters could be started in the school district concurrently. Each cluster could be positioned in a different part of the city. Also, the plan might be implemented in several cities, at the same time.

This plan should be viewed as one possible way startup could take place. I assume this plan will be changed to fit whatever the startup circumstances are. Even if the first startup years follow the plan laid out below, subsequent years undoubtedly should be modified from this plan in light of what has taken place during the first years. Thus, each step will inform the next step as to how best to progress. That's the ULS way. It's also the sensible way.

Now let's consider year by year how this plan might work:

Preparation Year

The backup organization's two startup leaders select pilot teachers, acquire space, and outfit two new elementary pilot schools.

According to this plan, startup preparations are begun as soon as the backup organization is under way and the contract with the district is signed. Establishing pilot schools has the highest priority once the backup organization's Director and two elementary pilot school Startup Leaders are hired. During the first year of the backup organization, the two Startup Leaders focus on doing these five tasks, all related to starting the pilot schools:

1. They familiarize themselves with the work of the district's preschool teachers and assistants with a view of offering some of them positions as new pilot school teachers. The ULS training will begin at the beginning of the next school year.

2. The two Startup Leaders select and lease pilot school space, with the help of real estate agents hired by the backup organization. The school sites are to be ready for development by the newly selected pilot school teachers during the first months of the next school year;

3. The two Leaders outfit the new pilot schools with furniture, books, used computers, and other basic items.

4. If the two Startup Leaders aren't already, they should learn to be skilled in individualizing the teaching of writing and reading, as explained in Chapters Four, Five and Supplemental Article #3 in this book. This might mean that during this preparation year one or both of the Startup Leaders would learn by teaching four- or five-year-olds drawn from the district's preschool classes. The selected children of course would be mature enough to handle this learning.

5. The two Startup Leaders finalize the selection of sixteen pilot teachers from those preschool teachers and assistants (and other likely candidates) who had been observed relating to children in the Urban Little Schools way. The newly selected full-time pilot teachers will begin the new school year in September, eventually to work in eight partnerships, four partnerships in each of the two pilot schools.

How the Partnership Idea May Work

Each partnership of two full-time teachers will be responsible for a phased-in group of twelve ULS children, as their key teachers. One of the partners might teach mornings and the other in the afternoons. The not-teaching partner thus would be freed, each day, to pursue further individualized training.

This partnershipping will create in each of the two pilot schools, a pool of four extra experienced full-time pilot teachers, over and above the four full-time teachers needed to teach in each of the two pilot schools. Thus three or four years later, experienced pilot school teachers from this pool will be available to train additional Urban Little School teachers—one of the trainers assigned to train the teachers selected to staff each of the new Urban Little Schools modeled after the pilot schools. Also from the pool of available experienced ULS teachers, two will be groomed to begin the secondary pilot schools needed when the first elementary children reach twelve years of age. [2]

Elementary Pilot Schools' Year One

Pilot Teachers, in Partnerships, Prepare and Begin with Children

Beginning the new school year, in September, the sixteen newly selected experienced preschool teachers will be assigned, eight to each of the two new pilot elementary schools. The two school sites will be ready for the teachers—outfitted with furniture, computers, basic art materials plus other supplies and equipment. One of the two Startup Leaders will guide the startup in each new school. The Startup Leader will work one to one with each of the eight new teachers assigned to that Leader's school.

After a few weeks, the Startup Leader in each school will help the eight teachers group themselves into four partnerships. Instead of four full-time teachers, as described in Chapter Four's illustration, each new pilot elementary school will be staffed by four partnerships of two teachers each. When the first children begin in March, each partnership will be assigned a group of three or four entering five-year-olds. The partner teacher who teaches the group in the morning will meet the other partner for lunch at noon, when they can discuss what went on in the morning. Often the afternoon teacher will telephone the morning teacher to share what happened in the afternoon. Non-teaching time can be used for training and to handle administrative tasks of the new school.

Prior to the March children's entry date, the backup organization's community representative will accompany individual teachers to meet parents of four-year-olds in the neighborhood. The two Urban Little Schools people will explain the new parent-choice school to nearby parents.

From September, when the newly selected teachers will begin, the Startup Leaders each will lead a team of eight teachers to develop its new pilot elementary school's facilities. The Startup Leaders, one to one will guide the new teachers to prepare themselves individually for the teaching job slated to begin in March. This individualized training can be continued during non-teaching time, as mentioned, even when the children begin to attend, starting in March. Partnershipping also will provide extra teachers who can take over if one of their number has to leave teaching for an extended time or if a teacher might have to drop out of teaching in the pilot school altogether.

I assume most or all the new teachers will need to learn how to teach five-year-olds to write and to read in individualized ways, as explained in Chapters

Four and Five and Supplemental Article #3. The new teachers can practice, when they begin in September, by teaching four-year-olds in some of the district's preschool classes (maybe the classes from which the teachers had come). At the same time, the new ULS teachers will be conferencing one to one and will be exchanging journals regularly with their Startup Leader. This is designed to lead to learning which is tailored individually to each trainee while at the same time introducing teachers to a conference and journal exchange they will be asked to do with each of their own students. As examples of individual training, one teacher might learn about using computers for writing and other uses; another might work in a library's children's room, part time, for a few weeks; and a third teacher might take courses at the nearby community college.

Elementary Pilot Schools' Year Two

Pilot Teachers Add More Children to Their Schools and
Continue Their Own Individualized Learning.

In September of year two, more children will be added as neighborhood children on the waiting list reach five-years-old. By the end of this school year there should be about eight children in each partnership's group. During non-teaching hours partnership teachers will continue their individualized training as well as helping with administrative jobs.

Elementary Pilot Schools' Year Three

Continued Development of Pilot Schools and Their Teachers.

By the time the third year ends each partnership should be working with a group of about ten children—bringing the school up to its capacity of forty-four students. At the end of the year, one of the partnership teachers, in each of the two schools, will be selected to begin the next school year as the school's lead teacher. The lead teacher then will be responsible for the school's child study program and for other leadership work. During this third year the Startup Leader will continue leading the child-study program. Thus a model will have been established for the new teacher leader to follow. In year four, explained below, the new lead teacher will be given full-time to work on administration and child study. Then in year five the lead teacher will take responsibility for a group of eight children as well as handling the lead teacher duties, while the other teachers work with twelve children apiece.

Elementary Pilot Schools' Year Four

The Two Pilot Schools Grow to Full Capacity; If Preliminary Assessment is Positive, Five of the Pilot Partnership Teachers will be Selected to Become Startup II Trainers.

During year four the new lead teacher will contact neighborhood parents of preschoolers, individually, to help people understand the Urban Little Schools kind of schooling which is different from when they went to school. Also, the new lead teacher will take over leadership of the school's child study program and other leadership duties, from the Startup Leader. To release the newly appointed lead teacher for this work during this initial year in the new role, the lead teacher's former partnership teacher will take over all day, teaching their group of children.

During this year, the two pilot schools will continue at capacity, still with four groups of eleven, each led by a partnership or by a single teacher—forty-four students in all. At the beginning of this school year, the backup organization's two Startup Leaders will phase themselves out of their work in each of the pilot schools, turning responsibility over to the two new lead teachers. Startup Leaders will then move to take over other training jobs, as explained below. Short-term assistant teachers and volunteers will be taken in to work part-time at the pilot school. They not only should help individualize the schooling for children but they might become trainees later for teaching in elementary Urban Little Schools.

The pilot schools will be evaluated at the end of this year to see if results so far warrant expansion to a group of Startup II Schools in the district. These Startup II Schools will be the next step in increasing the number of elementary Urban Little Schools modeled after the pilot schools. Assuming this preliminary assessment of the pilot schools is positive, at the end of this school year, five of the partnership teachers from the two pilot schools will be selected as Startup II teacher trainers. Then in Year Five, these former pilot teachers, now teacher trainers, will begin to prepare five more Startup II elementary Urban Little Schools and select the twenty full-time teachers to run them.

Elementary Pilot Schools' Year Five

The Startup II Teacher Trainers Outfit Five ULS Elementary Schools and Select Teachers for Startup II Urban Little Schools.

One of the backup organization's two Startup Leaders will lead the team of the five former pilot school partnership teachers selected now to begin their new full-time role as Startup II teacher trainers. During this school year these five new teacher trainers and their Startup Leader will select twenty teachers working in the district's preschool staff or others in other settings. The twenty will be needed to begin five more elementary Urban Little Schools, four teachers to a school, slated to start with their first children in January of Year Six.[3] The twenty selected will be teachers who show they relate to children in the Urban Little Schools way and are capable of doing the ULS job. As part of the selection process, possible Startup II teacher candidates will be given opportunities to observe in the two pilot elementary schools in order to help them decide whether they want to teach as they have seen pilot teachers doing, should they be offered a job. Also, during this school year, the Startup II team of five new teacher trainers will work with backup organization people in selecting the five buildings or other space for their new Startup II Schools. Then they will outfit the new Startup II elementary Urban Little Schools so as to be ready when the five newly selected teams of teachers begin preparing their new elementary Startup II schools in September of year six.

Elementary Pilot Schools' Year Six

Teacher Trainers Train Teams of Startup II Teachers as each Team Organizes and Begins its New Elementary ULS; Two of the Remaining Pilot Elementary Partnership Teachers will Staff Upcoming Pilot Secondary Schools

At the beginning of this year, in September, the five Startup II teacher trainers each will begin working with a team of four new teachers assigned to that trainer's new Startup II elementary Urban Little School. Thus five more Urban Little Schools will be started, this year, modeled after the pilot schools.

The Startup II teacher training will emphasize new teachers' learning how to individualize the teaching of writing and reading. The new teachers' training will be concurrent with their observations in the pilot schools, where they will be able to see experienced teachers tailoring the learning of reading and writing to each child. The Startup II teacher trainers will work with each of their four teachers in the same one to one way their Startup Leaders taught them when they began their training as new ULS teachers.

After the first of January, the first children will enter each of the new Startup II schools, one by one when they turn five-years-old. The school year will end in June with each new teacher leading a group of about four children who had entered from January to June.

During this year two of the teachers remaining as partnership teachers in the pilot schools will move from elementary teaching to begin two new pilot secondary Urban Little Schools. With guidance from the Startup Leaders, these two teachers will have been preparing themselves for the possibility of being a secondary pilot school teacher. These two teachers will be people who have shown they were particularly capable of handling the three key counseling roles of an Urban Little Schools secondary teacher's job: academic counseling, job-related counseling, and listening counseling, as explained in Chapter Seven.

Elementary Pilot Schools' Year Seven

Two Pilot Elementary Teachers Begin Preparing their New Pilot Secondary Schools

During the year, the five new Startup II elementary Urban Little Schools will continue to grow as more five-year-olds from the neighborhood are added. By the end of this year probably there will be about eight children working with each new Startup II teacher. Short-term assistant teachers and volunteers will be on the scene, too. During this year the Startup II teacher trainers will continue to guide their groups of four teachers in each new school. The Startup II teacher trainers will work sensitively with each team to decide on the person in the team who, next year, will begin as the lead teacher in that school.

During this year, also, the first major step will be taken toward establishing two pilot secondary schools. These new secondary schools will be ready for the first children from the pilot elementary schools who will be expected to enter their secondary schools during Year Eight.

To prepare for their secondary teaching role, the two former pilot elementary teachers will move from their partnerships and each will be trained to set up her or his own secondary pilot school. Their elementary partners will continue on with their groups in the pilot schools. The new secondary teachers will be trained by the backup organization's Startup Leader who is not leading the Startup II teacher trainers. The two new secondary teachers will work individually with their Startup Leader.[4] They will do the following:

1. They will locate and lease space plus outfit it for their secondary Urban Little Schools "learning headquarters" in cooperation with real estate people hired by the backup organization.

2. They will work with the backup organization's task group charged with selecting independent learning materials, in two ways: first they will help plan the new secondary Self-directed Learning Center, and second, they will try out some of the independent study materials themselves. The first Center will be located in one of the two new secondary sites.

3. They will talk with interested possible employers of secondary young people, who had been contacted by the backup organization people.

4. They will do individual study and other work needed to help them succeed in their new roles as secondary Urban Little Schools teachers.

Pilot Elementary Schools' Year Eight

The First Elementary Children Begin as Secondary Students

The first secondary school children will graduate from the two elementary pilot schools, now in their eighth year of teaching children. The number transferring to the new pilot secondary schools shouldn't be large this first year because of attrition during the previous seven years. [5]

The incoming young people and new secondary teachers should have a somewhat collegial relationship, as together they pioneer the new secondary school. The young people could take real responsibility for making the Urban Little Schools secondary idea work. They could participate with their teachers and the backup organization people in improving what was first tried. For example, young people could try out the Self-directed Learning Center's new independent learning materials. They then could give feedback to their teachers and the backup group which had prepared the materials. Also, the young people would try out the idea of a secondary schooling where they worked on jobs. Young people would share their experiences with their teachers in the young people's regularly scheduled biweekly conferences and journals.

Also, during this year, the Startup II elementary schools will continue to add children up to capacity of twelve per regular teacher with eight under the care of the lead teacher. The Startup II Leaders will phase themselves out this year, passing the leadership at each new school to the school's newly selected lead teacher.

Beginning of the Pilot Elementary School's Ninth Year

The Cluster of Urban Little Schools will be Established in the District; it will be Ready to Spawn More Urban Little Schools

By the beginning of the pilot elementary schools' ninth year the following will have happened: the pilot elementary schools will have graduated their first children; the Startup II elementary schools will have ended their second full year, each with about forty-four children from five- to eight-years-old; the two new pilot secondary schools will have been growing with more elementary ULS graduates who had been prepared for their self-directed secondary education when they were students in the pilot elementary pilot schools.

The two Startup Leaders can now turn their attention to support further expansion of the number of elementary and secondary Urban Little Schools. To staff these new Urban Little Schools, new teacher trainees will be selected from assistants, volunteers and from the ranks of those experienced teachers in the district who demonstrate that they relate to children in the ULS way.

More on Startup

Why Pilot Schools Might Start with Partnership Teachers

In the suggested pilot school startup plan, I used the partnership idea because it offered a way to provide extra full-time teachers who had learned how to teach in the pilot elementary school. Also the partners could go on with their own learning while teaching half-days.

In addition, the partnership teachers working with the same children can offer two perspectives on each child. Each teacher can contribute ideas that might help that child's learning. Also children might find it easier to relate to one of the partners than to the other. This allows for even stronger one to one "fits" between child and teacher.

Partnershipping also gives teachers the chance to take a brief time off when they need it. One to one teaching is demanding and exacting work. A

ULS teacher can't retreat behind the mask which typical teachers can wear. Open one to one relationships with children often reveal the emotional tone of both the teacher and the child. Rather than come to school feeling out of sorts, partnership teachers can take the day off. The partner can take over full-time for the day. There will be no substitute called who the children don't know. Life for the children will go on in its very special way.

Here are three more ways how partnershipping might help make Urban Little Schools even better: (1) partnerships would be the ideal staffing for many secondary Urban Little Schools where young people might better relate to one person than the other; (2) partnershipping opens the possibility for recruiting sought-after people who would be perfect as ULS teachers but couldn't or wouldn't teach full-time; and (3) utilizing partnerships of two full-time teachers, an Urban Little School could be kept open from 7:00 AM to 5:00 PM in order to accommodate working parents and to keep children from being prey to gangs and street violence. (This would require additional funding.)

Finally, another advantage of starting pilot teachers in partnerships is that it introduces the partnership idea—a valuable option for ULS staffing. Without such a meaningful practical introduction to the idea, I have found people in schools simply don't take partnershipping seriously. When these school people attempt to solve problems for which partnershipping might be an option worth considering, they don't entertain the partnershipping possibility.

I learned about partnership teaching when I directed the experimental training program for partnership teachers at Syracuse University, as described in Chapter Two. From this beginning it was natural for us to staff our new SIEE School with part-time people. It gave us all of the advantages I have just discussed.

Why the Author Suggests Replication of the Pilot Urban Little Schools at the End of Three-plus Years of Teaching Children

In the startup plan, I suggested that at the end of three-plus years operation, the preliminary decision should be made whether the pilot schools had been successful up to that point. If the pilot elementary Urban Little Schools were then deemed successful, five pilot schools teachers would move from their partnerships to begin preparing for their new role as Startup II teacher trainers. They would then select and train more teachers for new elementary Startup II schools patterned after the pilot examples.

Of course it would be better to wait, before replication, until the first pilot children had become about twelve-years-old. But I am assuming that the need for more Urban Little Schools in the district simply would be too great to wait that long. After three-plus years of pilot school operation, I feel that a projection could be made as to whether children were measuring up to the Urban Little Schools character goals and would meet the elementary ULS minimum academic exit criteria. These exit criteria stipulate the following, as explained in more detail in Supplemental Article #2: each child graduating to a secondary ULS will be able to handle the reading, writing and arithmetic of their secondary jobs; each child will be able to use the computer and library with ease; each child will be able to learn independently the basic high school academic subjects at the Self-directed Learning Centers; and finally, each child will be able to pass the standard sixth grade achievement tests at grade level or better.

This assessment projection at the end of three-plus years of operation with children builds on two other evaluations done on pilot school children at the ends of the two previous years. Therefore most likely there would no surprises when the word came in from the assessment done at the end of the third full year of pilot operation with children. Of course, the pilot schools would be assessed each subsequent year to check the projection.

The Quality-Money Balance

The more children admitted, the more money paid from the school district or from Charter School funding, but caution should be taken not to compromise the development of a new school. Startup teachers and people from the backup organization are likely to feel pressure to bring the newly formed startup schools to their full complements of forty-four children as soon as possible. One reason is that the more children attending, the more money comes from per-pupil funding from the host school district and/or from Charter School sources. The more money from per-pupil funding, the less needed from donor grants for startup given to the backup organization. Then there would be more backup organization funding available to start more Urban Little Schools.

But I caution people not to add too many children too soon in the face of this pressure. It might sound a bit soft-nosed (that's the reverse of "hard-nosed") to say that inventive school people need professional leisure to be able to think through what they are doing as they are doing it. But even if it sounds like a luxury, it is a necessity if ULS people are going to innovate soundly step by step. As explained in Chapter Two, when I set up the partnership teacher training program and then the SIEE School, a key part of our problem-solving process was that we had time to figure out what was needed next and then to do it even if we had to undo some of what was already done. This un-doing/re-doing process was so much easier when there weren't so many students involved.

Also, don't forget how important it is to add children to newly forming schools so that there won't be too many children in any one year. The school you are creating is a multi-aged school. You need to meter the children in at a rate that takes into account projected attrition and which will result in a school where older children work side by side with young ones. The levels I suggest in the plan should create such a multi-age school.

Begin Replicated Urban Little Schools with Two Teachers and Build to Four?

An option worth considering is to start new elementary Urban Little Schools modeled after the pilot schools, with two teachers, not four as laid out in the suggested plan above. Then it would be less complex to begin, in terms of relationships between new teachers. Things would be simpler. As the school grew with new children, new teachers would be added until there were four teachers and forty-four children. Also, fewer children would be needed at first, when the neighboring parents might not be all that sure about that new small parent-choice school down the block which used a schooling approach with which parents weren't familiar.

Further Thoughts on Helping Startup Teachers Learn and Practice Diagnosing a Child's Reading and Writing Needs

It is absolutely crucial that pilot and Startup II teachers begin their first full year with children, knowing how to individualize children's learning to write and read. To do this teachers need to be good at diagnosing and implementation—good at figuring out what each child needs and then how to provide that in ways which best fit the child. New Startup II teachers have the advantage of observing pilot school teachers diagnosing and then using that knowledge in their individualization of learning for each child. Pilot school teachers had learned diagnosis and implementation from their Startup Leaders.

Both pilot teachers and Startup II teachers have a training period before the children enter when they can learn how to do this—when they can learn how to find out what individual children know, what they don't know and the next steps to teach them what they need. One way some teachers might learn how to do this skillfully would be to enlist the help of young children from the neighborhood. Most of these would be four-year-olds who might then start as some of the first students in the nearby Urban Little School, after they turned five. I have found most children enjoy helping trainee teachers learn. For many of those children, it is like playing school.

I assume, as I write about this, all of the new teachers will study Chapters Four and Five plus Supplemental Article #3 in this book. This material, along with other explanations in the book, detail how writing and reading might be tailored to each child at the various stages of growth in independence. Trainees should check out numerous young children, to find out the stage at which each child is, in becoming independent in writing and in reading. For example, when children show signs of early independence, that is if the they can read and write a little on their own, then the trainees should check to see how the children can handle decoding the consonant-vowel-consonant basic phonic pattern (such as the word *cat*) to determine their phonetic skill. Also, at this point the new teacher should determine how many of the basic reading words each of the children can read. Then the children should be involved in learning games and perhaps exercises which might be useful in learning what the teacher trainee feels the children need to learn. Easy success in these learning activities can help confirm whether the trainees' diagnoses were accurate.

Subsequent Teachers, Who Will Start and Staff the Next Waves of Urban Little Schools, Might Improve on their Pilot Models

Maybe the Urban Little Schools patterned after the pilot schools will do a better job than is being done in those pilot schools. Instead of only having this book to guide them, as did the pilot teachers, the next wave of teachers will have both the book and experience in the pilot schools to point the way. These next wave teachers won't have to invent the wheel as much as did the pilot teachers—the basic ULS design will be in operation to guide them. Then they might fine tune the ULS idea even more.

Notes

1   My experience is that colleges of education accept any university student on their campuses with the requisite grade point average, and do not deny recommendation for the credential even if the student has had a difficult time as a student teacher. In my twenty years working in elementary teacher training at three colleges of education I have heard of only one student who a faculty member said should be asked to leave the program. That student eventually was recommended for a teaching credential.

2   See further discussion about partnership teaching in the last section of this chapter. Also see Chapter Two's "Professional Journey" memoir where I explain how I trained prospective partnership teachers to individualize children's learning while individually guiding the trainees to tailor their own learning to their needs as teachers-to-be.

3   One of the four in each new school, later will take over as the Lead Teacher who takes charge of the school's child study program and only teaches eight children one to one.

4   At this point it might be decided to begin only one secondary school, staffed in partnership with the two newly selected former elementary pilot teachers who have had experience as partnership teachers. This could depend on the teachers' preferences or the decision might be influenced by the number of elementary children expected to enter during the new secondary schools' first years.

5   Attrition is expected to lessen as more elementary Urban Little Schools become available in other locations, allowing children whose families move within the city, to transfer to another Urban Little School.

Supplemental Articles

University and Urban Little School Partnerships

Why Not Have an Urban University Start Pilot Urban Little Schools to Revitalize Declining Neighborhoods on its Fringes?

Many urban universities are experiencing decline in the neighborhoods which surround them. Urban Little Schools could be an important piece within these universities' efforts to reverse the downward slide of their neighboring communities and to reach out to their neighbors. These Urban Little Schools would fit hand-in-glove with living in the city, where difference is the norm. Their individualized learning would ensure that all children succeeded whether they were rich or poor, whether their parents had advanced degrees or had had to drop out of school, whether the children came to school most days with light or heavy hearts.

A university-sponsored backup organization could begin with two elementary pilot Urban Little Schools. The university might begin according to the startup sequence laid out in Chapter Twelve. Both these small schools, of not over forty-four children apiece, would be situated in declining neighborhoods which fringed the university campus.

The elementary Urban Little Schools particularly could be a major force in bringing about a revitalized sense of community on the university's urban fringe. These schools would provide a five-star schooling alternative for university and neighborhood parents who chose to begin their five-year-olds in the Urban Little School down the block. University urban studies and education students could study the project to analyze the differences between the Urban Little Schools total redesign approach to school reform as opposed to the typical quick-fix way of handling school reform. They also could study some of the ULS features such as the teacher-child relationship and the way learning to read, write and do arithmetic was tailored to each child.

The Urban Little Schools, through their university sponsored backup organization could report to the local board of education or they might organize as charter private schools if the local school district did not want to be a partner.

• • •

Some universities which are located in deteriorating parts of our cities are now making effective efforts to help adjacent inner city neighborhoods. A case in point is Clark University, a venerable institution enrolling 2700 students in Worcester, Massachusetts. Fourteen years ago many local people saw Clark's fifty acre campus as an "arrogant presence" in the words of one of Clark's retired faculty members.[1] Since then Clark has made a strong beginning in changing its image to that of a working partner with its neighbors. It has backed good intentions up with several million dollars in grants, secured from private foundations, including a $2.4 million grant from the federal Housing and Urban Development's Office of University Partnerships.

These funds supported the establishment of a local non-profit community development corporation in the Clark neighborhood, whose objectives for improvement fell in the following five areas: physical renovation, public safety, education of children, economic development, and social/recreation opportunities. So far, here are four of the results:

1. People who move to the area are being offered economic incentives to invest and remodel properties. By mid-1997 nine faculty and staff families plus Clark's president, Richard Traina, have moved into the neighborhood.
2. Clark's Hiatt Center for Urban Education is aiding a nearby new junior/senior high school project to succeed, with tutoring and other help; plus Clark has secured the funds to enable every graduate of this new secondary school a full-tuition college scholarship.
3. Neighborhood high school graduates, who have lived in the community for at least five years, can go to Clark for four tuition-free years if they qualify.
4. The local school district has begun work on a new $20 million school building in the neighborhood.

The kind of neighborhood revitalization which Clark is doing would be an ideal setting for Urban Little Schools. As a part of this spirit of community regeneration, elementary Urban Little Schools could help bring together people who had a stake in neighborhood vitality and cohesion. Parents in the immediate area, meeting with other parents and neighbors, could get to know each other at their new Urban Little School a few doors away or just around the corner. They could count on one another when it came to doing things that made their streets safer and made the neighborhood a more pleasant place in which to live. Then secondary Urban Little Schools could further bring the community and the university together as the secondary young people from the neighborhood worked alongside university technicians, librarians, maintenance people and researchers. When these young people graduated they would know what a university was all about, from the inside out. These university job placements would be in addition to their other community jobs.

Trusting relationships such as we have been discussing are a powerful force for security and stability in an urban neighborhood. This is especially so if the neighbors' cohesion results in their taking initiatives such as telling children to stop destructive behavior seen in front of their houses.

People's willingness to take neighborhood responsibility, seems to be a key factor which can lower violent crime and lessen destructiveness in declining neighborhoods. In a substantial study recently published in *Science Magazine* it was found that homicide rates were forty percent lower in neighborhoods where residents felt they could trust and count on their neighbors and with this backing, found themselves willing to intervene in bringing about safe and orderly life on their streets. Examples of such intervention were "monitoring of spontaneous play groups among children, a willingness to intervene to prevent acts such as truancy and street-corner 'hanging' by teenage peer groups, and the confrontation of persons who are exploiting or disturbing public space." The study's three authors surveyed 8,732 residents in 343 Chicago neighborhoods. [2]

Urban Little Schools could help enable this kind of individual responsibility to better the neighborhood because the Urban Little Schools easy atmosphere of welcome and trust encourages dialogue between people who have a stake in the neighborhood and its families . Meeting in their nearby Urban Little School, neighbors and ULS parents might come together with city officials and others who could be able to help them get needed jobs done. City trucks could help neighbors clean up vacant lots; city inspectors should respond to neighborhood pressure by enforcing building codes; agency workers could help neighborhood people secure remodeling grants. Initial contact for much of this could come about casually, when, for example, parents and other neighborhood persons might chat with city officials over soup and coffee in their Urban Little Schools' kitchen.

Thus Urban Little Schools could bring parents and neighbors together in ways that could heighten trust and effective working-together relationships. For parents, especially, the stake in the neighborhood is more than just a desire for a decent place to live. The stake is for a neighborhood which would support the success of their children's elementary Urban Little School which, in turn, would provide for their children an even chance at good jobs and a life of integrity.

Along with neighborhood parents, many university parents should see the value to their families of living in the neighborhood so their five-year-olds might start in an elementary Urban Little School. I would expect that many faculty, staff and student parents would choose these small schools where teachers responded to children individually and sensitively. It should be exciting for many university families to live in a rising city neighborhood within walking distance of their university. In Urban Little Schools, children of different backgrounds and ages learn side by side, often in individually tailored ways. A child from a more privileged home would learn alongside a child from a less privileged home and it would feel perfectly natural. The children would grow up seeing each other as they were—individuals of vast potential.

How might serious discussions begin for the establishment of Urban Little Schools on the university's fringe? Parents from the university and from the neighborhood might begin discussing how Urban Little Schools could be a catalyst in bringing together a university-neighborhood community. Then too, as is often the case unfortunately, dialogue between university and neighborhood people might arise because of a shocking incident or a study which showed the neighborhood was ready for violent incidents to happen. Individuals and study groups in these informal discussions might talk seriously about rethinking the education of neighborhood children and make a place for an Urban Little Schools backup organization in the university's urban studies department or in the university's school of education.

I am speaking here of a school of education whose key professors and dean wanted to be part of the solution to failing urban schooling through fundamental redesign rather than quick-fix. These people might see the potential for education reform in the Urban Little Schools idea and want an autonomous Urban Little Schools backup organization to work out of their college. It would be refreshing and enlightening for the college's teacher trainees to see first-rate urban schools at work—schools where there were no losers, where learning was tailored to each child.

Then too, if an urban studies department's faculty and students worked to develop strong pilot Urban Little Schools, they could study the resultant neighborhood change. Urban studies professionals could see and study the dynamics of revitalization - the change brought about when there was a personally oriented school which could bring residents together so they came to depend on each other and worked for better streets on which their children might live.

In whatever college or department it was located, the university ULS teacher training should be handled by its autonomous backup organization that helped its trainees learn the ULS way. Trainees would learn one to one with their teachers with the same kind of self-directing and individualized process which later the trainees would use in teaching their ULS children. This Urban Little Schools teacher training process is explained in Chapters Nine and Twelve.

The university's ULS backup organization might not find it difficult to obtain foundation grants because of the promise of the university's commitment.

The university and some Urban Little Schools teachers could both benefit by the university enrolling some of those ULS teachers who had not yet earned their undergraduate degrees. The university could offer a degree program to ULS teachers who were looking for ways to finish an undergraduate program while they taught. Costs for less well off teachers could be subsidized by foundation grants. The committed people who taught at nearby Urban Little Schools, would be people who should enhance the university's student body. They would have been recruited for Urban Little Schools teaching because they were outstanding individuals who were naturals at teaching the ULS way.

• • •

In conclusion, it seems a natural partnership—a university which needs to revitalize its fringe neighborhoods and the Urban Little Schools which could help make this possible. With this partnership, once more the university's community might extend out from its campus and bring an exciting quality life to its nearby neighborhood.

Notes

1 These faculty member's words are quoted in an informative article about Clark's partnership with its neighboring community: An aloof university learns how to be a good neighbor. (1997, September 11) *The Christian Science Monitor*, pp. 10-11.

2 R.J. Sampson, S.W. Raudenbush, and F. Earls. (1997, August 15). *Science Magazine, Vol. 277*, pp. 918-924.

The Academic and Job-related Exit Requirements List

In the Urban Little Schools design, definite minimum academic and job-related exit criteria for each student are specified. In this article these criteria are listed. The only exception is for students with disablements, which seriously limit their academic or job-related learning. This article also lays out a procedure for alternative ULS academic and job-related exit requirements for students who can pass the host district's requirements for high school graduation but who need special ULS graduation requirements to be tailored to their specific situation, over and above the district's graduation requirements.

The minimum exit criteria specified in this chapter are goals to be met before each of the students leave their elementary Urban Little School and before they graduate from their secondary Urban Little School. The exit criteria give substance to the ULS claim that every child, except for some severely disabled young people, will leave qualified for college, or for other more suitable training, and will have an even chance at good jobs.

Minimum Exit Requirements for Every Elementary Child

By the time children leave their elementary Urban Little School each of them needs to be able to do these two tasks successfully:

1. They need to be able to learn traditional high school subject matter independently at the ULS Self-directed Learning Center.
2. They need to be able to succeed on their first ULS secondary jobs. On jobs, this means handling ably such skills as writing, reading and arithmetic plus being able to work with others in effective honest straight-forward ways.

To achieve this academic and job readiness one child might need to remain in the elementary Urban Little Schools longer than other elementary children. That's okay. There is no stigma in an Urban Little School if you stay a year or so longer. Although most elementary ULS children probably will leave to go to a secondary Urban Little School around twelve years of age, some won't and we should expect that the children involved will feel okay about it. It should be okay to them because in an Urban Little School, what you do and how long you do it is a matter between you and your teacher. Diversity and individual-specific learning is all around as children work alongside others of all ages. Also, we should expect that children will have friendships with others at school of differing ages because the school's structure doesn't channel children into a same-age peer group culture. So just because one elementary Urban Little Schooler moves to secondary school at a certain age shouldn't mean that another, who happens to be about the same chronological age, would feel shame for not leaving at the same time. The point is for each student to move to secondary Urban Little School when the student is prepared. You leave for your next step when you and your teacher know you are equipped to handle it.

More specifically, in order to handle the literacy tasks, the mathematical tasks, and to be effective with computers and other tools necessary to study independently at the secondary Self-directed Learning Center, and to be successful on secondary jobs, each of the children who leave their elementary Urban Little School needs to be able to meet the following expectations:

1. Graduating elementary ULS children will be expected to score, on a standardized achievement test, at or above the sixth grade level in reading, writing, grammar, spelling and arithmetic. Such a test might be the Iowa Test of Basic Skills or The Metropolitan Achievement Tests. (Most children who graduate from the elementary ULS will be around twelve years old, the age of children in the sixth grade in conventional schools.)

2. ULS children will be able to use reading, writing and the library to prepare and write an essay on an unfamiliar subject. In writing the essay they will be able to write with punctuation, spelling, and usage which clearly communicate their ideas to the reader.

3. The students will be able to use basic research tools such as a standard elementary school dictionary and encyclopedia.

4. In arithmetic, by the time children leave their elementary Urban Little School they will be able to estimate correct answers in arithmetic problems before they do the calculation. They will understand the meaning of the decimal number system so they can explain place value and how it works in such operations as borrowing and carrying. They will be able to pass an achievement exam used to test sixth graders who have been learning the fundamentals of geometry and algebra.

5. Children leaving the elementary Urban Little Schools will know the organization of their local library. They will be able to find books and other materials they might need. For example, if a boy were asked where the biographies were kept, he could lead the questioner right to the spot in the library where they were shelved. Another example: the child will have learned to use skillfully such library tools as the computer-based catalog and the book numbering system.

6. The children who are ready to leave their elementary ULS and enter a secondary Urban Little School will know how to use computers. They will have learned to use a computer's word processing facility in their writing, how to create graphics and other visual elements that enhance their ability to communicate, and how to reach others in computer

networks to share information and ideas. In addition, they will know how to learn independently with a computer. Thus for example, a child might learn the arithmetic times tables through computer games.

Minimum Exit Requirements for Every Secondary Young Person

All of the young people at the secondary level must leave the Urban Little Schools able to take the steps which will eventuate in their being able to compete on even terms for jobs they see as fitting for themselves. This means they will need to learn how to train themselves for the jobs they might want, to judge themselves accurately as a worker and as a person, and know how to learn independently. It also means, they will need to be prepared to gain admittance to colleges and advanced training programs. Thus they will have to be able to meet the following two specific goals before graduation from their secondary Urban Little Schools:

1. After taking basic high school subject courses at the ULS self-directed Learning Center, each graduating secondary student will score, cumulatively, above the 50th percentile of all the young people passing the state or district's high school graduation academic examination (or the nation's, if this is a nation-wide test.) This means each secondary ULS student will score at least better than 50% of the students passing the examination. In no particular subject should the student score less than the 40th percentile of those who pass. These graduation tests should include the following academic areas: English and literature; history, geography and civics; general math, algebra and geometry; a foreign language; general science, plus an in-depth course in either physics, biology or chemistry.
2. *One year before expected graduation*, each secondary ULS young person will be expected to achieve a score on a college entrance exam profile in basic high school subjects which state college admissions officers rate above the 40th percentile as compared with their entering freshmen

that year. *Upon graduation*, a year or so later, the same ULS young person will score higher than the 50th percentile on the same profile rated in the same way.

Alternative Secondary Exit Requirements

The only exception to meeting all of the above criteria will be young people who should graduate because they are prepared to succeed at college and in an honest effective life, but who should do their preparation in their own way. These students require an alternative set of secondary exit requirements over and above the academic graduation requirements set by the state or local school district. Passing the state or local academic graduation requirements is a must, whether the student uses alternative exit requirements or not. But a student needn't score above the 50th percentile of college entering freshmen, upon graduation, if the student can show achievement which marks him or her as outstanding in some other basic way and the student has a ULS record which clearly shows the young person is able to succeed in a college which is right for that student.

Thus, for example, a graduating young woman might not score above the 50th percentile of college entering freshmen, required of other ULS graduates. But she will graduate from her secondary Urban Little School after passing the required state or local high school graduation exams. In this case the student is a talented writer, who has demonstrated her ability and commitment. She is able to graduate under alternative exit requirements because it is clear she will be able successfully to pursue college or other further learning when and if she needs it.

This is not to say that secondary young people will be graduated when they come of age. "Social promotion" is not practiced in the Urban Little Schools. When we speak of alternative exit requirements we are talking about both the student and teacher, working together, judging the student on the student's own merits, on close knowledge of the student's capabilities and character. We are talking about fashioning alternative exit requirements which will have a better fit for a particular student, but still will fit the ULS aim that every single graduating young person will have an even chance at good jobs and a decent life.

Here is a suggested procedure for setting up an alternative set of exit requirements: Assuming the young person passes the state and local exams for high school graduation, the case for graduating on one's own terms will be made in the young person's portfolio. The teacher and the young person will write why the young person should be graduated according to the alternative criteria presented and support this proposal with facts and examples. The case then will be reviewed by the parents and key people in the ULS backup organization. Both the parents and the backup people must agree with the teacher and the young person that ULS graduation has been earned and should be granted.

How Every Child Can be Helped to Learn to Write, Read and Use the Library with Independent Skill and Satisfaction

I am writing this article for people who will be teaching children to read and write in an elementary Urban Little School such as the Fircroft School depicted in Chapter Four. However, the information in the article can be used by anyone who wants to tailor learning to read and write to each child. My aim is to teach teachers to know the essential content a particular child might need to grasp in order to take the next best step in that child's learning. In the article you will find content broken down into four stages which contain the tasks most children need to master as they learn to be independent in reading and writing and learn to use their ability with skill and satisfaction. Along with the content at each stage, I shall suggest ways you might determine what a particular child needs to do next and then teaching methods to help you guide the child in individualized ways. Once you learn how to help children through the four stages you can deviate from this sequence as you see fit to help each child.

You of course also have to consider outside factors which sometimes interfere with children's moving ahead and take whatever steps you can to overcome or minimize these roadblocks. For example, perhaps one child might need an eye exam, which checks how well the student can handle the task of close-up reading and writing. Maybe another child needs a more wholesome diet. Perhaps, as with Norman in our SIEE School, a child needs to learn without feeling pressure to fit in; or as in the case of Barry, a child might need to learn within tightly prescribed behavior boundaries. (See pp. 59-60 in Chapter Two.)

The way presented in this chapter is quite different from how children learn in most conventional schools. There, the teachers don't have to know the content well enough to analyze a child's ability in a fine-tuned way. Teachers just need to know enough to determine where the child should start in the school's sequentially organized series of lessons laid out as the curriculum. Then those children who are seen as not keeping up with the recommended pacing in reading are sent to the remedial teacher to be helped to catch up. Children's not measuring up usually means low marks on their report cards and perhaps repeating the grade. The result, by about the third grade is a school where about twenty percent or less are seen as winners, ten percent or more are losers and the rest are seen as "just ordinary."

Here are the four stages mentioned above which most children need to go through, in learning to read and write independently as they learn to make books and reading a source of lifelong self-education and satisfaction:

Stage One: Coming to know writing and reading as talk-written-down;

Stage Two: Learning the fundamentals for writing and reading independence;

Stage Three: Building one's fluency in writing and reading, through practice;

Stage Four: Using and enjoying skillful reading, effective writing and library research.

First, I need to remind you that individual children's learning might be in two or more stages at the same time. For example, a child might come to school knowing the sounds of the consonant letters (a task in Stage Two) while intuitively not grasping the idea of reading and writing as being talk-written-down (Stage One).

These four stages are presented here to help the teacher know what might be done to help a particular child become independent and then to use that ability with increasing sureness. These stages are not intended as a mandatory sequence of instruction. The sequence laid out is meant to organize the content for the convenience of the teacher who wants to determine what an emphasis should be for a particular child—what step should be next. I'll begin by laying out the basics of helping children master the tasks at the first stage, the bridge from talking, to reading and writing.

Stage One: Coming to Know Writing and Reading as Talk-written-down

Somewhere during the time children learn to talk, most of them begin to learn at least a beginning awareness of how writing is talk-written-down and reading essentially is the reverse. Perhaps they pick this up from books which are read to them, or from television advertisements they watch or from other times when written words are coupled with what someone says. What's needed when these little children begin at school, then, is to develop and build on whatever intuitive awareness the child might have that writing and reading are talk-written-down.

Then children have the groundwork to write and read automatically, so eventually they can free their conscious awareness to think about what they are reading or to compose what they want to write. This kind of automatic intuitive process is similar to how children integrate the use of their vision, hearing and smelling senses, mostly below the levels of consciousness. Upon coming into a room, for example, a child picks up loads of clues from what is seen, what is heard and what is smelled. The child does this in an integrated way and mostly below the levels of consciousness. The conscious mind is left free for the necessary critical thinking.

In the illustrative example of the Fircroft School in Chapter Four, I have given examples to show how ULS elementary teachers can focus on helping beginners develop this automatic response to writing and to reading, to help the student cross the bridge from talking to writing and reading.

Newstime, as used in Fircroft School, is a superb way, I have found, to help children get the hang of how writing is talk-written-down if it is taught engagingly by a teacher, who listens carefully to what each child contributes. In Newstime, reading and writing are happening simultaneously in front of the children. Their interrelatedness helps build the child's growing independence and fluency. The content is relevant to the children's lives. Children can see—in discrete words set out in left to right sequence—how punctuation, spelling and other conventions are brought together to make what is written down easy to read and understand.

Through practice in Newstime, children begin to integrate the basics of literacy below the levels of their consciousness. Not only do children learn to spell and recognize commonly used words during Newstime; they begin to encode and to decode the common sound elements, such as the individual consonant letters, and so on.

Newstime in groups can lead naturally to individual Newstimes for the two or three five-year-old beginners in each elementary teacher's multi-age group of twelve. Daily many of these beginners can dictate one to one to an adult or older child who writes what they say on the computer or in cursive writing done by hand. The older person can help the process along just as the teacher leading Newstime does. That is, the older person can question, "What happened then?" and in other ways lead children to elaborate.

Perhaps also the teacher taking the child's dictation can help a young beginner to practice writing by providing story starters and story stems from the teacher's growing collection. Here are three of my favorites:

- "Look what's coming out of the sink," cried...
- One thing I've always wondered about is...
- A spaceship landed next to my house and...

Dictating in this way helps beginning children write what they want to say quickly enough so they are not frustrated. That is essential. Dictation can be taken on a computer or it can be written by hand by the older person. Gradually as the children become more skillful, full responsibility for writing can be passed to them. Also, children's individually dictated pieces can be read to the other beginners, say, once each week at a "writing sharing" session. Some of the pieces might be mailed to family members or others significant in a child's life if that seems appropriate.

Beginners can be helped to begin journal writing to their key teacher, by dictating the occasional journal to an adult or older child—someone other than their key teacher. Then the next morning the child receives a journal in return from the key teacher. Let this beginning of a journal exchange be a natural thing which grows from children's desire to use this avenue in their relationship with their key teacher. Some beginners will want to start right off because they see the older children using this way of communicating with the key teacher and the beginner will want to do that too. Some beginning children will want to dictate a journal almost every day. Others will only get into the swing later.

All of this emphasis on individual expression should be in a wider context of non-verbal expression at the school. As was described in Chapter Four and in my description of the SIEE School in Chapter Two, the school can be a place rich in non-verbal ways for children to express themselves— from the dressup corner, to the cafeteria-style art area, to the rhythm instruments at the ready for some children who might choose to sing along with piano accompaniment first thing in the morning.

Finally, loads of good books should be read to children, particularly the beginners. As was done at Fircroft School in the morning, beginners listened to a picture book read by a teacher in a cozy group; then right after lunch they heard the day's installment of a story being read to the whole school. Once a week or more often, beginners should be taken to the children's room of the nearby library where they might hear the librarian read a story or tell one.

Stage Two: Learning the Fundamentals for Writing and Reading Independence

The teacher's job at Stage Two, is to guide the children toward a fledgling independence. I'll give examples below so you can help children move from an awareness of how writing and reading are talk-written-down to students doing writing and reading increasingly on their own. I shall emphasize how you can help children learn the highest priority fundamentals leading to reading and writing independence.

Some children seem to learn analytically with a readily available phonetic sense. Others seem to learn to read and to write more intuitively. They might not seem regularly to use an easily applied phonetic sense.

Using what you can learn in this Stage Two section, you can help children who seem to learn best analytically and systematically. You can help them memorize the essential phonetic sound elements, the most common words (is, and, then, etc.), and the mechanics of writing. Mechanically and logically, in a step by step sequence, you can help these children to build on their increasing knowledge in order to became able writers and readers.

For children who learn in a more intuitive fashion without as much attention to the individual sound units or memorizing the basic sight words, you can provide plenty of opportunities for them to pick up the way elements in words sound—pick up this kind of knowledge while they are using writing and reading to communicate as they do in their journal exchange with you and in Newstime.

In my teaching I have found almost all children learn to read and write with both approaches—intuitively *and* by analysis, logic, and rote memorization. It's just that some students seem better at doing one than the other. In addition, because all children need to learn how to approach words phonetically in order to deal effectively with spelling, dictionary use and other sounding-out tasks, we need to make sure every student learns to read, write and spell with at least a functional phonetic skill. Therefore I suggest that your policy should be that all children stand to benefit not only from memorizing common words but also from learning the analytical decoding and encoding process explicitly—if children learn the mechanics of phonetic word analysis in ways that are fun, ways which don't make children who don't take to phonetic analysis easily feel they doesn't measure up in their schoolwork.

You can use games to help children practice analyzing words skillfully and to memorize common words and sound elements. The logical and analytical learners learn the process and content elements they need for their breakdown of words and subsequent synthesis. The more intuitive, non-analytical learners aren't frustrated by failing in interminable school exercises done for the teacher's approval. Before beginning a group games, be sure all players are introduced effectively to the material they will be practicing in the game. This will insure that every child plays the game with a sense of satisfaction.

Games not only make it fun to memorize the key elements for logical analysis, they bring people together. Games are used as enjoyable and powerful teaching tools even for children who don't seem to have a natural bent for word analysis or the learning of sight words. Some games can be played by a group of children like Consonant Bingo which I'll explain later; other games can be played individually on the computer. Also I'll speak later more about using the computer to learn and to practice key phonetic and sight word elements which need to be memorized.

This doesn't rule out the more traditional ways to teach phonetic elements and sight words. Use anything which works for a particular child. A good workbook is often prized by children, who will labor over the pages until they take the completed book home proudly. Select phonics workbooks which are carefully sequenced for systematic learning and which teach phonic elements useful in unlocking words at least half of the time. (More about which elements these are below.) Another good way to teach children to make the sounds phonetic elements "say" is by having the child mimic your lip and mouth position as you make a particular phonetic sound element. Thus when you sound out the *-tuh* sound of the consonant *t* the child can see the way you hold your lips and where your tongue is. The next step is to have the child use a mirror to make her or his facial expression match yours. When sounding the consonants such as *-tuh* emphasize the *t* sound and minimize your sounding of the *-uh*.

So whether a child seems to learn intuitively, systematically, or uses both avenues to learning equally well, the essential task for almost all children at this stage, is to master four fundamentals at an unconscious or automatic level of skill and awareness. These four fundamentals cover the essentials of becoming independent in reading and writing. Children who master these four fundamentals will be able to write everyday thoughts and read simple communication with ease. Here are the four fundamentals:

1. Contextual Clues

When I say "context clues" I mean the reader's ability to determine what word might fit, in light of the reader's understanding of the story's plot or the narrative so far. Context acts as a prompter, narrowing the possibilities of what the unknown word might be. Thus with a sense of context, when children sound out the word or see already known word bits within the longer word, they can choose the correct sound for the whole word—the sound that makes a word that fits what is being read. Much of the teacher's writing talk-written-down in Newstime and in taking individual dictation from beginners can help children develop this sense.

In order to use the power of the context in predicting what a word should be, children need to read material in which they are caught up and read fast enough to keep the story alive. Therefore, you need to make sure beginners are reading simple books that they can move through with ease.

As you work with children at this stage you will soon find which books labeled "easy to read" fill this bill and which do not.

When you are with your beginning readers at the library teach them how to size up a book the library labels "easy to read" by trying a few selections to determine if they can read it fast enough to keep the story line moving so they will be able to puzzle out new words phonetically. I have found many books labeled "easy to read" are too difficult for the just-beginning reader to maintain all-important reading speed. We shall analyze a truly easy to read book, below. This exercise should help you see why some "easy to read" books are in fact easy for fledgling readers and some are not.

2. Conventions and Form

Basic to both being on one's own in reading and in writing at the fledgling level is the child's beginning skill in using the conventions of form. Here, I am speaking of developing the following abilities:

- moving from left to right on a page intuitively;
- pausing and giving appropriate emphasis according to punctuation marks;
- writing letters and words legibly in manuscript printing;
- writing appropriate periods, commas, question marks, capitals, and apostrophes.

I hope you can see how the language experiences I have been talking about so far—Newstime, taking dictation and reading it back with the child, and other daily reading and writing experience—all build the beginning awareness and integrative ability necessary for developing this fundamental skill. I'll say more later about fine tuning these abilities.

3. Sight Recognition and Spelling of Common Words

The third fundamental is the child's ability to recognize on sight and spell the most common words. I separate these common words into two groups. First are the Top Twelve Words. These are the most common and are about one fifth of the words one finds in the easy-to-read books that are best to use to start children reading. These are the first 12 words, in order of commonness, from a list of the 188 most common words. These 188 were the most repeated words in sixty-five favorite children's books. After these first 188 Basic Words all the other words in the children's books didn't show up often enough in the tabulation to warrant children's memorizing them for instant recognition. Here is a list of the Top Twelve Words starting with *the*, which is the most common word found in the books surveyed. (The most common words are in the first column, ending with *I*.)

the	to	and	was
a	you	it	said
I	he	of	in

Here are the rest of these 188 Basic Words, listed vertically. The most common words are in the first column (beginning with *his* and ending with *have*.)

his	go	my	your	away	two	school	friend
that	we	would	time	man	or	still	next
she	one	me	from	old	head	much	open
for	then	will	good	by	door	keep	has
on	little	big	any	their	before	children	hard
they	down	mother	about	here	more	give	enough
but	do	went	Mr.	saw	eat	work	wait
had	can	are	father	call	oh	king	Mrs.
at	could	come	around	turn	again	first	morning
him	when	back	want	after	play	even	find
with	did	if	don't	well	who	cry	only
up	what	now	how	think	been	try	us
all	thing	other	know	ran	may	new	three
look	so	long	right	let	stop	must	our
is	see	no	put	help	off	grand	found
her	not	came	too	side	never	start	why
there	were	ask	got	house	eye	soon	girl
some	get	day	take	home	took	made	place
out	them	very	where	thought	people	run	under
as	like	boy	every	make	say	hand	while
be	just	an	dog	walk	tree	began	told
have	this	over	way	water	tell	gave	than

Children will find around sixty to seventy percent of the words in truly easy to read books are these Basic Words, with over half of that number falling in the Top Twelve Words and the words in the first two or three columns. I find newspaper copy is roughly fifty percent Basic Words.[1] As with the language conventions, our beginners usually don't have to learn most of these words laboriously in exercises. They learn them naturally because they see these words being used and use them themselves so often in the rich ULS reading and writing experiences, such as Newstime, in which they participate.

4. Phonetic Skills

The fourth and final reading and writing fundamental for the child to master with automatic response, is the ability to sound out the regular consonant-vowel-consonant pattern (*c-a-t*) in all its ramifications. I advise teachers to teach this one powerful phonics or sounding-out rule to virtually all of their children except perhaps for the small minority (less than one percent?) who don't seem to have any phonic sense at all. It is the only phonics rule that applies more than half of the time—as opposed to other rules where there are more exceptions than occasions when the rule works. Here is this powerful phonics rule:

> When a consonant-vowel-consonant word or word segment has only one mid-point vowel, (like in *cat*) try the "short" sound of that vowel as in *mat* or *sit* unless the word ends in silent "*e*," in which case try the "long" sound of the vowel as in *mate* or *site*. (Some people say that the long sound of the vowel is when it "says its name.")

Again, because our beginning children have been using this fundamental so much as they read and write (Newstime, writing on their own and similar experience), they learn most of the regular phonic, or sound elements involved by using them rather than by learning through traditional exercises. But, as in learning the Basic Words, it is worthwhile to reinforce this learning by practice, so the child becomes automatic in instant sight recognition and spelling. You can do this reinforcement, as I mentioned, by having children learn in games, by having children work on the computer with interactive learning programs and in more traditional ways such as in workbooks.

The regular phonic elements which the child must be able to encode and decode in using our c-v-c rule are the following:[2]

The sounds of the nineteen consonant letters:

s	m	h	j	r	z	x	t	l
g	p	b	w	f	k	d	n	c	v

The sounds of the common consonant blends such as:

st	cl	sn	spl	bl	gl	sm	str	pl
fl	sw	spr	fr

The sounds of these common consonant digraphs (consonant blends in which you don't hear the sounds of the individual letters):

ng	sh	wh	ph	nk	ch	ck	th

The sounds of common syllables, especially these:

ent	est	ail	ight	ay	ain	ide	er	ill
tion	ter	ide	con	ock	ed	ell	kni	cen
ake	ile	en	ly	cig	qu	cas	wro	re
pro	pre

The sounds of the following common vowel elements (each introduced here and sometimes ended by a consonant to make a nonsense syllable):

fay	taw	zoar	dee	meer	moy	roat	oot	kour
maup	eap	mair	fow	kai	foi

The four common suffixes:

y	(e)d	s	ing

Demonstrating the Power of these Four Fundamentals

First we'll look at the task of reading. After showing the power of these fundamentals in helping children to get on their own in reading, it should be easy to see what's needed for the child to master the task of being independent in writing. It's the reverse of reading.

I'll demonstrate on a page copied from *The Boxcar Children.*[3] I have found this old book to be one of the most appealing and best written easy-to-read book of the many available. By using this page I'll not only be able to show you the power of our four fundamentals, we shall get a glimpse of the format and story of a good easy to read book to help children practice these fundamentals.

The Boxcar Children is a story about how a family of four children run away from The Children's Home, an orphanage. While on their journey, Jessie and Henry, with their younger brother Benny and sister Violet escape during the night from a man and woman who want to exploit the older children's labor in their bakery. Along the way, they befriend a homeless dog who becomes one of them. The children's adventure-filled trip in the darkness brings them to an off-the-beaten-track woods. Here they find a deserted railroad boxcar situated on an unused rusty spur track. A small stream flows nearby. They find all sorts of items at a dump not far away, which with ingenuity they use to set up housekeeping in their new home—the boxcar. Their adventures living on their own, how they can count on each other, a pervading element of mystery and suspense, all make this a story that I have yet to see a fledgling reader want to leave. *The Boxcar Children* is 154 pages long.

On page fourteen in the book, pictured here, we find the children escaping from the exploitative bakers. On this page, I have framed a segment of fifty words which I chose at random. Below I shall explain how by analyzing the words within the framed area we can show the power of our four fundamentals in providing the child with beginning independence in reading.

Now let's examine that boxed segment of 50 words to demonstrate and confirm what I have just said about the power of the four fundamentals. I shall do this in a way you might replicate if you wish to use this method to analyze other children's books. I have used it many times on segments taken from books and newspapers. It has helped me to ground myself in the task children face in getting on their own in reading.

Within the framed segment of 50 words, I have put a circle around each of the Top Twelve Words and have crossed out each of the other Basic Words from our list. It turns out that 70% of the words (35/50) are on our list of Basic Words, of which 18% (9/50) are in the Top Twelve Words.

The remaining 15 words (30% of the segment) primarily can be decoded by using the c-v-c fundamental assisted by the story context to narrow

14   *The Boxcar Children*

"You must carry Benny," said Jessie. "He will cry if we wake him up. But I'll wake Violet.

"Sh, Violet! Come! We are going to run away again. If we don't run away, the baker will take Benny to a Children's Home in the morning."

The little girl woke up at once. She sat up and rolled off the bench. She did not make any noise.

"What shall I do?" she whispered softly.

"Carry this," said Jessie. She gave her the workbag.

Jessie put the two loaves of bread into the laundry bag, and then she looked around the room.

"All right," she said to Henry. "Take Benny now."

Henry took Benny in his arms and carried him to the door of the bakery. Jessie took the laundry bag and opened the door very possibilities. Let me explain by first separating the 15 remaining words into two columns below. The first column contains the words *Benny, home, woke,* etc., which easily can be decoded using the c-v-c pattern. (I call these "Regular c-v-c Words.") Then in the second column I shall list the words that require more effort—*Sh, Violet, going* etc. These "Other Words" are words that essentially can be decoded with the basic sound pattern and elements children have learned, but most of these words in the second column require that children lean more heavily on context clues—what makes sense according to the story line—to help them figure out the unknown words.

You can see how the "Regular c-v-c Words" all can be decoded rather easily using the child's knowledge of the c-v-c rule above and the sounds that the child expects the elements to say. As the rule directs the child to expect, the single medial vowel in almost all the words has the "short" sound (like the *a* in *mat*). (*Children* is broken into two segments, each of which can be decoded with our c-v-c rule.) Four of these ten words use the rule's direction that when a c-v-c word ends in an *e* make the medial vowel "say it's name" (the "long" sound of the vowel, like in *mate*). One word (*noise*) uses a medial vowel element on our list of common vowel elements. Four more of the words (*Benny, shall, bench* and *child*) use consonant digraphs or blends of two or three consonants. The suffix *y* in *Benny* is one of the common suffixes from our list.

Regular C - V - C Words   Other words

c	v	c	+	suffix		Other words
B	e	nn		y		Sh
h	o	m		e		Violet
w	o	k		e		going
s	a	t				once
b	a	k		er		rolled
sh	a	ll				
b	e	nch				
m	a	k		e		
n	oi	s		e		
[ch	i	ld				
r	e	n]				

Now look at our second column above—at the remaining five words that do not fit the c-v-c pattern expectations neatly. The first word *Sh* can be decoded easily by the child who can use the four fundamentals. It is one of the digraphs the child has learned.

The next word, *Violet*, probably was learned when the child was introduced to this easy to read book. (Try to insure that a fledgling reader can read the names of a book's main characters easily before handing the book to the child to begin reading.) But *Violet* can be decoded, with the aid of the context, too. Children can be expected to know the sound of *V*. They can decode *let* which is a simple c-v-c patterned segment.

Next we have the word *going*. This is another easy one: *go* is a Basic Word and *ing* is one of the four common suffixes.

The word *once* is harder to decode using our four fundamentals. The child needs to lean heavily on context clues. *Once* follows *at*, which the child knows as a Basic Word. It should help because "at once" is common usage.

Finally, the word *rolled* shouldn't be too big a challenge if the child can use the context to help. Aside from the irregular sound of "o" (it is "long" in this word instead of "short" as the child has been led to expect for medial vowels) the rest of the word is consistent with our fundamentals.

Now to apply this to writing: The task essentially is the reverse from the task of reading. Basically, for children to be on their own in writing, they need to be able to use our fundamentals (all except using context clues, which is just for reading) as encoding skills rather than in decoding. Thus, the typical child has to know how to handle the conventions listed above (as Fundamental Two), how to spell the Basic Words, and how to sound out the spelling of basic elements in words that follow the c-v-c pattern. Finally, as in decoding, the child needs to be able to handle these fundamentals with ease, increasingly making decisions automatically as to spelling, and other conventions.

You can monitor the child's writing growth easily in the journal exchange you and the child have. As soon as the children are on their own in writing and not writing their journals through dictation, you will have feedback each week as to how each child is getting on with writing.

Using Games to Teach Basic Reading Words and Sound Elements

As I have been saying, for fledgling independence it is vital that you help the child to be able to use *with ease* the Basic Words, the sound elements and the rest that are delineated in our four fundamentals. As mentioned, I find that computer games and group games are the best way I know of to help the child practice and practice, using these key words and sound units until they become automatic responses. I don't use group games to teach the elements as much as to practice them—to memorize phonetic elements and sight words by using the elements until the process becomes as automatic as breathing in and out. Be sure players in a group game are practicing elements which they already have learned to recognize but need to practice. This will guarantee every player a satisfying and educational experience.

My favorite group game to teach the Basic Words is Fish, a card game where each card has a Basic Word written on it. A Fircroft teacher and a few children, in Chapter Four, were playing Fish in the morning as the children drifted in from 8:30 on. Deal out five cards per player with the rest of the cards stacked in the middle, face down. The object is to put down pairs of cards until the winning player doesn't have any more cards. If the cards in the middle are all taken, then the winner is the person with the most pairs down. Children have to read every card aloud as they put it down. George may ask Sarah for a card needed to complete a pair when it is his turn. For example, "Sarah do you have a 'said'?" If she doesn't have the word she tells George to "go fish," and he has to draw a card. The skillful player remembers who asks for what card. Teachers make the first Fish deck to use the first thirteen Basic Words (4 x 13 = 52) in place of the usual symbols on playing cards. The simplest way is to tape slips of paper with words on them to the faces of playing cards. Then teachers make a deck using the next thirteen words and so on until they get decks that contain all the most common Basic Words—listed in the first two columns above.

Concentration is another good card game to teach the Basic Words. Maybe you remember playing it as a child. As with Fish, children can play it with a deck which has thirteen of the Basic Words (4 x 13 = 52) instead of numbers and face cards. To begin play, lay out all or half of the deck in a few columns. Then the first player picks up two cards and reads out loud what is on them. If they are a pair, that player can have them as one "book"—so long as the player can read the words on the cards out loud. A player who doesn't draw a pair, turns the cards over again in place while all the players try to remember the Basic Word on each card turned down. The game continues like this. Soon it becomes a challenge to keep the location in mind of each word that is face down. If players can remember when it is their turn, they simply turn over a pair and then they'll get a "book" and a second turn. The player then turns over one more card and tries to remember where its pair is located under the columns of card backs that all look the same. The player who remembers and can read the new pair of cards, gets another turn, and so on.

Bingo is my favorite game to teach the consonant elements, common syllables, and common vowel elements. Each Bingo game you prepare should have a set of bingo cards containing a different group of these elements, at an increasing level of difficulty. Thus you can have one game that uses a set of cards with the nineteen initial consonants for those children who need to practice these and another set using common syllables for students who need practice to become automatic with these. Children have to call out the sound of what they cover up on their cards, as they cover them. Then the winner reads aloud each of the list of winning sounds that were uncovered. Again, be sure each child has an even chance to win—that each is familiar with the phonetic content being practiced in the game.

In addition to these two favorites, use a variety of snaky path board games. You can get the boards at garage sales. Paste over a Basic Word or a common sound element in each box on the snaky paths. Then when children move according to their throw of the dice, they have to say the words or common elements that they cross. As in the other games we have been discussing, load the first games with the easiest words and elements. For more skilled children, in subsequent games, present the less common words and sound elements.

Stage Three: Building Fluency in Writing and Reading, Through Practice

Here are some ways to help children practice reading and writing in order to build their fluency quickly. These ways fit naturally with their growth at school in using reading and writing as meaningful communication.

Help Children Learn to Choose the Right Books for Themselves

One way you can build reading fluency is to help children learn to choose books they like and can read quickly enough to let the context help them unlock unknown words. Usually, when I do this with children, the two of us take time to try out several easy-to-read books until the child chooses one. Along with looking at the pictures to get a feel for the story line, I encourage the children to try reading a sentence or two to confirm that they can read the book. I do this in a way that teaches the children to do this for themselves. I call this a "build in."

When I taught young children this way in my second grade class, typically I would sit next to the child, perhaps reading the first few pages or so and ask the child to read a bit in the book to help the book hold the young reader's interest through to the end. In doing this—asking ourselves if the book is easy enough to read and reading a bit—I reminded children that there was no use trying to read a book unless they could read it fast enough to use the story's context to help them decode words. If it looked like this might be the right story for a child, we took turns reading on a bit, introducing the book's characters, the setting, and getting some idea of the problem or story line which would lead the reader toward the book's climax. I didn't do an elaborate "build in" with children who only needed a quick introduction—just for those who needed this help to keep reading up to speed. I was pretty sure in advance, before we began our "build in," whether the child would be able to read the book with ease. I knew this from my experience with the other reading the child had done. I also knew which easy to read books were likely to hold a child's interest.

Not only did I get to know children's reading level from being with them as we choose book after easy reading book, periodically each of the children and I would sit down together and check their reading level in the progressively more difficult passages of an informal reading inventory.[4] This, in turn, helped me learn the difficulty level of the various easy to read books. For example, *The Boxcar Children*, which I used with almost every one of my beginning readers once they were on their own, can be read, after a "build in," by a child who was above the second grade level passage in an informal reading inventory.

I can't say too much about your helping children to select books they can move through at a pace fast enough to use the context to help figure out unknown words. I feel sure the reason some children who have mastered the fundamentals we have been discussing, cannot read the daily newspaper or other adult writing effectively, is that they are so slowed down by unfamiliar vocabulary and usage, they simply lose track. Then they cannot use the logic and thought line—the context clues—to help figure out unknown words. It is not that they don't know the conventions or that they cannot sound out words and read the common sight words.

Set Things Up so Children can Practice Reading Seriously

Children, at this stage, should have an uninterrupted half hour each day for reading practice, as illustrated in Chapter Four's Fircroft School schedule. You might recall how, during this time, the Fircroft children got three different kinds of support to read independently: introduction to independent reading; almost-independent reading for children who might need to ask help with an occasional unknown word; and independent reading for children who didn't need help but might benefit from solitude, to soak themselves into their book.

Please read carefully the description of those three Fircroft groups. Those groups were a far cry from children doing reading lessons in the conventional schools' reading groups. In Fircroft's three groups, the emphasis was on function. In deciding on the best group for a child teachers asked themselves and each child, "What does this child need to read independently?" Children and teachers worked it out; they talked about which kind of a situation would most help the child to move through a book. Sometimes a child tried one kind of support, then another, in determining the best fit. Being in one group or another, then, had nothing do with who was better than whom. The point was for each of the children to get the help they needed to read books independently.

To sum up, our overall goal in helping children to be fluent readers is to help children to become independent in a fast, sure, automatic way. Now, similarly, our goal in helping children toward fluent writing is for children to write with ease so that they can do it automatically, so that the processes have become so habitual children handle them largely below the levels of consciousness. Also, in both reading and writing it is key that each of the children develop pride and satisfaction in using their skill as a reader and craftsmanship as a writer. All this follows the same natural route as the children took to learn to speak. In learning to talk, children first caught on to the idea of putting thoughts in verbal code—spoken words—then they became fluent at doing so, by a great deal of motivated practice. As they did this, they could feel satisfaction in doing it well.

Helping Children to Practice their Writing

Introduce children to writing with a pencil or pen when they are ready, as I mentioned. It is important that you *not* ask children to write by hand before they can do it with a beginning sense of ease. If children are pushed too soon to write by hand—before their small hand muscles and coordination are adequately developed—they likely will become at least a bit frustrated. When your hand can't handle a pencil with ease, it is painstakingly hard to write by hand each letter and each word. It can be frustrating when one lags too far behind the flow of thoughts in one's head. Perhaps one reason so many adults find themselves shying away from writing personal letters is they were started to write in school before they could handle the mechanics of letter formation and writing down whole words with ease.

So wait to introduce children to handwriting if it appears they don't have the physical maturation and the requisite eye-hand coordination for writing. When they are ready they can learn how to write the manuscript (printing) alphabet and then practice doing it to improve speed. Then later you can introduce cursive (longhand) writing. You can do this with workbooks which emphasize simple consonant-vowel-consonant patterns in their practice material.

Begin Most Children's Serious Writing on the Computer

For writing on one's own, the computer's word processing facility is very helpful. It takes children far less eye-hand coordination and small muscle development to work the computer's keyboard than it does to write by hand. So start most children with writing on the computer. Children usually begin with one finger, as their little hands won't span the keys on the keyboard. Later they can learn to touch-type using one of the commercially available software programs. Also there are small scale keyboards available so young children can be taught to touch type from the beginning.[5]

Using the computer to write seems to fit as a natural route to fluency. It's so special for children to see their words and thoughts come out of the computer's printer. Children are able to read the printout better than manuscript printing too, because the printer letter font you can use is similar to the font used in the child's books. [6]

Use the computer's spell-check to help students decide on correct spelling for misspelled words. Students can increase their spelling sense as they puzzle over alternatives the computer suggests. Have students keep a list of their misspelled words the computer highlights. These can be their weekly spelling words to learn which then should be re-tested monthly. Periodically ask students to let you see their journal drafts before the spell-check was used. This will enable the two of you to monitor the student's growth in spelling ability. Then, if needed, you can have the student do separate lessons to increase spelling power. Good programs, often in game format, are available to help students increase spelling sense. (See more on these software programs and on using the computer's word processing assistance, pp. 278--80.)

The Child's Journal Exchange with You is so Important at this Stage

Every few days, perhaps every day, you will exchange a journal with those children in your group who are coming to be on their own in writing. This will be in addition to the journals you receive from your more independent students. What good practice this is for your fledgling writers who are at the stage when they need loads and loads of meaningful practice and can model after your writing in the journals they receive from you.[7] Don't correct the journals you receive from your students. This is not the place for them to feel judged as writers. It is a place for them to practice with more and more ease as they use their writing to share ideas, feelings and their thoughts about their own learning.

But you can use their journals to help them learn needed conventions. To do this, use their journals diagnostically as well as an act of communication. That is, use their journals to determine where the students are in their development as skillful writers. Then you will be in a position to guide the students, if need be, to fine tune their writing, perhaps to learn more about punctuation, grammar and usage.

Journals also give you and each student a marvelous chance to share your spontaneous side, in writing. Let your ideas and feelings pop out onto paper via your journals. Students will get the idea and do likewise. Even though writing on a computer allows you two to revise and edit, in most cases don't emphasize that. At this stage journals are primarily intended as spontaneous narrative writing somewhat similar to how people share casually via e-mail.

In your journals to your students you teach by the example of what you write, both by your clearness in communication and by the tone and subtlety of your writing. Journal writing often fuels itself. When you write one thought or idea, others are given freedom to assert themselves. It's sometimes good just to start writing even if what you write seems a bit trivial. So just start. Don't wait for the right phrase or the attention-getter.

Getting started writing a journal seems a particularly difficult thing for some teachers. When I sense an old lingering fearful association to writing, in some teachers' questions concerning getting a journal started, I often suggest they turn and look out the window—maybe at the sky or a tree—then ask the teachers to begin to write what they see. If any associations, thoughts or feelings present themselves, write those too. I urge these teachers to let themselves join their writing with all their senses—what they see, smell, feel. This seems to make it clear that journal writing is not an exercise to be judged, but a chance to tap whatever current runs inside each of us.

As you write your journals to children, feel free to muse and reflect if that is what seems to come up as you sit at your desk. I am talking of your speaking from your heart, often in response to something a child has brought up in a journal. You might share a bit of your own poetry in your journal to a child. Don't expect a child to share inner feelings unless you open yourself to what matters to you, in your journals.

I am not talking here about making journal writing some sort of psychological self-disclosure. I am talking of writing about feelings and thoughts which are honest and important even if they seem unconnected or if they seem what some people might judge to be "not important."

Stage Four: Using and Enjoying Skillful Reading, Effective Writing and Library Research

Each student's journey is quite different from here on out. They now read and write independently. Independence in reading means the child scores at or above the sixth grade level on an informal reading inventory. When I speak of independent writers I mean children who are able to write a simple story with coherent plot, characters, setting and flow. Also children write with the conventions of punctuation, usage and spelling correct enough for easy communication. Your goal becomes to help these independent readers and writers fine tune their new fluency as they use their independent skill in rewarding ways. You are helping them to begin their lifelong process of self-directed learning using reading, writing and the library.

In writing, your goal is to help students learn to take pride both in the substance and craft of their writing. You are there to guide them as they grow in ability to express themselves clearly and use grammar, usage and spelling conventions correctly; as they write in fiction, poetry, narrative and expository form. I use "narrative" form to mean telling something, such as when students write to their teacher regularly in journals. An "expository" piece teaches the reader—with an explanation which is ordered by logic, whose sequence develops the subject.

Guide students to explore the library with satisfaction and deepening insight as they come to know authors and find lasting value in books and reading. In this process you will be introducing them to literature, science and the social studies—subjects which they will study systematically in their succeeding years. This includes beginning each student in meaningful research in the library. Also, in their seeking knowledge, help students use textbooks with independent thought and questioning rather than just passively memorizing for a test.

Coming to Know and Value the Library as a New ULS Teacher

First let's talk about how you, a new teacher, can increase your knowledge and enjoyment of a good children's library. Once you, yourself, catch the library bug you will find that the children under your care tend to follow suit. It's contagious.

If you haven't really immersed yourself in the world of the children's library, do it. Go out and enjoy the children's library and the adult collection, too. You can learn a lot and come to know yourself a bit better, perhaps. The library holds so much of the content you will use to guide your students to learn. All through children's lifetimes it won't cost them anything to avail themselves of this treasure house. It's free for the asking.

 Get to know a few really good children's librarians. You won't have to go far to find some. I have found almost all children's librarians to be caring people who want to help children and their teachers explore the world of children's books. I sometimes think, how can they be otherwise after living with the richness in so many of the beautiful and informative children's books all around them. Children's authors so often speak directly from what matters most to them. Illustrators give forth from those special places within themselves. It's OK to be idealistic and openly hopeful about life, as an author or illustrator in the world of children's books.

As you observe the librarians at morning story times, watch the children's faces as the librarians tell the story in some of their favorite books. When the older children come in after school and on Saturdays, you might drop in to observe how the librarian helps child after child turn their curiosity into questions which can direct the children to information-packed and colorful books. Be sure to listen as the librarian talks with parents about the right books for reading out loud at home.

I remember recently asking a children's librarian to recommend an important children's book my wife and I might read together. I asked her to suggest a book which she enjoyed reading. The librarian suggested *The Satanic Mill*, by Otfried Preussler.[8] The tale is set in the early seventeen hundreds in Germany. As in so many good children's fiction books, this story brought my wife and I close to the mysteries and fearful dilemmas of living. It also brought us to a lovely young man, Krabat, and to a lot of enjoyment in the reading. We were with Krabat as he was drawn in to learn the evil arts which would give him power over others. He found himself with other young men who were following an evil master and seemingly felt good about having their new power even though they had lost their freedom in the bargain. Krabat didn't know he was coming under the master's spell until he was virtually powerless to leave. In subtle ways Krabat began to find out he was losing his freedom to be himself. His individuality was almost taken over by the evil master. It took all Krabat's clear thinking to figure out the situation he had stepped into, all his will to face his fear of meeting the evil master as an equal; all his ingenuity to break loose from the dark spell. A beautiful friendship gave him the final strength of heart to face the master.

Enjoy books which speak to your life. Take home piles of children's books you might come across as you shelve books as part of your helping the librarian. I took home all sorts of books when I was a teacher and for years afterward. I didn't agonize over whether this or that book might be one which I would enjoy. If after a quick look and a read on a page or two, I was drawn to the book, I'd take it. Then at home I'd select the books from the pile which I wanted to read to myself or wanted to read to my children out loud.

That's another way you, a new teacher, might come to explore and enjoy the children's library—do it with your own child or with another child. Reading aloud can go far beyond your children's first few years. As your children get older some of the books will come from the children's room and some from the adult collection in the library. I remember reading *Watership Down*[9] to my ten-year-old daughter each evening when she went to bed. Maybe I looked forward to the reading each night even more than she did. As we read a chapter or so each evening, the two of us could be with our rabbit friends as they sought to build a new society and way of life after having to flee from developers who gassed so many of their family and other community members. I remember once looking up and seeing she had drifted off to sleep. What a lovely way to end the day—with a good story and the love of your father.

Let the librarian help you to read about the lives of the authors to whom you find you are drawn. I remember being drawn to Armstrong Sperry after reading his *Call it Courage*.[10] The book touched something special in me. Sperry wrote about his life when he won the Newbery Medal for the best children's book in 1940. As I read his autobiographic account I found myself close to him. He told about leaving his job in New York shortly after World War I and traveling to the South Seas long before the islands were romanticized by popular fiction writers. I inferred from what he said that he found himself fed up being an advertising illustrator. During the several years he spent in the South Seas, he spent a year living with a community of islanders, soaking up their myths and sharing their day-to-day life. Out of this grew *Call it Courage*.

From the beginning of his book I sensed Armstrong Sperry was a kindred soul. During my adolescent years I yearned to build my own sailboat and sail it single-handed around the world—especially to the places where I had heard people lived simple straightforward lives. I too wanted to get away. Later I did just that. I left my university job and, instead of sailing around the world, I drove around the country with my dog, finally ending in England at a lovely retreat center where, indeed, life was simpler and more meaningful to me than what I had experienced before.

Use Your Regular Conferences and Journals to Discuss and Guide Students' Reading, Writing and Library Research

Use your regular weekly journal or conference to discuss the books and authors your fluent readers are reading, the fiction and poems they might be writing, along with their current library research projects. Guide them to be able to use their independent skill and knowledge for enjoyment and wisdom. Also their skill and knowledge will serve as an introduction to the basic subject content they later will learn systematically at the secondary Self-directed Study Center.

Bit by well-discussed bit, during this last stage of learning to use their reading and writing independence, you will be grooming each of your students to take more and more responsibility for their own learning which they will continue to pursue under the guidance of their secondary teacher. Reading, writing, and using the library are basic tools to do this. But perhaps even more important, as you discuss the books each student is reading in conferences and journals, you will be setting the stage for a lifetime habit of reading and satisfaction from using the library.

Be Discerning and Articulate when Discussing Fiction

In your conferences and journals you can help your students become more discerning about the books they read. You can help them increasingly to develop an understanding and appreciation of meaningful and well written fiction. Out of these discussions students can distinguish better between a well crafted book which speaks to them, which they might find themselves cherishing, as opposed to a book which is much like most TV videos—momentary diversion, a few laughs perhaps, maybe some sensation and it's all over.

Reading many good children's books yourself should make you experienced in looking at a piece of children's fiction discerningly. Another way to help yourself discuss good books is to know and use vocabulary and concepts which can allow you and your students to become articulate about the elements in fiction. I am speaking of words and phrases which will allow the two of you to reflect and share your impressions, your judgments. This wording also can help you and your students talk about their own fiction writing.

Some vocabulary and concepts are listed below which you should understand and be able to help your students use in their thinking and in communicating with you about the fiction they are reading and perhaps writing. The idea here is to provide a language with which you and your students might discuss fiction sensitively. It certainly is not my intention to ask you to teach students the technical vocabulary of literature criticism as an end in itself. It is presented here to help you and your student to be more articulate about what you read. My intention is to assist you to put into words the subtleties, the fleeting feelings, the exciting thoughts which a good piece of fiction can inspire in the reader. [11]

1. A book's *theme* or point: A good piece of children's fiction says something; it always has a point. Perhaps the point is to explore what freedom means as was done so well in *The Satanic Mill* I mentioned before; perhaps it is more subtle and general such as to illustrate what friendship is all about, as is done is *Charlotte's Web*. [12]
2. It is important for the discerning reader to be aware of the author's options in positioning her or himself to tell the story—the author's

choice of *point of view* or *focus of narration*. Typically the author can choose one of these points of view to do this:

The Scenic Narrator: Here the author is positioned within the character who is acting. This limits the author to staying within the limits of the character's senses for the information and insights to be reported to the reader. Taking this point of view enables the author to write so the reader might readily identify emotionally with the character—be right there as the character deals with the story's challenges and rewards. A disadvantage is that the reader can only assume what might be going on with other characters. What lies around the corner in the story can only be surmised.

The Omniscient Narrator: Taking this position, the author can describe what is going on within and without all of the characters. The advantages are obvious. A disadvantage is that the reader is separated from any one character by a kind of impersonal distance.

The First Person Narrator: Here the storyteller is a character in the story. "When I saw him coming I began to feel strange inside," might be a line from the story. Using this point of view, typically the author has the chance to bond the reader and the character more than by using either of the above two points of view.

3. The *plot* is the progression of action in a story. Usually this is the sequential unfolding of the story.

4. Often in children's fiction the difference between a well written story and one which is not, rides on *characterization*. If the author uses stereotypes (the smiling mailman or the always nurturing grandmother) the story can go as flat as the shallowness of these characterizations. In some well written stories, on the other hand, one or two characterizations are made real and vital against a backdrop of less uniquely drawn characters whose actions seem defined by the roles and social categories assigned to them. This is OK when done well. It can allow the reader to focus fully on the one or two characters whose characterizations are drawn perhaps with more subtle realism than the others.

5. In the *setting* the author provides the reader with a sense of context—the world in which the story takes place. In some stories the setting is so important it becomes the point of the story, it's heart, as for example a story about what life is like in a small town which is apart from the modern mainstream

6   *Conflict and resolution*: Typically near the beginning in the plot, the author writes in a problem or conflict situation which faces the characters. In a well written piece of fiction this often simply is a kind of intuitive awareness the author develops in the reader. Then as the plot progresses the reader finds the seeds or clues to the initial problem's resolution.

7.   In most good fiction pieces there is a point in the story where the reader senses the general lines and basic form of the resolution. This is called the *moment of illumination.* It typically is not the climax but is the point in the story where the reader is given a meaningful perspective which integrates all which has gone before and suggests the lines of resolution which will follow.

8.   Finally, in the book's *climax*, the resolution typically takes place with the reader's full attention perhaps riveted on the crucial detail which puts to rest the tension of the initial problem situation. Usually the book's ending tails off quickly from this point.

Creative Writing: A Time when Young Writers Listen to Themselves

In discussing this topic let me tell about one teacher, Hughes Mearns. He drew each of his students toward an increasingly deeper sensitivity to their individual creative spirit.

Mearns was a writer and poet who took a job teaching English at Teacher's College, Columbia University's famous Lincoln School of Experimentation when it was being organized right after World War I. He had just returned from being an army psychologist during the war. Mearns turned down an offer to be the superintendent of a large school district. Instead he wanted to see if he could help young people respond to their essences as feeling and thinking people.

At Lincoln School Mearns asked for a job teaching eighth graders—the adolescent age when so many parents and teachers saw little hope of reversing teenagers' paths toward wanting be like the others in their cliques or other peer groups. He said he wanted to see if he could bring teenagers closer to their genuine selves through writing.

He did this beautifully. He guided his young teenage students to find their own worlds to talk about in their creative writing. He shared his and other young people's writing with the students. He invited them to write about what they knew, to write from their hearts. He emphasized how form in poetry and other self-expressive writing wasn't nearly as important as genuineness—that rhyming, for example, might ornament a poem but wasn't what poetry was all about.

Traditional form had a place for Mearns, but that was not the priority. Bringing out each child's individuality was—that deep current which ran inside, as he put it. One day while explaining and reading poetry to a group of eight-year-old children he found himself saying, "Poetry is when you talk with yourself." Instantly he sensed his young audience understood. Poetry came from one's inner recesses where subtle individuality resides, where special thoughts seek to inform one's being.

Hughes Mearns seemed to have the kind of an accepting relationship with his students which made it easy and comfortable for them to share their personal writing with him. His students didn't see him as the teacher who judged what they wrote but instead saw their teacher as one who felt privileged to be allowed to read their pieces that so often came from a dialogue with themselves. At one point he kept the small bottom drawer of his desk just for written pieces his students might want to slip in. In his classes he spent a great deal of the time sharing with the students his own life as a creative writer—how sometimes, for example, he got up in the middle of the night to write just the phrase which had eluded him all day.

Try to take some pointers from Hughes Mearns' style of teaching creative writing. For example, encourage your students to write as if they were speaking with themselves, as they allow out inner feelings and wisdom. Read them pieces you value where the authors do this. Accept what students write, with due respect. Here I am not advocating overly personal self-disclosure which might make a student feel vulnerable afterward. But I am encouraging writing that has a deep connection to the writer.

Also you can bring in writers whose writing comes from their essential humanness. At school they can share their work and their craft with your students. Take advantage of your elementary Urban Little School's weekly Friday afternoon cafeteria-style learning Events Time when children choose to go to whatever class they fancy. Invite writers to come to the Friday afternoon Events Time "writer's corner" to share poems and segments from their other writing along with discussing how they work. Invite people who resonate with Hughes Mearns' "Poetry is when you talk with yourself." [13]

I remember participating in such a class once a week when I was at a retreat center in England. Our group's teacher simply read a poem he loved and stopped. Often the quiet would last a few minutes. Then someone would say something the writing brought forth in that listener. Maybe no one else would share or a few more would comment, usually leaving plenty of quiet space between speakers. When all who wanted to speak, had spoken, the teacher would read another favorite piece of his. When I left each of these weekly classes I felt the door to my special inner self was a bit further ajar.

Help Students Write Clearly with Correct Grammar, Spelling and Usage

You won't have to begin from scratch to teach your students how to use the writing conventions. Your independently writing children will have been doing so for years in their journals. They have been modeling their writing after their teacher's, in the journal they received every few days. Your journals to them now, will model good use of conventions. Also your students have participated in hundreds of Newstime sessions, when they were beginners, where teachers modeled how to use punctuation, spelling and some other conventions. So by this time—when they are independent in writing—they should understand the importance of spelling, grammar and usage in written communication and have a clear sense of how to go about it correctly. Also they will have sensed how good authors were using correct conventions in their writing. Your students will have heard read or will have been reading themselves, an increasingly large volume of well written books. So the problem for you, in guiding most of your independently writing and reading children, is to decide how to top up and fine tune what they already know and sense.

If you feel it is needed, double check to make sure students can spell correctly all of the Basic Words which are listed in this chapter. Help them learn to spell any which they spell incorrectly. You will know easy-enough if one of your students has trouble with sentence form, the fundamentals of punctuation and other basics because this will be apparent in their journals. If they need to be helped with any of this you can do it but not on the journal sheets.

The journals are not an exercise in how to use the conventions as we discussed in Task Three, above. Journals are one of the best ways to practice using conventions. Any red marks or other criticism of writing on the journals inevitably will take from students' freedom to say what they want to say spontaneously. Having said that, one way you might help students to polish their journals themselves, is to use the computer's word processing aides such as its spell-check and its grammar check facility. The computer's thesaurus can help students select just the right word. These computer tools should only be used when students feel confident as a writer of journals. Let students decide when and if they want to use these computer aides to writing. Probably they will want to use the computer's spell-check facility from the beginning of their journal writing to help them change the spelling of any word the computer program thinks they might have misspelled. This is so different from those red marks from the traditional English teacher. Here the computer helps students help themselves toward better communication and more pride in a well-crafted written piece before they offer it to a reader.

You will know easily what students need to learn just by reading their journals. If the student might benefit from more systematic instruction in the use of conventions, you might try the student in a computer program which teaches sequentially the fundamentals of grammar, punctuation, usage or spelling. In addition to teaching needed skills these kinds of interactive computer programs give the students a foretaste for the kind of self-directed learning activities they will use in the secondary years to learn basic high school content. For example, the following programs, among others, are available from Learning Services Company's 1999 catalogue:[14]

- *I Love Spelling* (Grades 2-5) "Six exciting spelling games, packed with hundreds of hilarious animations and jokes make learning to spell more fun than it's ever been! Children can customize the games by choosing special word groups to play with names of their favorite animals, parts of the body country names and many more. Teachers and parents have access to more than 50 spelling k-pattern word groups that target key spelling problem areas. And intelligent tracking software allows children to target words they have problems with."
- *Elementary Writing Skills* "Students practice basic writing skills in biographies, reports, essays and paragraphs. Students learn editing skills, sentence combining techniques, punctuation rules and more."
- *Mastering English Grammar* "This collection of 46 best selling programs on CD-ROM is designed for grades six and up and remedial college

work. Includes: Working with Sentences, Capitalization and More, Punctuation, and Practical Grammar I, II, and III. Learning Parts of Speech Package—which is highly rated for accuracy, clarity logic appropriate difficulty, from error, and directions."

As Your Students Become Sure of Themselves as Writers, Help them Edit and Revise their Work

The computer's word processing facility is a godsend for editing and revising. When I feel I am nearing completion of a draft I sit in front of the computer and read every word in the piece out loud to myself, line by line. As I read along I pay attention to the sense which tells me when a phrase isn't quite right, when a sentence within the paragraph should be the lead sentence in the paragraph, when the paragraph isn't bridged from the last paragraph. It's so simple with the computer's word processing facility to let my fingers almost effortlessly make the deletions, type the changes, "cut and paste." If a word doesn't sound just right I can highlight it on the computer screen and click to the computer program's thesaurus for synonyms. Not only does this give me other word possibilities, it helps me to think through just the right connotation for the word in question as I refine what I want to say.

With children, the trick is to help them to revise with satisfaction. It is hard work usually to polish a piece. Writers talk about finishing a piece and feeling that it is DONE. They simply don't want to take apart that gift of their writing which is now on the computer's disk. I know I feel that way after a lot of work writing a piece. Be careful not to overburden your students with revision when they are just getting used to looking at their work to see if it is clear, concise enough and communicative. Help them polish until the piece shines but not so they burn out in the process.

This guidance of your young writers isn't as hard as it might sound. Because you will be teaching in an individualized way you can encourage some students to revise rigorously while with others this might come later in the young writer's development. And some students will take to revision. They will find satisfaction in finely crafting their writing. I can't emphasize too much how an individualized approach to teaching fits so well with writing which comes from the student's individuality.

One way to help students see the value in revising and editing a piece, even though they might feel satisfied with it, is to help them get it ready for publication. Typically this is done by the school having a magazine which comes out periodically. I prefer the "direct mailing" approach because it allows you to "publish" virtually all the really polished pieces a student of yours might write. With this approach you and the student can send the polished pieces to a select group of readers who might be interested. Each student can make up her or his own mailing list for distribution. Thus former teachers might get the piece in the mail, the children's librarian who helps the student might receive a copy in the mail. Perhaps grown sisters or brothers should receive a copy. What about the child's grandmother? Try to mail the piece to people who know the value of honest praise, so if they are impressed or learn something special they might tell the young author.

Help Students Learn to Use the Tools of Efficient Library Research

Keep a checklist for each of your elementary ULS students to make sure they have the skills and knowledge needed to research and write an expository piece on an topic which is not familiar to them. Informed by this checklist you can consider how best to help students learn and develop the library research skills and knowledge they need. Here is a list of the basic knowledge a student should come to have in order to do proficient library research which is fruitful and satisfying. The student should be able to:

- Use alphabetically organized material
- Use an elementary school English language dictionary
- Use a book's index
- Use encyclopedia
- Use parts of a book such as the introduction and subheads
- Use maps, globes and atlases
- Use *World Almanac* and other yearbooks
- Use *Who's Who* and other biographic reference books
- Use on-line encyclopedia and atlases
- Use the library's on-line catalog
- Locate library books using call numbers

Help your Fledgling Library Researchers Learn to Narrow and Clarify their Library Research Questions

Have short one to one conferences with your students daily when they are involved in their first few library research projects. Then as the students become more self-reliant they can move ahead without your checking-in so often. I am speaking of short five or ten minute pop-in conferences to help the student move from a general interest in a topic to a final written piece which clearly speaks to questions of significance involved in the subject being studied. These short pop-in conferences tend to make each step in the library research and write-up job yield satisfaction and interesting content knowledge for the student. They can help you to determine if the student needs to learn specific skills too, such as how to skim an encyclopedia article, or how to take brief notes. Some of these kinds of skills can be learned in self-directed ways by the student using computer software.

Help your students to develop and extend their initial orientation to the subject which incorporates the students' interest—to get a more thorough understanding of the topic— beyond the recognition of key concepts used in the field. This background can come partly out of the talks you have with students about what they want to know. It might come from students reading simple books which summarize the subject, often with colorful illustrations and diagrams. With this context, your students often can come to grasp the big ideas and understand the specialized vocabulary involved. Perhaps this might be followed up by students' writing an initial sketch explaining what they might want to know. For some students you will sense this is as far as really they are interested in going. That's fine. No sense in making a serious inquiry into something the student isn't drawn to pursue any further.

Once your students feel a serious sense of direction about what they want to learn and write up, they can approach the consequent library research job in a step by step way with your support in pop-in conferences and with your regular conferences and journal exchange. I call this the "narrowing and clarifying task" for the serious young library researcher.

The students might read encyclopedia articles dealing with the subject in question and discuss with you which key guide words, noted during their reading, could lead to further information. As students read further in the areas delineated by the guide words—perhaps read in more encyclopedia articles—you can help them draft a set of questions which incorporate their curiosity and which eventually will be honed to become the main topics of their write-ups.

For example, for a student who doesn't know about engines and wants to find out, the list of study questions might begin with, "What does a carburetor do and how does it work?" That might be followed by "What makes the engine piston go down?" Key guide words for further study might be "internal combustion," "crank shaft," and so on. These words could lead to articles and books which should contain other key words to look up in indexes, further encyclopedia articles and on-line sources. Somewhere in the process might come this title for the written piece: "How the automobile engine turns gasoline into power."

Using these kinds of guide words breaks up the subject into manageable parts which then can be narrowed further to focus on the questions which carry students to the heart of their inquiry. Without breaking the subject into manageable parts which can be pursued relatively easily, many beginning library researchers find it daunting to wade into a great deal of unfamiliar information. They need all the help they can get to clarify what precisely they want to learn. Beginning library researchers sometimes need help to be sure they know the needed vocabulary and organizing ideas used in the topic area; to get the information they need in each topic area; to note the key information and ideas they might want to include in their write-up. [15]

Some students find it helpful to narrow and to clarify their library research problem using a form you can easily prepare, which guides them to answer the following four questions:

1. In general, I want to find out the following:
2. Here are some key guide words and/or subtopics that should be useful in beginning to look up information in encyclopedia, the on-line library catalog, tables of contents, indexes, etc.
3. Here are some books, magazines, on-line resources etc. I might use:
4. These are some questions which might guide my study; (perhaps they will be the major headings of my eventual writeup outline):

To facilitate students' library research, you should have these books available in your school

- Two sets of an elementary school encyclopedia, such as *Comptons* or *World Book*
- Several elementary school dictionaries
- Three copies of the latest *Webster's Collegiate Dictionary*
- One copy each of a biographical and a geographical dictionary, a world atlas, a world almanac and two local atlases
- On-line CD Rom disks holding complete adult encyclopedias and atlases
- Reference books giving biographical background on children's authors
- *Who's Who* references and other reference books recommended by a good children's librarian
- A world globe

Help Students Actively Think their Way Through a Textbook

Finally, a word about helping your independent readers and writers learn actively from textbooks. By that I mean teaching them to stay in charge of their learning while drawing upon the textbook's information and ideas in ways which efficiently will let the text teach them what they need to know. Essentially the students ask themselves three questions after they leaf through the material laid out in the textbook's pages which is relevant to their question:

1. What additional help do I need such as vocabulary study or an overview introduction to the subject?
2. How much of the text's information and ideas do I already know?
3. What is it, then, I need to know as I proceed through the text material guided by what I want to know?

The first few times a student goes through this process it might seem awkward—much easier just to proceed through the text and memorize the information in the text. But after two or three times, perhaps working on one chapter from a different textbook in each case, most students who are independent readers and writers will get the hang of it. They then will be able to apply this process for textbook study in any way that works for them, according to what they want to find out.

If the text deals with a subject which is not familiar to the student, almost always students will profit from an overview or introduction to the subject matter. This helps them set a context for themselves. Then they will have a big picture, a sense of the subject which gives them a place to hang the bits of factual knowledge and ideas they encounter as they go through the text.

As in the overview stage of library research, you can help your student understand this general introduction to the subject being studied in the textbook. Maybe the first step is for you to talk with the student to get a feeling for yourself whether the student has a working knowledge of the subject and its vocabulary.

Perhaps you, as the teacher, don't know enough in the subject area to carry on an informed discussion. Then the two of you will be off together, learning a context of general knowledge, vocabulary and perhaps history which is relevant to the text material. If your students or you need more introduction, probably the encyclopedia should be the first stop, as it usually is when the students begin to narrow and clarify their research questions. Then, depending on the subject, don't forget those well written and illustrated children's non-fiction books. So often the purpose of the non-fiction children's books is to give the reader just what is needed: a general introduction to the subject.

Ask the librarian for help identifying the right non-fiction books from the children's collection. I think of a beautiful children's history of World Civilization I looked through the other day. It contained a timeline which gave a sense of sequence and proportion to the saga of history. It was chock full of fascinating details which brought to life the nitty gritty of living in past times. And it made it fascinating. The illustrations and layout made events like the plague, the industrial revolution, and the advent of popular democracy exciting moments in a remarkable story—as of course they are. What a wonderful background this children's book might be for a student who wants to ferret out factual elaboration and ideas from a well-written textbook on world history.[16]

A Last Word

And that word is *practice*. If you are a new ULS teacher, practice over and over again with children you know well. Get sure and fast about handling the basics we have discussed. Many children like to help new teachers do this. It's fun for them when they know how important their role is in making you a good teacher.

The idea here is to come to be able to work with children one to one quickly so the two of you can have more time to listen to each other, to plan, to take each other seriously. With practice, you will have confidence based on experience that can help you decide on a child's best next step, that will allow you to pick up little clues which will help you fine tune the child's work.

Notes

1   The study to find out this list of Basic Words was done in the 1960s financed by a grant from the federal Office of Education. Therefore, it is "in the public domain" and can be replicated without copyright restriction. You can photocopy this list to see what words beginning readers can read to get an idea of the words children know and the ones they need to learn. Sorry to say, I have been unable to find the name of the research group which did the study. Whoever you were, thanks, for such a helpful piece of work.

2   A particularly revealing study shows that only this rule, of all the traditional phonics rules, applies more than half of the time. With other rules such as "When two vowels go walking the first does the talking," there are more exceptions than regular applications. [Clymer, Theodore. (1963). The utility of phonic generalizations in the primary grades. *The Reading Teacher, 16*, p. 253 - 258.] This is further supported by the work of the linguist Charles C. Fries. His book lists hundreds of examples of words that follow the c-v-c and c-v-c plus silent "e" rule—all to make his point that if children can recognize this pattern automatically, they have taken a giant step in learning to read and spell. Fries, C.C. (1962). *Linguistics and Reading*. New York: Holt, Rinehart and Winston.

3   Warner, Gertrude Chandler, *The Boxcar Children*, Copyright 1942,1950, 1977, by Albert Whitman and Company. Used with permission.

4   I used: *The Spache Diagnostic Reading Scales*. (1981). Del Monte Research Park, Monterey, CA 93940: McGraw-Hill.

5   "Little Fingers" keyboards allow young children to learn to touch type. In addition there are several touch typing computer programs out, some in game format. Also some teachers use "SpeedSkin" key covers so children won't be tempted to peek. These kinds of aids in teaching touch-typing are described in the Learning

Services catalog. Write Learning Services Company for a copy (PO Box 10636, Eugene, OR 97440-2636).

6   For word processing, use older computers which can be purchased for $100 or less apiece. I am speaking of systems such as the Apple Macintosh SE. These are simple to operate and can allow you to buy several to place at different spots in your school. Then you will have money left over to buy a couple of the more state-of-the art systems with larger screens on which students can use CD Rom Disks.

7   In order for your writing to model the best possible form as well as substance, you might need to brush up on your technical skills. Self-teaching computer exercises are listed in "Stage Four", pp. 278-279.

8   Translated from German by Anthea Bell. (1971). New York: The Macmillan Co.

9   Adams, Richard. (1972). *Watership Down*. New York: The Macmillan Co.

10 Sperry, Armstrong. (1940). *Call it Courage*. New York: The Macmillan Co.

11 In the 608 page classic, *Understanding Fiction*, Cleanth Brooks Jr. and Robert Penn Warren use the vocabulary and concepts introduced here as they discuss short stories. (New York: Appleton-Century-Crofts, 1943.)

12 E.B. White. (1940). *Charlotte's Web*. New York: Harper-Collins.

13 For a real treat read Mearns' 1929 account of helping young adolescents to write creatively: Mearns, Hughes. (1958). *Creative Power*. New York: Dover Publications Inc.

14 Learning Services, Box 10636, Eugene OR, 97440-2636. Also write for information on "Editor in Chief Software" for interactive CD Rom computer learning. Send query to Critical Thinking Books and Software, PO Box 448, Pacific Grove, CA 93950-0448.

15 To learn more about helping students in this narrowing and clarifying process, and in beginning library research, see Newman, Robert E., *Reading Writing and Self-Esteem,* op. cit., pp. 206-224. These pages contain suggested forms and lists which can help children do the job in a satisfying and manageable step by step way.

16 Millard, Dr. Anne and Jonags, Patricia. (1985). *The Usborne Book of World History*. London: Usborne Publishing Ltd.

AskERIC

An example of how this free information-searching service can help locate independent learning software, videos and other relevant information.

Where to start looking for available independent learning software, video lessons, and other self-directed learning materials for secondary students? In Chapter 9, I suggested starting with AskERIC. (ERIC stands for Education Resources and Information Center.) AskERIC is a free educational information service, located at Syracuse University and funded by the federal government, which opens up a wealth of information. Simply send an e-mail detailing your request to <askeric@askeric.org>. Within 48 hours you will receive an acknowledgment. Then in a short time they will send you a listing of suggested sources, which you can use to begin your search. Sometimes the AskERIC hub center at Syracuse University forwards a request it receives to another center in the country which might specialize in locating the kind of information requested.

This supplemental article contains an abridged version of my response from AskERIC when I sent an e-mail asking for what was available in secondary school independent learning materials suitable for a ULS Self-directed Learning Center. I also asked for background articles about others' experiences helping young people to learn the high school basics independently. To be explicit in my request, I gave two examples of the kinds of materials I wanted to find: (1) IBM's K-12 computer programs for learning high school basic courses independently; (2) The Teaching Company's videotaped high school lectures. (Both of these independent learning resources are cited in Chapter Nine.)

Within 48 hours of the time I sent it, I received an acknowledgment from AskERIC. Then the next e-mail I received from AskERIC came with the information I requested. That came within two days of their acknowledgment. Following is the shortened version of the second e-mail I received from AskERIC. I have deleted what looked to me like non-relevant data and reformatted the e-mail style to make it consistent with this book's format.

• • •

From: Tracey Bremer <tlbqa@stny.lrun.com
Subject: Secondary School Level Self-instruction software and videos
To: renewman
Subject: Secondary School Level Self-instruction Software and Videos

Robert,

In response to your request, I conducted a sample search of the ERIC database. Below I have appended my search strategy, citations with abstracts, and directions for accessing the full-text. These citations may represent an introductory, rather than exhaustive, search for information on your topic.

If you would like to conduct your own free ERIC database searches via the Internet, please send a request for directions to askeric@askeric.org or go directly to http://www.askeric.org/Eric

In addition, I have attached some related resources that may also be helpful. Thank you for using AskERIC! If you have any questions or would like further assistance, please send another message.

Cordially,
Tracey Bremer, AskERIC Network Information Specialist

ERIC Clearinghouse on Information and Technology 4-194
Center for Science and Technology Syracuse, NY 13244-4100
URL: http://www.askeric.org • E-mail: askeric@askeric.org
Phone: 1-800-464-9107 < 315-443-3640

SOFTWARE LISTSERV
Electronic. Mailing Lists:

- ACSOFT-L
  Educational software discussion.
  To subscribe, address an e-mail message in the following manner:
  To: listserv@wuvmd.wustl.edu
  subscribe ACSOFT-L

SOFTWARE GUIDES—REVIEWS
Internet Sites

- PEP: Resources for Parents, Educators, and Publishers
  Contains 350+ pages of content and over 3,500 linkages relating to children's software. Includes news, reviews, ratings, a software evaluation instrument, teacher resources, a national directory of computer recycling centers, shopper resources, and the PEP Registry of educational software publishers.
  http://www.microweb.com/pepsite
- Newsweek's Parents Guide to Children's Software
  Provides parents with a resource for children's software reviews and recommendations, news columns & bulletin boards.
  http://www.newsweekparentsguide.com/
- TIC: Technology in the Curriculum
  TIC Online, the California Technology in the Curriculum [TIC] Evaluations Database, has information on 2,000+ computer software, CD-ROM, computer-interactive videodisc, and instructional video programs rated as Exemplary or Desirable by the California Instructional Technology Clearinghouse over the past six years. Searchable by subject, material category, platform, language, grade level.
  http://clearinghouse.k12.ca.us
- TechShopper
  Contains wide range of product reviews, including hardware, software, peripherals, games, internet application software, etc.
  http://www.techweb.com/shopper/

- Review Booth
  A clearinghouse for published hardware and software product reviews.
  http://www.reviewbooth.com/
- Open Computing Products
  Contains reviews, news, more. Ceased publication in 1995, but still
  contains useful information.
  http://www.wcmh.com/oc/products/products.html
- CHORUS
  CHORUS is an international "meta-resource" exploring and supporting the use of new media in the arts and humanities. It is composed of
  several sections presenting software reviews, original research, bibliogra-
  phies, annotated links and Shockwave demonstrations.
  http://www-writing.berkeley.edu/chorus/
- Thunderbeam
  Contains over 2,000 reviews, demos, shareware, parenting tips, contests,
  forums, and a large kids' software store.
  http://www.thunderbeam.com/w/m/index.html
- Benchin'
  Reviews of over 100,000 software products submitted by average users.
  http://www.benchin.com/
- Children's Software Reviews
  This collection of WWW documents is intended as a repository for
  volunteer reviews of children's software produced by the users of the
  newsgroup misc.kids.computer.
  http://qv3pluto.leidenuniv.nl/steve/reviews/welcome.htm
- Children's Software Revue
  http://www2.childrenssoftware.com/childrenssoftware/
- School House Software Reviews
  http://204.96.11.210/wv/school/html/scholrev.htm
- Sources for Reviews of Educational CD-ROMs and Software
  A bibliography of periodicals containing software reviews.
  http://www.unc.edu/cit/guides/irg-31.html
- SuperKids Educational Software Review
  Contains software reviews written by kids, parents, teachers.
  http://www.superkids.com/

- Tips on Choosing Software for Your School
  http://www.siec.k12.in.us/~west/article/soft.htm
- Software Evaluation Instrument from Children's Software Review
  A checklist of items to consider when reviewing software.
  http://www.pepsite.com/Revue/evaluation.html
- Seven Steps To Responsible Software Selection. ERIC Digest.
  http://ericir.syr.edu/ithome/digests/software.html

ADDITIONAL RESOURCES

- *Only the Best: The Annual Guide to Highest Rated Educational Software*
  (1997 edition)
  http://www.ascd.org
  ASCD Association for Supervision and Curriculum Development
  1703 North Beauregard Street, Alexandria, VA 22311-1714 USA
  (800) 933-ASCD (2723) • (703) 578-9600
- *The Latest & Best of TESS – The Educational Software Selector*
  (updated every 6 months)
  http://www.interhelp.com/epie_tess.htm
  By EPIE Institute (Education Product Information Exchange Institute)
  1996 Price: $79.95
  103 West Montauk Highway #3 Hampton Bays, NY 11946-4006
  Phone: (516) 728-9100 • Fax: (516) 728-9228
- *The Educational Software Preview Guide*
  This guide lists favorably reviewed, commercially available, microcomputer
  software for instructional use in preschool through grade 12. (1999 edition
  available)—call 800-336-5191 to order.
  http://www.computerlearning.org/books/EdSWPrev.htm

FILM AND VIDEO
Directories

- Audio Video Market Place. New York: R. R. Bowker. A directory of
  production and distribution services which provide audio and visual
  materials. Not a subject or rental guide.
- The Directory of Video, Computer, and Audio-Visual Products. Fairfax,
  VA: The International Communications Industries Association.

- Educational Film Locator. New York: R. R. Bowker, 1978.
- Educational Video and Film Rental Catalog. Kent, OH: Kent State University, Audio Visual Services, 1988–. A listing of videocassettes and 16mm films available for rental to schools and qualified individuals. All subjects and audience levels. Selected videotapes available free of cost to schools, libraries, and industries.
- International Directory of Interactive Multimedia Producers. Santa Clara, CA: Multimedia Computing Corporation.
- The Knowledge Collection, vol. 3, 1988. New York: McGraw-Hill, 1987. More than 6000 special-interest educational, informational and instructional videotapes (VHS only) covering a wide variety of topics.
- Recommended Videos for Schools. Santa Barbara, CA: ABC-CLIO, 1992. Includes title, subject, and price indexes, and a list of producers and distributors.

ADDITIONAL SOURCES

- Brown, James W., Richard B. Lewis and Fred F. Harcleroad. AV Instruction: Technology, Media, and Methods, 6th ed. New York: McGraw-Hill, 1983. Textbook for using all forms of audio-visual instructional media in the classroom. Chapters on selection of materials, methods of use and operation of equipment.
- Foster, Harold M. The New Literacy: The Language of Film and Television. Urbana, IL: National Council of Teachers of English, 1979. PN 1995 .F64
- Gallant, Jennifer Jung. Best Videos for Children and Young Adults: A Core Collection for Libraries. Santa Barbara, CA: ABC-CLIO, 1990.
- Romiszowski, A. J. The Selection and Use of Instructional Media, 2nd ed. New York: Nichols Publishing Company, 1988.

INDEXES

- Film and Video Finder. Albequerque, NM: Access Innovations, 1989. A bibliographic guide to 16mm films and videotapes. Approximately 160,00 entries accessible by subject or title.
- Index to AV Producers and Distributors. 7th ed. National Information Center for Educational Media. Medford, N.J.: Plexus, 1989.

- Media Review. Pleasantville, NY: Media Review. Professional reviews and ratings of instructional media for use in classrooms, K- college.
- Media Review Digest. Ann Arbor, MI: Pierian Press, 1974-. An annual index to and digest of reviews, evaluations and descriptions of all forms of non-book media.
- MiddleWeb's Teaching Strategies resources
  http://www.middleweb.com/CurrStrategies.html
- Teaching Methods
  Contains an annotated list to aid you in finding relevant educational resources on the World Wide Web on Teaching Methods.
  http://lib.upm.edu.my/iistem.html

OBTAINING THE FULL TEXT OF MATERIALS CITED IN ERIC

Eric Documents: (Citations identified by an ED number) are available in microfiche form at libraries or other institutions housing ERIC Resource Collections worldwide; to identify your local ERIC Resource Collection, connect to: http://www.ed.gov/BASISDB/EROD/eric/SF. Documents are also available selectively in a variety of formats (including microfiche, paper copy, or electronic) from the ERIC Document Reproduction Service for a fee: tel. (800) 443-ERIC, email service@edrs.com, online order form: http://edrs.com/Webstore/Express.cfm

Eric Journals: (Citations identified by an EJ number) are available in your local library or via interlibrary loan services, from the originating journal publisher, or for a fee from the following article reproduction vendors: CARL UnCover S.O.S.: email sos@carl.org, tel. (800) 787-7979, online order form: http://uncweb.carl.org/sos/sosform.html; or ISI Document Solution: email ids@isinet.com, tel. (800) 336-4474,(215) 386-4399, online order form: http://www.isinet.com/prodserv/ids/idsfm.html

---

Please refer to citation for other specific availability info

ERIC
AN: ED414318
AU: Shrader,-Vincent-E.

TI: Designing a Teacher/Course Assessment Instrument for Distance Education. PY: 1997

DL: http://orders.edrs.com/members/sp.cfm?AN=ED414318

DT: Reports-Research (143); Speeches-or-Meeting-Papers (150)

PG: 9

DE: *College-Students; *Course-Evaluation; *Distance-Education; *High-School-Students; *Independent-Study; *Item-Analysis

DE: College-Faculty; High-Schools; Higher-Education; Measurement-Techniques; Student-Attitudes; Test-Construction ID: *Brigham-Young-University-UT

AB: Independent Study (IS) at Brigham Young University (Utah) enrolls nearly 17,000 high school students and 13,000 college students each year. Results of student evaluations are used to help determine to what extent the IS courses and instructors are meeting student needs. IS administrators decided to redesign the student forms to provide a better measure of course effectiveness and student attitudes toward registration, service, and course materials. A study of about 300 completed forms helped identify trends in the data. Data from this analysis and from student interviews were used to construct new items that were assimilated into a possible item pool. Faculty members were asked to evaluate these items grouped into subscales. Approximately 50 faculty members responded to the request, and about 75 later replied to a request to evaluate a revised instrument. The developed instrument was then sent with each final examination packet until over 500 student forms were returned. An error in the key provided with the form resulted in a second field test with 116 forms for item analysis. This analysis showed that almost all the items had moderate to high adjusted item-total correlation coefficients. A refinement resulted in five subscales, and another item analysis supported these subscales. The instrument was accepted for use in IS evaluations. (Contains eight tables and eight references.) (SLD)

ERIC

AN: ED345523

AU: Curtin,-Constance; Shinall,-Stanley

TI: An Example of the Use of Microcomputers in Foreign Language Learning and Teaching from a High School for the Academically Talented.

PY: 1987

JN: IDEAL

DT: Reports-Descriptive (141); Journal-Articles (080)

PG: 8

DE: *Academically-Gifted; *Computer-Assisted-Instruction; *Curriculum-Design; *Microcomputers-; *Second-Language-Learning; *Student-Motivation

DE: Cultural-Awareness; Demonstration-Centers; Feedback-; High-Schools; Independent-Study; Instructional-Effectiveness; Program-Descriptions; Second-Language-Instruction

ID: *University-of-Illinois

AB: Results of two studies of microcomputer use for second language instruction at the secondary level are reported. The investigation is based on observations made at the University of Illinois' University High School, which serves academically talented students from the surrounding area. The school's computer laboratory uses software packages for French, German, Russian, and Spanish. It allows whole classes to use microcomputers simultaneously and permits use of a variety of software formats. It is concluded that computer-assisted language instruction is an excellent tool in the promotion of independent study and review that can result in better or more efficient learning. Learner characteristics seen as contributing to achievement are discussed in relation to previous research done at the university. The best software appears to be that which capitalizes on positive learner attributes. Programs that permit self-direction, provide appropriate feedback, encourage discovery about the language, and expand student awareness of the target culture are recommended. (Author/MSE)

ERIC

AN: ED345043

AU: Houdek,-Elizabeth; and-others

TI: Independent Study Program Profiles 1990-91. Final Report.

CS: National Univ. Continuing Education Association, Washington, DC. Independent Study Div.

PY: 1992

AV: Independent Study Program, 305A Tupper Hall, Ohio University, Athens, OH 45701-2979 ($10.00).

DT: Reports-Research (143)

PG: 126

DE: *Distance-Education; *Enrollment-; *Faculty-; *Fees-; *Independent-Study DE: Curriculum-Development; Enrollment-Trends; High-Schools; Higher-Education; National-Surveys; Noncredit-Courses; Postsecondary-Education; Profiles-; Program-Development; Student-Costs

ID: National-University-Continuing-Education-Assn

AB: This final report represents the responses of 76 institutions to the 1990-91 annual survey of the Division of Independent Study, National University Continuing Education Association (NUCEA). Data describe enrollments and program practices in college-level, high school, and noncredit programs. Eight tables and five figures provide information on course enrollments, course fees, staff size, course development, and faculty stipends. Format and contents of tables follow an established pattern to maintain comparability between years. Part 1, Total Program Scope, contains an executive summary. Figures and tables illustrate the following: independent study program, 1990-91 profiles; independent study enrollments, NUCEA member institutions 1990-91; independent study enrollments, miscellaneous enrollment information; college, high school, and noncredit course information; independent study faculty and staff; and special fees. Part 2, College Programs, provides tables and figures that illustrate information on college enrollment and college programs with a semester hour, quarter hour, and other fee basis. Part 3, High School Programs, contains tables and figures showing program information and enrollments. Part 4, Noncredit Programs, presents tables and figures illustrating noncredit program information and noncredit enrollments. Part 5 provides the survey instrument. Footnotes for college, high school, and noncredit information are appended. (YLB)

• • •

Index

About the Author

Robert Newman is a teacher, writer, and emeritus professor at Syracuse University in the United States. After graduating from Antioch College, he taught children ages six to fourteen in a one-room school in the California hills and then grades six and two at a suburban school. He trained teachers at a year-long demonstration classroom in an inner city elementary school. After receiving his doctorate at Stanford University, he taught at three other universities. He was principal of The University of Chicago Laboratory Schools' Lower School, and for ten years, while teaching at Syracuse University, he directed an experimental small school similar to The Fircroft School described in this book. He is author of *God Bless the Grass*: *Studies in Children's Self-Esteem* (R & E Research Publishers), *Reading, Writing and Self-Esteem* (Prentice-Hall), and the pamphlet series, *The Language Arts of Individual Inquiry* (Science Research Associates). His latest work is a pamphlet, "The Still Small Voice, Fear, and Me" (Quaker Universalists, 7 Barewell Close, St. Marychurch, Torquay, Devon TQ 4PS, England).